Turtles & Tortoises For Dummies®

D0796199

Turtle and Tortoise Vocabulary

This book has been written so that even beginning turtle and tortoise owners can understand it; however, some words may be new to you. Here are some of the words used in reference to turtles and tortoises. Appendix A gives a more complete glossary.

- **Aquatic turtle:** A turtle that spends all or the majority of its time in the water
- **Basking site or basking area:** An area for a turtle or tortoise to absorb warmth from sunshine or another heat source
- **Brackish water:** Fresh water that receives some salt water from the ocean during high tides, making it more salty than fresh
- **Carapace:** The top shell covering the back
- **Carnivore:** A meat eater
- **Carrion:** Decaying flesh that may be used for food
- **Chelonians:** All turtles and tortoises
- **Clutch:** A nest of eggs
- **Estivates:** Hibernates in summer
- **Hatchlings:** Baby turtles or tortoises
- **Herbivore:** A plant eater
- **Keel:** A ridge in the carapace, usually from front to rear so that it is over or parallels the spine
- **Omnivore:** Eats both meat and plants
- **Plastron:** The lower shell
- **Scute:** A single surface section of the shell; each shell is made up of many scutes with underlying skeletal bone
- **Semi-aquatic turtle:** A turtle that spends about half of its time in the water and half of its time on land
- **Semi-terrestrial turtle:** A turtle that spends most of its time on land but also goes into the water once in a while
- **Side-necked turtle:** When this type of turtle shelters its head, the neck folds to the side but does not disappear into the shell
- **Terrarium:** An aquarium or cage that contains live plants, a higher humidity, and no swimming water
- **Terrestrial turtle:** A turtle that lives on land but bathes or soaks in water or goes into the water to escape predators
- **Tortoise:** A land-based chelonian that can't swim and only goes into shallow water to drink or soak; a tortoise never voluntarily enters water over its head
- **Vent:** Equivalent to an anal opening
- **Vivarium:** An aquarium divided into two sections — one for water and one for land

For Dummies™: Bestselling Book Series for Beginners

Turtles & Tortoises For Dummies®

Your Chelonian's Records

Keeping records is a necessity. Do you remember exactly when you bought that turtle or tortoise? Was it three years ago or four? When were those eggs laid? Was it the day Grandma came to dinner or the day your son dropped your favorite lamp? In addition, with so many species protected by law, you need to be able to show where, when, and from whom you got each pet. Records and photographs can also help you identify your pets if one is stolen or escapes.

Animal's name, number, and identification _____

Species common name _____

Latin name _____

Physical description in detail _____

_____

Date acquired _____ From whom _____

Age at time of acquisition _____

Other information regarding acquisition _____

_____

On the following lines, keep track of other pertinent information, including illnesses, injuries, changes in habits, sexual maturity, breeding information, and anything else that's important to you. Weigh your hatchlings and measure their lengths weekly; weigh and measure adults monthly. Attach up-to-date photographs of your pet, too.

_____

_____

_____

_____

_____

_____

_____

_____

_____

Hungry Minds™

For Dummies™: Bestselling Book Series for Beginners

Turtles & Tortoises

FOR

DUMMIES®

by Liz Palika

Hungry Minds™

HUNGRY MINDS, INC.

New York, NY ◆ Cleveland, OH ◆ Indianapolis, IN

Turtles & Tortoises For Dummies®

Published by:
Hungry Minds, Inc.
909 Third Avenue
New York, NY 10022
www.hungryminds.com
www.dummies.com

Library of Congress Control Number: 00-110835

ISBN: 0-7645-5313-5

Printed in the United States of America

10 9 8 7 6 5 4 3

1O/RW/QT/QR/IN

Distributed in the United States by Hungry Minds, Inc.

Distributed by CDG Books Canada Inc. for Canada; by Transworld Publishers Limited in the United Kingdom; by IDG Norge Books for Norway; by IDG Sweden Books for Sweden; by IDG Books Australia Publishing Corporation Pty. Ltd. for Australia and New Zealand; by TransQuest Publishers Pte Ltd. for Singapore, Malaysia, Thailand, Indonesia, and Hong Kong; by Gotop Information Inc. for Taiwan; by ICG Muse, Inc. for Japan; by Intersoft for South Africa; by Eyrolles for France; by International Thomson Publishing for Germany, Austria and Switzerland; by Distribuidora Cuspide for Argentina; by LR International for Brazil; by Galileo Libros for Chile; by Ediciones ZETA S.C.R. Ltda. for Peru; by WS Computer Publishing Corporation, Inc., for the Philippines; by Contemporanea de Ediciones for Venezuela; by Express Computer Distributors for the Caribbean and West Indies; by Micronesia Media Distributor, Inc. for Micronesia; by Chips Computadoras S.A. de C.V. for Mexico; by Editorial Norma de Panama S.A. for Panama; by American Bookshops for Finland.

For general information on Hungry Minds' products and services please contact our Customer Care department; within the U.S. at 800-762-2974, outside the U.S. at 317-572-3993 or fax 317-572-4002.

For sales inquiries and resellers information, including discounts, premium and bulk quantity sales and foreign language translations please contact our Customer Care department at 800-434-3422, fax 317-572-4002 or write to Hungry Minds, Inc., Attn: Customer Care department, 10475 Crosspoint Boulevard, Indianapolis, IN 46256.

For information on licensing foreign or domestic rights, please contact our Sub-Rights Customer Care department at 650-653-7098.

For information on using Hungry Minds' products and services in the classroom or for ordering examination copies, please contact our Educational Sales department at 800-434-2086 or fax 317-572-4005.

Please contact our Public Relations department at 212-884-5163 for press review copies or 212-884-5000 for author interviews and other publicity information or fax 212-884-5400.

For authorization to photocopy items for corporate, personal, or educational use, please contact Copyright Clearance Center, 222 Rosewood Drive, Danvers, MA 01923, or fax 978-750-4470.

Hungry Minds is a trademark of Hungry Minds, Inc.

About the Author

Liz Palika met her first reptile as a teenager when she brought home a long, sleek, black racer snake and her mother promptly locked her out of the house! That snake was immediately released back into the wild, but Liz's fascination with reptiles continued.

Today, Liz and her husband, Paul, take in numerous abandoned, neglected, or escaped turtles and tortoises. The chelonians are evaluated as to their state of health, nursed back to health, and then adopted to new homes. A few who need special care remain with Liz and Paul for as long as needed. A few stay forever! Onyx, a Gulf Coast box turtle, was the first chelonian taken in after Liz and Paul decided (almost 20 years ago) to do rescue work. Onyx was so personable and so old (she is ancient) that she has remained a permanent resident. She and seven of her offspring are the rulers of the box turtle outside enclosure. Besides Onyx's contribution to the world, the Palikas have established a breeding colony of leopard tortoises and a colony of sulcatas.

Liz is an award-winning author; her books have won honors from ASPCA, Purina, Dog Writers Association of America, Cat Writers Association, and the San Diego Book Writers. Her more than 30 nonfiction books include *The Consumer's Guide to Feeding Reptiles* (Howell Book House), *Your Bearded Dragon's Life* (Prima), *Your Iguana's Life* (Prima), and *The Leopard Tortoise; He said, She said* (Green Nature Books).

Author's Acknowledgments

First and foremost, I want to thank my husband, Paul Palika. He is so patient, following me to turtle and tortoise shows, educational seminars, and rescue group meetings. He puts up with turtle egg incubators on the kitchen counter, baby turtles in sweater boxes, and gigantic tortoises mowing the grass in the backyard. (Come to think of it, I think he actually likes the help with mowing!) He helps me dig up tortoise eggs when I holler for help. He has driven hours, one way, to help me pick up a tortoise hit by a car. His patience seems limitless. Thank you, Paul.

Thanks, too, to my sister Mary Welther and my friend Petra Horn. Both are also serving as board members for the Watachie Reptile, Turtle & Tortoise rescue group and, like my husband, have spent hours at seminars, meetings, and educational displays, answering thousands of questions about turtles and tortoises. Thank you, Mary and Petra; I couldn't do it without you!

Publisher's Acknowledgments

We're proud of this book; please send us your comments through our Online Registration Form located at www.dummies.com.

Some of the people who helped bring this book to market include the following:

Acquisitions, Editorial, and Media Development

Project Editors: Tere Drenth, Pamela Mourouzis

Acquiring Editor: Kira Sexton

Technical Reviewer: Richard C. Paull

Editorial Administrator: Michelle Hacker

Cover Photo: FPG International LLC/
   © Gary Randall

Production

Project Coordinator: Maridee Ennis

Layout and Graphics: Amy Adrian,
   LeAndra Johnson, Jackie Nicholas,
   Jacque Schneider, Jeremey Unger

Special Art: Kristin Doney, illustrator;
   Bill Love, color photographer

Proofreaders: Andy Hollandbeck,
   Susan Moritz, Nancy Price,
   York Production Services, Inc.

Indexer: York Production Services, Inc.

Hungry Minds Consumer Reference Group

   Business: Kathleen A. Welton, Vice President and Publisher; Kevin Thornton, Acquisitions Manager

   Cooking/Gardening: Jennifer Feldman, Associate Vice President and Publisher

   Education/Reference: Diane Graves Steele, Vice President and Publisher

   Lifestyles/Pets: Kathleen Nebenhaus, Vice President and Publisher; Tracy Boggier, Managing Editor

   Travel: Michael Spring, Vice President and Publisher; Suzanne Jannetta, Editorial Director; Brice Gosnell, Publishing Director

Hungry Minds Consumer Editorial Services: Kathleen Nebenhaus, Vice President and Publisher; Kristin A. Cocks, Editorial Director; Cindy Kitchel, Editorial Director

Hungry Minds Consumer Production: Debbie Stailey, Production Director

About Howell Book House

Committed to the Human/Companion Animal Bond

Thank you for choosing a book brought to you by the pet experts at Howell Book House, a division of Hungry Minds, Inc. And welcome to the family of pet owners who've put their trust in Howell books for nearly 40 years!

Pet ownership is about relationships — the bonds people form with their dogs, cats, horses, birds, fish, small mammals, reptiles, and other animals. Howell Book House/Hungry Minds understands that these are some of the most important relationships in life, and that it's vital to nurture them through enjoyment and education. The happiest pet owners are those who know they're taking the best care of their pets — and with Howell books owners have this satisfaction. They're happy, educated owners, and as a result, they have happy pets, and that enriches the bond they share.

Howell Book House was established in 1961 by Mr. Elsworth S. Howell, an active and proactive dog fancier who showed English Setters and judged at the prestigious Westminster Kennel Club show in New York. Mr. Howell based his publishing program on strength of content, and his passion for books written by experienced and knowledgeable owners defined Howell Book House and has remained true over the years. Howell's reputation as the premier pet book publisher is supported by the distinction of having won more awards from the Dog Writers Association of America than any other publisher. Howell Book House/Hungry Minds has over 400 titles in publication, including such classics as The American Kennel Club's *Complete Dog Book,* the *Dog Owner's Home Veterinary Handbook, Blessed Are the Brood Mares,* and *Mother Knows Best: The Natural Way to Train Your Dog.*

When you need answers to questions you have about any aspect of raising or training your companion animals, trust that Howell Book House/Hungry Minds has the answers. We welcome your comments and suggestions, and we look forward to helping you maximize your relationships with your pets throughout the years.

The Howell Book House Staff

Contents at a Glance

Cartoons at a Glance

By Rich Tennant

page 7

page 191

page 55

page 145

page 255

Cartoon Information:
Fax: 978-546-7747
E-Mail: richtennant@the5thwave.com
World Wide Web: www.the5thwave.com

Table of Contents

Introduction

●●●

As I sit in my backyard enjoying the flowers and the songbirds, something steps on my toes: something heavy and very hard. It's Pearl, my 35-pound leopard tortoise. As Pearl tries to climb up my leg, I hand her a rose blossom; after all, that's what she wants. I've had Pearl since she was a hatchling, and she's a bit spoiled. Pearl, who has beautiful cream-yellow coloring with black splotches, is bright, alert, vigorous, and healthy. (I'm especially proud of her being healthy because many people have a difficult time keeping leopard tortoises in good health.)

My addiction to turtles and tortoises began over 20 years ago when my husband and I adopted two desert tortoises. We soon became involved in turtle and tortoise adoption, joined several *herpetological societies* (groups of reptile and amphibian hobbyists) and turtle and tortoise clubs — things just seemed to escalate from there. We've discovered a lot over the years, and this book is a result of that education, giving you all the information you need to choose the right turtle or tortoise and keep him healthy and happy.

About This Book

In our turtle and tortoise rescue work, my husband and I took in many *chelonians* (turtles and tortoises) who had been cared for improperly — either kept in incorrect environmental conditions or fed an incorrect diet. We found that many people simply didn't know how to care for their turtles or tortoises or had been given the wrong instructions as to how to care for them.

If you're a beginning turtle and tortoise keeper, this book will get you started right. You can find out what you need to know to house, feed, care for your chelonian, and much, much more. You can even discover how to find a reptile veterinarian.

If you're more expert at keeping turtles and tortoises, you may find some of this information rather basic. But in these pages, you can still pick up some new ideas. As you probably already know, keeping reptiles is an ever-changing experience!

You can read this book cover to cover, but you don't have to use it that way. Instead, feel free to use this book as a reference. If you want to know something about a particular topic, go straight to that chapter for the information you need.

Conventions Used in This Book

Scientists have identified about a dozen different families of turtles and tortoises. All 250 different *species* (or types) of turtles and tortoises are identified by a common name, such as eastern box turtle, and a Latin scientific name, such as *Terrapene carolina carolina.* For simplicity's sake, I refer to the turtles and tortoises in this book by their common names. However, to keep misunderstandings and misidentifications to a minimum, I also have to give you the species Latin name. So, in the sections where I discuss specific species, I use both the common and the scientific names. Although the scientific names may seem quite complicated, they actually simplify identification sometimes. For example, several different types of tortoise have been called spur-thigh tortoises. However, if the particular tortoise is identified as a *Geochelone sulcata,* you know that this refers to the really big, 200-pound tortoises from Africa.

In addition, I show temperature in Fahrenheit, not Celsius. If you're used to the Celsius scale, use the following table to convert:

°F	°C	°F	°C
105	40.5	88	31.1
104	40.0	87	30.5
103	39.4	86	30.0
102	38.9	85	29.4
101	38.3	84	28.9
100	37.7	83	28.3
99	37.2	82	27.8
98	36.6	81	27.2
97	36.1	80	26.6
96	35.5	79	26.1
95	35.0	78	25.5
94	34.4	77	25.0
93	33.9	76	24.4
92	33.3	75	23.9
91	32.7	74	23.3
90	32.2	73	22.8
89	31.6	72	22.2

°F	°C	°F	°C
71	21.6	51	10.5
70	21.1	50	10.0
69	20.5	49	9.4
68	20.0	48	8.9
67	19.4	47	8.3
66	18.9	46	7.8
65	18.3	45	7.2
64	17.8	44	6.7
63	17.2	43	6.1
62	16.7	42	5.6
61	16.1	41	5.0
60	15.5	40	4.4
59	15.0	39	3.9
58	14.4	38	3.3
57	13.9	37	2.8
56	13.3	36	2.2
55	12.8	35	1.7
54	12.2	34	1.1
53	11.7	33	0.6
52	11.1	32	0.0

Foolish Assumptions

In writing this book, I made some foolish assumptions about you, dear reader:

- ✔ You may be considering buying a turtle or tortoise but don't know what species would be the right pet for you.
- ✔ You may be considering buying a turtle or tortoise but aren't quite sure what care he may need — you want to know what it will take to keep your pet healthy.

- ✔ You already have a turtle or tortoise (or two or three) and want to know more about caring for your pets.

- ✔ You found a turtle or tortoise wandering through the neighborhood or crossing the street and want to know more about the animal you found.

- ✔ You are a pet professional and want to get the lowdown on our shelled friends.

- ✔ Your kids have been bugging you for a turtle, and you want to know what you would be getting into prior to saying yes or no.

How This Book Is Organized

I've organized this book into five distinct parts, plus some appendixes and a colorful photo section. This section gives you the lowdown on what you can find in each part of this book.

Part 1: Deciding Whether a Turtle or Tortoise Is Right for You

Keeping a turtle or tortoise as a pet is different from keeping a dog or cat. This part helps you decide whether a turtle or tortoise is the right pet for you. In addition, you find out how to choose between a turtle and a tortoise — and how to choose the right one for you and your family. I also talk about whether you should keep one, two, or three turtles or tortoises — after all, they can be addictive!

Part 11: The Who's Who of Turtles and Tortoises

This part describes some of the most popular species of pet turtles and tortoises: where they came from and how much care they need. You can find information about aquatic turtles, who spend most or all of their time in the water; semi-aquatic turtles, who spend most, but not all, of their time in the water; semi-terrestrial turtles, who spend most of their time on land but do go into the water; and last but certainly not least, terrestrial turtles, who spend most of their time on land. Not all turtles are alike; in fact, some are more different than alike. Before you choose a turtle, you need to know something about them.

Tortoises vary from tiny little guys who weigh less than 1 pound to great big giants weighing 500 or 600 pounds! Some are colored with earth tones and subdued markings, while others are bright yellow and black. Tortoises are more similar than different, especially when compared to the varieties of turtles; however, they do have individual needs.

Part III: Welcome Home! Creating a Safe and Healthy Environment

This part explains what your turtle or tortoise needs for a cage, aquarium, terrarium, or outside enclosure. I take a look at the pros and cons of various types of cages and enclosures and show you how to choose the right one. This part is the place to find out about heat — how to supply it and why it's important. I also discuss lighting, humidity, water, and a number of other important concerns.

Part IV: Open Wide! Turtle and Tortoise Health

How do you know whether your turtle or tortoise is healthy? What are some signs of illness? In this part, you discover how to take care of your turtle or tortoise's health as well as how to recognize potential problems. I also discuss about how to find a veterinarian who can help you care for your shelled pet, how to figure out what to feed your chelonian, how to help your pet hibernate, and how to decide whether to breed your turtle or tortoise.

Part V: The Part of Tens

This part is full of little bits of information, from the ten best turtle and tortoise pets to ten not-so-great pets to ten common mistakes that turtle and tortoise owners make. You can also find ten tips on how to keep your turtle or tortoise healthy and safe.

Appendixes

Appendixes are like parting gifts that you get just for showing up. The glossary defines all those somewhat mysterious terms — such as *carapace* (the top shell), *plastron* (the bottom shell), and *ectothermic* (cold-blooded) — used in the text. The resource list shows you some places to continue your research and includes some Internet sites that provide good information.

Color photo section

The color photo section gives you eight pages of brightly colored turtles and tortoises that are fascinating to look at. Whether you're deciding which type of turtle to purchase or you've had tortoises wandering your backyard for years, the color photo section is sure to inspire you.

Icons Used in This Book

Icons, little pictures in the margins of this book, are meant to guide you to information that's specific to your needs. Here's what they mean:

The tips, tricks, and techniques that this icon highlights make life with your pet turtle or tortoise a little more enjoyable.

This icon points out bits of information that you'll want to store in the back of your mind. Think of this icon as the literary equivalent of sticking an interesting article to your refrigerator door.

Turtles and tortoises can be pretty easy to take care of, but this icon tells you when to proceed with caution.

This icon directs you to in-depth information that's meant for the turtle geek in you. Feel free to skip these if you want to.

Where to Go from Here

If you're thinking about getting a turtle or tortoise and need all the information you can get, start at the beginning of this book and work your way through it. If you have a turtle or tortoise and are confused by some of the conflicting advice you've seen or read, read carefully through the specific chapters that answer your questions. If you're a turtle and tortoise owner already and you need to research a few different subjects, go for it! Take a peek at the index or table of contents and then start wherever you want.

Part I

Deciding Whether a Turtle or Tortoise Is Right for You

The 5th Wave   By Rich Tennant

"I'll have the baked ziti, and just the salad bar for my tortoise."

In this part . . .

Do you enjoy the unusual? Do you treasure the different and unique? Do you like causing a reaction? If you answer "Yes!" to these questions, you probably enjoy different pets, too. Not the average Joe Dog or Miss Kitty for you!

If you enjoy the different and unusual, a turtle or tortoise may just be the right pet for you. However, you need to think about some things before you go shopping.

The four chapters in this part can answer all your questions. What are turtles and tortoises? What can you expect from a turtle as a pet? What does turtle ownership require of you? How much time does turtle ownership require? What type of turtle or tortoise is right for you? Where can you buy your new pet? And much, much more.

Chapter 1

Understanding Chelonians

*W*hen you think of turtles, do you think of the tiny quarter or half-dollar–sized turtles that used to be sold in pet stores (and in some places still are)? If so, you're not alone. That image is the one that comes to mind when many people think of turtles. However, those tiny little turtles (most of whom died shortly after their purchase) are only one of many different types of turtles and tortoises, many of which can be long-lived, healthy, hearty pets.

Turtles and tortoises are known as chelonians, from the Greek word for "tortoise," *chelona. Chelonian* refers to all turtles and tortoises, no matter whether they live in the ocean, in fresh water, or on land.

✔ The term *turtles* applies to chelonians that live in or around water. Sea turtles, for example, never leave the ocean except to lay their eggs. Other turtles are more or less aquatic, depending on their species. The sliders, mud, bog, and leaf turtles are all found close to fresh water. Terrapins are aquatic turtles that people frequently eat. Many terrapins live in and close to brackish salt water. Box turtles are primarily *terrestrial* (land roving) but are almost always found within walking distance of water. See Figure 1-1 for an example of a turtle.

✔ The term *tortoise* refers to chelonians that live on land and rarely venture into water except to drink or bathe. Tortoises range in size from tiny little guys weighing less than 1 pound to gigantic, weighing over 600 (or more) pounds. Size aside, tortoises have many things in common. They are primarily *herbivores* (plant eaters), although many will scavenge, given the chance. Tortoises also usually have hard shells, often with high domes, to help protect against predators. Take a look at Figure 1-2.

Figure 1-1:
A turtle.

Figure 1-2:
A tortoise.

In this book, I focus on the species of turtles and tortoises best suited for pet ownership. Although more than 250 different species of chelonians exist, many are impossible to keep as pets. Think of the size aquarium and the filtration system you would need to keep a 200-pound green sea turtle! However, many species of turtles and tortoises do quite well in captivity and make good pets.

Understanding Life in the Original Mobile Home

Turtles and tortoises are in the reptile family, which means that they are *ectothermic,* or cold-blooded. Cold-blooded animals rely on external heat sources, such as warm ground, hot rocks, or sunshine, to warm their bodies. Turtles are the original sun worshippers and can often be found sleeping on rocks or logs, soaking up the sun's rays.

All turtles and tortoises share a similar characteristic: their shell. No other animal on Earth has a shell quite like this. A turtle's shell is a boxlike *exoskeleton* (a word that refers to a part of an external skeleton) with the spine and ribs fused to the top shell. These bones are, in fact, a part of the *carapace,* or top shell. The shell itself is made of bone, and the outer covering of the shell is made of *keratin,* much like human fingernails.

Each shell is made up of sections called *scutes.* As the turtle grows, new layers of keratin are formed around the outer edges of each scute, looking much like the growth rings of a tree. Some people count each of these rings in an effort to tell how old a turtle may be. This can give only a rough idea, however, because just like a tree, if food is plentiful a turtle may have two growth spurts per year, or in a bad year may grow very little. Also, as a turtle gets older, the shell becomes worn and smooth, and the rings may be difficult to see.

The type of shell and the degree of protection offered by the shell are based on the turtle's lifestyle and habitat. Sea turtles, for example, have a light, streamlined shell covered by a leathery skin. Freshwater turtles usually have a hard shell, but in some species, it's too small to protect the entire body. Land turtles and tortoises that rely on the shell for protection have a hard, domed shell.

The stay-at-home type

When Zeus held his wedding feast, all the animals were invited. Only the tortoise arrived too late. Zeus wanted to know why, so he asked her the next day why she was the only one who did not arrive in time for the banquet. Her answer was, "My house is dear to me; my house is the best." Zeus was angry at her answer and ordained that the tortoise should always have to carry her house around with her. In just this way, many people prefer to dwell simply under their own roofs rather than live luxuriously in the homes of friends. (from *Aesop's Fables*)

This turtleneck comes in green

When a turtle pulls its head into its shell for protection, its neck either folds to the side or into a vertical S shape, and the skin of its neck bunches up — hence the name *turtleneck* for shirts and sweaters with bunched-up necks.

Many turtles and tortoises can pull in all four legs and their head so that the shell protects them from predators. With many species, the outer skin of the legs is hard, rough, and, in some tortoises, armored, giving the turtle even more protection.

Some turtles and tortoises can even close their shell, giving additional protection. Box turtles (hence their name) have a hinge across the bottom shell (the *plastron*). This hinge can close both front and rear, hiding the turtle completely inside. The muscles holding the shell closed are incredibly tough, and after the hinge is shut, you can't open it without harming the turtle. A type of tortoise can close its shell, too, although not as completely as the box turtle. Hinge-back tortoises have a hinge across the top of their top shell (the *carapace*) and can close in their back legs, protecting them.

Although the shell, made of bone, seems to be the ultimate protection, it is vulnerable. Predators can chew and break the shell. A larger bird of prey can pick up a small turtle and, flying high, drop the turtle on rocks below, breaking the turtle's shell like an egg. The shell can protect a tortoise from a small, fast-moving wildfire, but larger, hotter fires will kill a turtle or tortoise caught in it. Domestic dogs — Fido and Fluffy — have been know to treat turtles like chew toys, with disastrous results!

The skin on the legs of tortoises is hard, with scales made of keratin protecting it. Some of the keratin scales are quite large and pronounced; on some species, the scales create spurs or spikes that help protect the tortoise from predators and also help desert tortoises retain water. Because aquatic turtles usually dive into water when threatened, their skin is much softer with fewer protective scales. Most turtles and tortoises have five toes (although they sometimes have four or as few as three) with hard nails on the toes. Aquatic turtles have webbing between their toes.

Most chelonians have a birdlike beak, which enables them to bite off chunks of food. They don't have teeth, but hard, bony plates enable them to *masticate* (chew) their food. Most food, however, is swallowed whole.

TECHNICAL STUFF

Survivors from the age of dinosaurs

Turtle (and tortoise) fossils have been found linking them to the Mesozoic era in the Triassic period. Because of the mass of bone found in the shell, finding fossilized tortoises is actually quite common (compared to finding other creatures of the same size and era).

This Triassic turtle, called *Triassochelys dux*, is remarkably similar to turtles found today. It had an armored shell with ridges, tough skin with spurs, and spinelike projections on the tail. One marked difference, though, was that this turtle had teeth, whereas today's turtles have hard bony mouths or beaks instead of functional teeth.

The Cretaceous period, when dinosaurs became extinct, was the age of sea turtles. The turtles of this era had large gaps in the bony mass of their shells, making the shells lighter for swimming. The largest marine turtle ever found came from this era. The *Archelon ischyros* had a carapace measuring over 18 feet!

Toward the end of the Mesozoic era, land tortoises developed. In what is today central Europe, land tortoises evolved that look much like tortoises found in Indochina today. These tortoises had (and have) thick bony shells.

It is probably totally scientifically incorrect, but I can picture in my mind a gigantic dinosaur, looking like something out of the movie *Jurassic Park,* striding along, roaring and drooling, while at its feet a herbivorous tortoise munches calmly on greens!

Treasuring the Unusual

Most tortoise owners seem to enjoy the fact that their pets are different. Obviously, your tortoise won't chase a tennis ball like Fido will, but that's okay because your tortoise is different. Because turtles and tortoises came in a variety of sizes, shapes, and colors from an assortment of environments, there's something for everyone willing to care for them.

- ✔ The Spix's snake-necked turtle *(Platemys spixii)* is from eastern Brazil and has a black plastron, a long, heavily armored neck (complete with spikes), and a face that looks like a fish's.

- ✔ The big-headed turtle *(Platysternon megacephalum)* has such a large head — out of proportion to the rest of its body — that it can't retract its head fully into its shell. The big-headed turtle also has powerful jaws and has been known to bite.

- ✔ Side-neck turtles have exceptionally long necks; a few have necks as long as the rest of their bodies. The matamata *(Chelus fimbriatus)* has a long neck and a long nose that it uses as a snorkel. The matamata eats whole fish, using its powerful neck to help reach, grab, and subdue its prey.

> ✔ Box turtles don't vary much in size or physical conformation, but their colors can be quite striking. Some have yellow or red spots, stripes, or patterns on the skin and yellow or gold patterns on their shells. Red-eared sliders *(Trachemys scripta elegans),* western painted turtles *(Chrysemys picta belli),* and eastern painted turtles *(Chrysemys picta picta)* can be quite colorful and striking.

If you enjoy and treasure the unusual, you can find a turtle or tortoise that will strike your fancy.

Make sure that you don't choose a turtle or tortoise entirely for its looks, markings, or body conformation. Many turtles or tortoises require special conditions or care. You need to understand what this particular species requires before you add it to your family. See Part II for information on many species of turtles and tortoises.

Battling Extinction

Over the centuries, turtles and tortoises have evolved on every continent except Antarctica. Temperate or tropical climates are most popular, with southern North America, South America, Africa, southern Europe, and Asia being home to the most numerous species.

Although turtles and tortoises have flourished for millions of years, their future survival is not so certain. Many species have been wiped out or threatened with extinction because they have been used as food sources, or their eggs are routinely dug up and eaten.

Habitat destruction has threatened many species. Many South American tropical turtles and tortoises have been killed during the destruction of rainforests. In North America, gopher tortoises in the south and desert tortoises in the west are finding it harder and harder to survive as more people move into their territories. The situation is no different in Africa, Europe, or Asia.

In many parts of the world, warfare is killing turtles and tortoises. Landmines blow up tortoises as well as people. Tanks and heavy vehicles crush tortoises and collapse burrows. Vegetation necessary for survival is destroyed. During times of famine, a heavy tortoise is food for the hungry.

Future survival may be based on humankind's ability to step in and change what's happening now in many parts of the world. If sections of land can be set aside as preserves and protected from poaching, some species may be able to survive. Captive breeding populations may also hold hope for the future. Some species breed quite well in captivity, and the offspring of these turtles and tortoises may prevent some species from disappearing entirely.

Dwindling numbers

The California desert tortoise *(Gopherus agassizii)* used to range the Mexico, California, Arizona, Utah, and Nevada deserts in great numbers. This medium to large sized tortoise could live and even thrive in the hostile deserts. Unfortunately, loss of habitat and off-road recreational vehicles have threatened this hardy tortoise. An equally dangerous but much less visible threat is a respiratory infection known to infect most captive desert tortoises. This potentially fatal disease is treatable with antibiotics but is not curable, and has been spread to the wild population by captive tortoises set free by caring but ignorant owners.

Captive breeding can serve another purpose: to provide the pet-owning public with a source of animals already adapted to captivity. When wild-caught turtles and tortoises are captured, transported, and then sold to pet owners, the animals are traumatized. They have been removed from their natural habitat, stored somewhere (during which time they were probably not fed, or at least not properly fed), shipped one, two, or even three times, and then held again at the pet store or animal dealer's facility. When the unsuspecting pet owner brings home this traumatized turtle or tortoise, the chelonian may or may not adapt to its new home. As a result, say many experts, fully 90 percent of wild-caught chelonians die within their first year of captivity.

However, when chelonians are bred in captivity, they grow up exposed to people, the foods normally fed in captivity, and captive conditions. These turtles may feel some stress at shipping and during changes in their environment, but after they're sold, they are then re-exposed to what are, to them, normal captive conditions. They experience far less stress and thus have a greater chance for survival. Captive breeding also produces more animals for the pet market, reducing the need for animals to be caught in the wild. If more people request captive-bred animals and refuse to buy wild-caught animals, there will be again less need to capture chelonians in the wild.

The tortoises on the Galapagos Islands are a good example of the good that captive breeding can do. By the late 1960s, the number of Galapagos Islands tortoises was decreasing rapidly. Harvesting by sailors took a great many tortoises, but the introduction of feral cats, goats, rats, dogs, and other predators was decimating entire *clutches* (litters, with all eggs laid at one time) of eggs as well as any hatchlings that managed to finish incubation. The future looked bleak.

However, the Charles Darwin Research Station was built on Santa Cruz Island, and the remaining 14 Hood Island tortoises — all that remained of that subspecies — were relocated to the station. In 1971, the first eggs were incubated. Young hatchlings (of Hood Islands tortoises and other island subspecies) were *head-started* — fed regularly and grown to a size that can survive most predators — and then relocated to their ancestors' islands. Although some Galapagos subspecies are still decreasing in number, others are now thriving thanks to captive breeding.

Turtles in mythology, legend, and art

Turtles and tortoises have had a special place in many ancient cultures. In China, in 2,500 B.C., the symbol of a snake entwined with a tortoise was said to protect against evil spirits. The Emperor Hwang-ti had flags with this symbol lead and follow his armies to protect them from danger.

Eastern mythology said that the Earth was supported by a tortoise. East Indian legends said that a tortoise supported an elephant, which in turn supported the Earth. In Japan, the tortoise carried the mountain Horai (the home of the immortals) on its back. Also in Japan, turtles were considered symbols of happiness and good fortune, primarily because of their longevity. Tortoise art was frequently given at weddings to wish the newlyweds long life and happiness.

The legend of extreme longevity isn't true for all turtles and tortoises but certainly is deserved by some. The explorer Captain Cook is reputed to have given the King of Tonga a radiated tortoise. When the tortoise died, it is said to have been at least 189 years old. French explorer Marion de Fresne planted five Seychelles tortoises on the island of Mauritius in 1776. The last of these five died in 1918. The turtle had been in captivity for at least 152 years and was an adult when taken into captivity, so this chelonian may have been over 200 years old.

Perhaps because of their longevity, several cultures also associate tortoises with reincarnation. In one South American legend, if a person who was dying was laid on or next to a special tortoise's shell, the spirit of that person would live on and be transferred to a living person. In a Native American legend, a giant water turtle leads the dying person to his or her next lifetime.

Some Native Americans compare the tortoise shell with the night sky. The three bright stars that make up Orion's belt highlight the tortoise's back. In the story, these three stars, because they are always present, show the traveler the way home.

Turtles and tortoises also appear in many art forms, including paintings and sculptures. The favorite art form for turtles and tortoises seems to be that of small storage boxes, with the back shell coming off to reveal a storage area inside. Turtles and tortoises have also been depicted on stamps and coins: Japan released a nature conservation series of postcards with stamps, the ninth issue of which features a Spengler's turtle; Cuba, Vietnam, Yugoslavia, and Italy all released stamps with sea turtles on them; and Brazil, Kenya, the Cayman Islands, New Guinea, and several other countries released stamps with a variety of different species featured. The Fiji Islands released a sixpence coin with a loggerhead turtle on it. The Cayman Islands issued a 10 cent piece with a green turtle, and the Tonga Islands featured a radiated tortoise on a 1 senti coin.

Collections of turtles and tortoises in ceramic, porcelain, glass, and stone are still very popular. Modern depictions may be realistic, down to the small details in the scutes or skin wrinkles, or may be funny, with the turtles or tortoises having exaggerated characteristics. Some collections include hundreds or even thousands of chelonians.

The African spur-thigh tortoise, commonly called a sulcata *(Geochelone sulcata),* was rarely found in the pet trade as little as 20 years ago. Today, breeders have successfully raised generations of these large, friendly, and active tortoises. Although their survival in the wild in question, these tortoises will survive in captivity.

Making a Difference by Preserving Turtles and Tortoises

When I adopted those two desert tortoises many years ago, I did so because I knew that they were threatened in their native habitat (in this case, the Mojave Desert of California). I was doing something to help, and I felt good about that.

In today's society, we feel a little helpless sometimes. With so many problems in the world, we can do so little to change things. Sure, we can recycle. We can conserve gas. We can build a compost pile in the backyard. We can try to raise our kids right so that they don't contribute to the problems of our world. But even while I was doing those things, I often asked myself, "Isn't there something else I can do?"

By myself, I can't save a rainforest or prevent a highway from going through delicate desert lands. But by taking in those two misplaced, threatened tortoises, incubating their eggs, and raising their babies, I actually felt like I was doing something real to save a threatened species.

Since then, my husband and I have concentrated on five threatened species: two from North America, one from Eurasia, and two from Africa. We have had breeding success with two species and have enjoyed watching the babies grow and develop. The individuals from the three species that have not yet bred are still young but are healthy, active, and showing breeding behaviors, so we're anticipating the day when they, too, reproduce.

I can't think of much of anything that's more exciting than watching a baby turtle or tortoise break open its shell. A perfect miniature of the adult, complete with tiny little toenails, a baby turtle or tortoise from a threatened species is hope for the future. Chapter 21 shares more information about breeding.

The Tortoise and the Hare

Nearly every child reads the story called *The Tortoise and the Hare*. This fable from Aesop appears to have had its origins in African legends. In the African story, an eagle and a tortoise race to win the hand in marriage of a fair young woman. The tortoise won through prior planning, intelligence, and deceit and suffers for using deceit by being banned to the ocean forever — hence the origin of marine turtles. In the modern version, the tortoise wins due to hard work, steadiness, and reliability, whereas the hare takes his abilities for granted, goofs off, and, as a result, loses the race.

Chapter 2

Understanding What Turtle and Tortoise Ownership Requires of You

A lot of people come by their first turtle or tortoise accidentally. Perhaps you wandered into a pet store to look at that cute little puppy in the window and happened to see a baby turtle that was "Oh so cute!" I got my first two tortoises when I answered an ad in the paper to adopt rescued desert tortoises. Those first two, more years ago than I would like to admit, were the start of an addiction. And turtle and tortoise ownership really is addictive.

But before you get addicted, you need to know what turtle and tortoise ownership is all about. Owning one (or two or three) of these creatures is different from owning a dog or cat. Turtle or tortoise ownership makes some demands on you — for your attention, your time, and your pocketbook. Many a new pet owner has bought an inexpensive small turtle only to find out that the small turtle requires a large aquarium, a complicated filtration system, lights, heat, and food. What was at first glance an inexpensive pet turned into quite a financial investment.

Before you add a turtle or tortoise to your household, make sure that you can — and are willing to — do what's necessary for your pet. What is required, really, to care for turtles? I have a 20-gallon-long aquarium set up for box turtle hatchlings. I have potting soil in the bottom, several potted house-plants, and a plant saucer for water. Daily care includes the following: In the morning, I turn on the lights, wash the water bowl, refill it with clean water, and feed the baby turtles. In the evening, I turn off the lights, remove uneaten food, and wash the saucer on which the food was served. Several times a week, I go out in the backyard and hunt for insects for the turtles to chase and eat. Once every two weeks, I totally clean the enclosure, including replacing the potting soil and washing the glass.

Unless you live alone, you must include your family in your decision whether to keep turtles or tortoises as pets. Although chelonians are quiet pets that won't jump on someone's lap or bark at the neighbors, they do require care and attention, and they can make a mess. There are also some potential problems, especially the threat of salmonella, associated with owning a turtle. If a family member objects to the turtle or tortoise, life could become difficult, especially for the turtle or tortoise, and that isn't fair. All family members (or roommates) need to agree to the new pet before you add a turtle or tortoise to your household.

Growing Old Together

Turtle and tortoise ownership is a long-term commitment; hopefully, the two of you can grow old together. Many turtles and tortoises are known to live for 75 to 100 years or even longer. The following are some known or estimated life expectancies:

- Aldabran tortoise (*Geochelone gigantea* or *Aldabrachelys gigantea*): 200+ years
- American box turtles *(Terrapene carolina):* 75 to 125+ years
- Bolson tortoise *(Gopherus flavomarginatus):* 60 to 90 years
- California desert tortoise *(Gopherus agassizii):* 60 to 90 years
- Eastern painted turtle *(Chrysemys picta picta):* 30 to 50 years
- Florida gopher tortoise *(Gopherus polyphemus):* 60 to 90 years
- Galapagos giant tortoises *(Geochelone elephatopus):* 100 to 200+ years
- Leopard tortoise *(Geochelone pardalis):* 75 to 100 years
- Radiated tortoise *(Geochelone radiata):* 90 to 100+ years
- Red-eared slider *(Trachemys scripta elegans):* 30 to 50 years
- Western painted turtle *(Chrysemys picta belli):* 30 to 50 years

Because many species are new to science or have just recently been bred in captivity, no one really knows how long they can live. With new knowledge about nutrition, their environmental needs, and breeding, scientists may find that many species live even longer than was first thought.

Because of this, when you decide to add a turtle or tortoise to your household, you must be prepared to keep and care for this living creature for a long time. If you get a turtle and then find you can no longer keep her, finding a home for an adult turtle or tortoise can be very difficult, if not impossible. As with many pets, most buyers want a young animal. Many people assume that their local zoo will take their treasured turtle or tortoise, but that isn't necessarily so. Most zoos refuse to accept pet turtles or tortoises: Zoos concentrating on breeding threatened or endangered animals want, for the most part, *known* animals. That means the exact bloodline (pedigree or genealogy) and species or subspecies must be known for the animal. An unknown may also introduce disease or parasites to the zoo population.

Something else you need to think about is who will care for your tortoises when you have grown old and can no longer care for them. In California, thousands of desert tortoises live in captivity, and many of those thousands have been passed down from parents to children to grandchildren.

To protect my tortoises, I have been indoctrinating my nephew Alan to the uniqueness and special qualities of turtles and tortoises. When he comes to visit, he wants to visit the tortoises in the backyard first, and then he greets the rest of the family. His mother thinks it's rude, but this pleases me to no end! If he continues to treasure them as I hope he will, I won't have to worry about my pets in the future. Meanwhile, a special clause in my will specifies my instructions as to how to care for my turtles and tortoises should something happen to me.

Managing Expenses

Turtle and tortoise ownership does require a financial commitment, as this section describes.

Some turtles are very affordable; you can probably find a young red-eared slider *(Trachemys scripta elegans)* for $10 to $30. A small, captive-bred eastern box turtle *(Terrapene carolina carolina)* may run $20 to $40 in those states where selling them is legal.

Most tortoises will cost you more, but some are still quite reasonable. A young captive-bred sulcata *(Geochelone sulcata)* will probably sell for $50 to $200. A juvenile leopard tortoise *(Geochelone pardalis)* will go for $100 to $150. Many tortoises are much more expensive, however. A beautiful radiated tortoise *(Geochelone radiata)* may cost you $1,000 to $5,000, and a star tortoise *(Geochelone elegans)* may cost $500 to $3,000. And the purchase price of the turtle or tortoise is just the beginning of your expenses!

An aquatic turtle needs an aquarium — a minimum 20-gallon tank for a small turtle — to live in. This tank needs to be furnished with a strong filtration system that can keep up with the messes turtles can make. The aquarium also needs a water heater, a cover, and a light. Depending on the size of the aquarium, you can purchase this setup for $100 or $200 and up. (See Chapter 13 for more on aquariums.)

Tortoises need a different type of cage, although a very young or small tortoise can live in a dry aquarium until she outgrows it (see Chapter 14). Most tortoises need a cage much larger than most aquariums. A general rule says that a tortoise needs, at a minimum, 3 square yards of space for every 12 inches of length. The cage also needs a heat source or two (see Chapter 17), a cover, and a light (discussed in Chapter 16).

Some terrestrial turtles and tortoises do better outside (see Chapter 15). They need a secure, escape-proof enclosure with either wooden or concrete block walls. Rarely is the fence around your yard secure enough (or strong enough) to keep a turtle or tortoise safe.

Daily upkeep costs money, too. Aquatic turtles eat some plant material but also need protein foods: live fish, worms, trout chow, and a balanced turtle food. If you live in a temperate climate, tortoises can graze in the backyard but also need a selection of vegetables and tortoise food to eat. Turtles and tortoises need vitamin and mineral supplements added to their food on a regular basis.

Something else you may not have thought about is your utility bill. The heat lamp over a tortoise uses a lot of power. The water heater, filtration system, and light on an aquatic turtle's aquarium use electricity, too, which will show up on your bill! If you add multiple turtles and tortoises to your family, you may greatly increase your power usage.

You may also need to budget for occasional visits to the veterinarian. Although turtles and tortoises are, for the most part, fairly healthy and hearty, they do get hurt or sick sometimes. It's a good idea to have a veterinarian on call who specializes in reptiles, including turtles and tortoises.

Making Sure That Your Significant Other Is on Board

My husband and I share our home with many pets: We have dogs and cats and share equally in their care. Reptiles, however, are a little different. The turtles and tortoises are mine, and the iguanas are his. I am responsible for all of the care, feeding, and cleaning of my pets, and he takes care of his. However, we have agreed that prior to adding any additional pets, we will consult with one another.

If we each take care of our own, why do we make a point of asking about new ones? We do so for several reasons. First, each additional pet is a potential financial obligation. Feeding and caring for a pet takes money, as does veterinary care. Also, if I'm sick or out of town, he has to take care of my pets, and I do the same for him in similar circumstances. Also, either one of us could easily turn our home into a zoo (more so than it already is!). Together, we can work as a balance and counterbalance to make sure that we can take care of the animals we have.

Before you add a turtle or tortoise to your family, make sure that your significant other is aware of and approves of your plans. Share with him or her what you know about the pet you want, what the costs will be, what care the chelonian will need, where you will keep your pet, and how your new turtle or tortoise will affect your life. In most instances, it's better to prepare your significant other ahead of time for the realities of turtle ownership than to sneak your new pet in, hoping that he or she won't notice!

Coexisting with Other Pets

Many pet owners have a number of different pets because they love animals in all their assorted sizes, shapes, and personalities, much like my husband and I do. We have dogs, cats, turtles, tortoises, and iguanas, as well as other small reptiles. However, you must take some precautions if you share your home with a variety of pets.

Dogs, cats, and ferrets are predators — something you must keep in mind in regard to your other pets. Although cats are no danger to larger tortoises, cats can easily torture and kill small turtles, hatchling turtles, and hatchling tortoises. Ferrets, too, are small but have sharp teeth and can be quite tenacious.

Dogs are a bigger danger. Not only can a medium-sized to large dog kill small turtles and tortoises, dogs have also been known to kill or severely injure larger tortoises. Dogs can, and do, cause so much damage that many turtle and tortoise rescue organizations won't allow families with dogs to adopt their turtles or tortoises. Dogs, turtles, and tortoises can live together peacefully, though, if you take the time to safeguard your turtles and tortoises and train your dog.

Aquatic turtles who live inside your house in an aquarium are pretty safe from your other pets. A cat may play pat-pat on the glass, but that will be as far as most cats will push it. Other chelonians living in the house will also be safe as long as their aquarium(s), cage(s), and enclosure(s) are covered securely. Also, make sure that the cage is secure enough that a dog can't push it over.

Find the turtle, Ursa!

I have trained one of my dogs to help me with my turtles and tortoises. Ursa, an Australian Shepherd, helps me find hidden turtles. When I tell her, "Find the turtle!" she uses her sense of smell and finds all the turtles in the turtle yard. If I have an escapee or can't locate all the turtles, she finds them for me. Her sense of smell is so good that she has found newly hatched babies, buried eggs, and turtles hidden under leaves, buried in the ground, and burrowed under firewood. When she finds a turtle, she takes me to the turtle rather than trying to pick the chelonian up.

If you have turtles and tortoises outside and your dog normally spends time outside, too, take some precautions. I have a securely fenced turtle yard. The dogs can look in and the tortoises can look out, but the two are separated and therefore protected from each other — see Figure 2-1.

Figure 2-1:
Keep dogs and chelonians separated by a fence.

Don't assume that your friendly, well-behaved pooch won't bother your turtle. To most dogs, especially the ones left at home alone all day while you're at work, a turtle or tortoise is simply another toy. Your chelonian is something to play with, something to occupy your dog's time until you come home. The dog doesn't know that chewing on a turtle's shell or legs will kill the turtle!

All my dogs have been raised with tortoises. In fact, some of my tortoises are older than my oldest dog. My dogs have been trained to ignore the tortoises. When I'm at home and can supervise, the dogs are allowed in the yard with the tortoises while the tortoises graze on the grass. However, I don't allow myself to forget for even a moment that my well-trained, wonderful dogs are predators by nature, and I make sure that my tortoises are safe and secure in their own yard, away from the dogs, when I'm not there to supervise.

Mixing Chelonians and Children

During the television and movie days of the *Ninja Turtle* superheroes, thousands of children wanted turtles as pets. After they got the turtles, though, the kids found out that the turtles couldn't perform martial arts, didn't live in a sewer, and weren't in any shape or form superheroes. Not only that, the turtles didn't like pizza!

Although many kids had their bubbles burst by the realization that television and movies aren't real life, the turtles suffered even more. Thousands of small turtles were cared for improperly and died at the hands of children whose parents didn't supervise them.

I started doing turtle and tortoise rescue work during the height of the *Ninja Turtle* craze. Some weeks, I accepted 10 to 12 small turtles from people — usually the parents of small children — who no longer wanted them. Many of these turtles had cracked or broken shells because the kids were trying to get them to perform martial arts. Other turtles had holes drilled in their shells, were malnourished, or were suffering from neglect.

Some experts say that over 90 percent of all turtles die within their first year of captivity. That is a horrible statistic, especially when you consider that many turtles are relatively easy to keep as pets. Because of this, a turtle should never be considered a child's pet. The child may enjoy watching the turtle, or perhaps feeding her under a parent's supervision, but the child shouldn't care for or handle the turtle without supervision. The danger to the turtle is too great.

Turtles also pose some risks to the child. Most box turtles, for example, will eat just about anything placed in front of them and, in the wild, aren't at all hesitant about eating fruits, plants, berries, insects, eggs, or small rodents. A box turtle may bite a small child's finger, not out of aggressiveness but because it looks like something good to eat.

Although very few turtles or tortoises are aggressive, a few may bite accidentally or in self-defense. Unfortunately, after a turtle or tortoise bites, getting your finger back may be very difficult! Even if the bite hurts (and it will!), don't try to wrestle with the turtle. If frightened, the turtle will withdraw her head, taking your finger with it. Instead, try to hold still; as soon as the turtle realizes that she bit you instead of dinner, she'll let go.

The common snapping turtle *(Chelydra serpentina)* and the alligator snapping turtle *(Macroclemmys temmincki)* are two turtles who bite, sometimes quite readily. These two species aren't suitable pets, not just because they bite — and bite hard! — but because they grow quite large (especially the alligator snapping turtle) and have specific care needs that can be difficult for the average turtle owner to provide.

> ### *Ninja Turtle* craze in France
>
> During the early 1990s *Teenage Mutant Ninja Turtle* craze, an estimated 300,000 to 1 million red-eared sliders *(Trachemys scripta elegans)* were imported to French pet shops from the United States. When the kids got tired of the turtles, they were released into local waterways, where they now thrive.

Children can learn a lot from pet ownership. Watching a turtle or tortoise can connect a child to the natural world in a way that television never can. However, even the most responsible child should never be left in sole charge of a turtle or tortoise. A parent must always supervise the relationship and be ultimately responsible for the health of the child and the reptile.

Recognizing That Chelonians Aren't Soft and Fuzzy

Do you like to cuddle with your pets? Turtles and tortoises aren't particularly cuddly; in fact, some don't care for cuddling at all. In the wild, when another creature touches a turtle or tortoise, that contact usually constitutes a threat. A turtle and tortoise may *hiss* (expelling the air from its lungs) and draw in its head anytime something moves toward it. Tortoises rarely bite, and when they do, it's usually an accident — perhaps grabbing your finger when eating something from your hand. Many turtles, however, actively defend themselves against a *perceived* threat — which may be you!

In captivity, especially with captive-bred turtles and tortoises, individuals may get used to being touched but rarely solicit touching. My leopard tortoises will put up with having their heads rubbed in exchange for a strawberry. However, my Russian tortoises are an example of a species that sometimes likes touching; in their case, all four are captive-bred tortoises who have been touched gently and carefully from the time they hatched.

Too much touching of an animal that doesn't appreciate it results in stress. If an individual feels threatened by touching and petting, it may refuse to eat, may withdraw into its shell for long periods, and may even die from the stress.

However, you can gain considerable satisfaction simply by watching a turtle or tortoise live her life, especially when you're a vital part of that animal's survival. I really enjoy watching my tortoises. Watching them eat, explore their environment, react to each other, bask in the sun, and even sleep can be therapeutic for me. When the world around me is busy and frantic, the slow pace of these animals is so relaxing! I enjoy watching their personalities develop, too. When I offer them different foods, I can see how each tortoise approaches something new. Some are eager to sniff, taste, and eat new things. Others are more reserved and cautious. There's also nothing like watching a baby turtle or tortoise hatch that has come from your pets, that you have incubated. Such a tiny, perfect little life is absolutely amazing!

So if you need a pet that will allow you to pet her several times a day, get something other than a turtle or tortoise. However, if you can be satisfied with minimal touching but maximum observation, and if you will take pleasure in watching your turtles or tortoises live their lives, perhaps you will enjoy sharing your home with a turtle or tortoise.

Taking Time and Energy to Provide a Safe and Healthy Environment

Turtles and tortoises require your time and energy — some more than others.

Aquatic turtles in an aquarium require daily feeding. Every day, you also need to check the aquarium's filter, heater, and light to make sure that they're working properly. Doing so takes only a few minutes each day, though. Weekly, you need to clean the filter and perhaps do a partial water change in the aquarium. This may take an hour or two, depending on the type of filter you have and how the aquarium is set up. Several times a year, you need to empty and clean the aquarium. If you have a big aquarium, this chore can be extensive, requiring a full day's work.

Indoor tortoises need to be fed daily. You also need to pick up uneaten food and feces, but doing so takes only a few minutes each day. Indoor tortoise cages need to be thoroughly cleaned weekly. This can take from 30 minutes to an hour, depending on the size of the cage. Outdoor tortoises may need to be fed a few times a week (rather than every day) if you can provide adequate grass for them to graze on. Feces need to be picked up daily. (A dog's pooper scooper works well.) This, too, takes only a few minutes each day.

As you're deciding whether you have enough time to care for turtles or tortoises, remember that part of the fun of having them is watching them. Although turtles and tortoises don't like to be cuddled, they don't care if you watch! I have found, by watching my pets, that some are bolder than others and some are more cautious. Some like red flowers, while others like yellow. Some of the males are very macho, while others are more romantic. Watching the turtles and tortoises has been great fun over the years — much more so than television!

Keeping in mind that housetraining and obedience training aren't required

When you add a pet to your household, the pet is usually required to adapt to a certain respect. Dogs and cats are housetrained and learn that eliminating in the house is unacceptable. Birds are rarely housetrained but do learn not to bite the hand that feeds them. Dogs, cats, and most birds learn to respond to your voice and their own names. Some even learn tricks, complex behaviors, and commands.

Most reptiles, however — turtles and tortoises included — never master the concept of housetraining. Turtles and tortoises believe, "When ya gotta go, ya gotta go!" You, as the owner, are simply required to clean up after them — all the time!

Speaking of cleaning up: Tortoise feces can be amazing in a weird sort of way. As herbivores, tortoises eat a lot of plant material — high-fiber stuff — and that means what comes out is also high in fiber. In simpler terms, tortoises pass big (sometimes huge) feces in relation to their size. Before you add a tortoise to your household, you'd better be sure that won't gross you out!

Some turtle owners can second-guess when their turtles will need to relieve themselves and plan for it. Some relieve themselves in water; others after they eat. However, cleaning up after a turtle or tortoise who isn't house-trained is a fact of life.

Turtles and tortoises aren't avid fans of obedience training, either. No walking this pet on a leash! "Heel," "sit," "stay," and all the other obedience commands have no meaning to a turtle or tortoise. You may let your tortoise graze on the front lawn while you follow it around, but don't leave it out there alone or it'll be gone. And tortoises do not come when called!

Turtles and tortoises, like all reptiles, lack the enlarged cerebral hemispheres of the brains found in mammals. Because these areas of the brain control learning and reasoning, most reptiles don't have the brainpower that warm-blooded creatures have.

Now, this doesn't mean that turtles and tortoises are stupid. They aren't the most intelligent pets I've ever owned, but they're smart in the ways of things important to turtles and tortoises. When I bring over a bowl of mealworms to feed my box turtles, they recognize the bowl and react differently than if I am simply checking on them with empty hands.

One of my leopard tortoises, Pearl, likes the blossoms of one of my roses. When I go to that particular bush, Pearl follows me and begs for a blossom. Yes, she begs! She lifts one front leg up onto my leg, and as she tries to levitate her 30 pounds of shell upward, she cranes her head up as far as she can so that she's looking up at me. When I pick a pink rose and she can see it, she opens her mouth. I, of course, fall for this every time and feed her. She has trained me very well. My Russian tortoises (*Testudo* or *Geochelone horsfieldi*), also known as Horsfield's tortoises, are very personable little tortoises. When they see me in the backyard, they come charging over (literally!) and start climbing all over my feet. I may offer them a nasturtium blossom or a strawberry from the garden, but often I simply rub a little head or top shell. I may be imagining things, but I think they simply like the attention.

It's fun to grow your own flowers and vegetables to feed your turtles and tortoises; however, many common garden products are poisonous to your pets. Don't feed flowers, fruits, or vegetables if you've used any insecticides, pesticides, or fungicides on the plants. Also, make sure to wash any fertilizer residues off the plants.

Before you add a turtle or tortoise to your household, you need to understand that although the turtle or tortoise may train you, you will not train the turtle or tortoise!

Steering clear of salmonella and other threats

Oprah Winfrey mentioned salmonella from pet iguanas as a hidden household danger. The headlines in a large city newspaper said, "Reptile Salmonella Kills Infant." Is salmonella really a threat? Do turtles and tortoises carry salmonella? Unfortunately, the answer to both questions is yes. Yes, salmonella can be a danger to your family; and yes, turtles can carry salmonella. But I said *can.* Not all turtles carry salmonella, and it can be prevented and/or treated.

Salmonella is a type of bacteria found in the intestinal tract of many animals, including many reptiles. The animal carrying the bacteria may have it for years and not appear sick. If a healthy adult human comes in contact with the feces of an animal carrying salmonella (perhaps when cleaning a cage), he or she may have no reaction at all. If you're healthy, with a good immune system, your body may fight it off, and you may not even know it. Or you may think that you ate something that didn't agree with you because the symptoms are similar to those of food poisoning.

However, young children, senior citizens, and people with compromised immune systems can be at risk. In severe cases, the salmonella may move to other parts of the body and may cause other serious diseases, such as meningitis. Salmonella can be fatal.

The Center for Disease Control estimates that about 50,000 cases of reptile-related salmonella occur each year. A few, such as the visitors to the Denver Zoo who got sick after touching the enclosure walls near the Komodo dragon exhibit, are profiled by the media. Despite these high-profile health alerts, reptiles (including snakes, lizards, and turtles) can be blamed for only 10 to 15 percent of salmonella cases. Poultry, eggs, and milk can be infected with it. In Chicago, in 1984, more than 200,000 people got sick after drinking salmonella-contaminated milk. That's four times the yearly number of reptile-caused cases!

You can take some easy steps to minimize the risk of picking up salmonella from a reptile pet:

- ✔ Never use the kitchen sink to wash your turtle's cage, dishes, or accessories.

- ✔ Never use the kitchen sink as a swimming pool for your turtle.

- ✔ Wash the turtle things outside, and have a scrubber set aside just for the reptile's stuff. You can also use bleach to disinfect the turtle's things; just make sure that you rinse them very well before putting them back in the turtle's cage.

- ✔ Keep your turtle's environment clean to reduce the risk of salmonella. For aquatic turtles, a good water filtration system using a charcoal filter helps keep the water clean. For all turtles, clean the cage or aquarium regularly. A good general rule is that if it smells, it needs to be cleaned!

- ✔ Quarantine new turtles in a separate aquarium or cage for a minimum of six weeks before introducing them to other turtles. For extra safety, your veterinarian can test the new turtle to see if it is carrying salmonella.

- ✔ Wash your hands well after caring for your pet. Use an antibacterial soap and scrub your hands for at least 30 seconds. Teach your children (and other family members) to do the same.

- ✔ Make sure that your children don't kiss the turtle or touch the turtle to their faces. Nor should they get in the habit of touching things in the turtle's tank or enclosure: Kids may forget to wash their hands afterward (and you never know when the turtle may think that little pink finger is lunch!).

CAUTION

Keeping an eye on your chelonian's health

A turtle or tortoise owner must become familiar enough with the animals under his or her care to notice when something is wrong. When appetite declines or behavior changes, you must pay attention. Sometimes the symptoms of an injury or illness are very subtle, because in the wild, an animal showing weakness falls prey to predators!

CAUTION

Although few (if any) diseases can be transmitted between people and turtles, some parasites can be shared. *Ascarids* (roundworms) can be found in many mammals and reptiles. Hookworms and pinworms can also be found in reptiles and mammals. Some amoebic organisms and protozoan agents, especially giardia, can also be transmitted to people. You can prevent almost all, if not absolutely all, of the possible threats to human health from reptile ownership by practicing good hygiene:

- ✔ Pick up feces regularly and dispose of them properly, ideally in a sealed plastic bag.

- ✔ Clean cages well with a bleach solution and rinse thoroughly. Clean food dishes and other cage accessories regularly (not in the kitchen sink!).

- ✔ Always wash your hands thoroughly after handling a reptile or anything in the reptile's cage.

Avoiding Common Mistakes

Turtle and tortoise ownership requires knowledge, forethought, and common sense. Listed in this section are some mistakes that real turtle and tortoise owners have made. By sharing their experiences, perhaps you can keep from making the same mistakes.

- ✔ Janet adopted a Florida gopher tortoise *(Gopherus polyphemus)* through a tortoise adoption group. She was so enamored by this tortoise's personality that she put her name back on the adoption list. She adopted several more tortoises and, at the same time, bought four tortoises of several different types. Within a few months, she had 12 tortoises of various species. When one of the tortoises came down with an upper respiratory infection, she treated it quickly; however, it soon spread throughout her tortoise herd. A parasitic infestation followed, and by the end of the summer, Janet was overwhelmed by veterinary bills and the amount of care that her charges required.

"I took on too many tortoises too quickly," Janet admitted. "I didn't know enough about the care they require and how much the veterinary bills could be. I love my tortoises, but I'm going to place several of them so that I can keep my herd a manageable size."

✔ Tom had bought a rare aquatic turtle that was an exquisite example of her species — beautifully marked and very healthy. This turtle thrived in his care, and Tom enjoyed caring for the turtle, so he bought another. Unfortunately, he didn't quarantine the new turtle, and within a few weeks, both turtles were ill. He took both turtles to a local veterinarian and after one day of treatment, both turtles were dead.

"I made two mistakes," Tom said. "I didn't quarantine my new turtle, and I hadn't done any research about veterinarians specializing in reptile medicine. The vet I used is super with cats and dogs. He's treated my dog for years. But he admits he knows very little about turtles. Before I buy any more turtles, I will find an experienced reptile veterinarian."

✔ Sarah adopted a hatchling tortoise from a friend who bred them. She set up a good indoor enclosure for the baby and took great care of it. Unfortunately, the baby failed to thrive. When she questioned the breeder about the health of the baby tortoise, the breeder, knowing her friend, asked her how often Sarah touched or handled the baby.

"I am a touchy person," Sarah said, "and my friend knew that. She told me I was to touch or pet my tortoise only once a day. Once I stopped handling the baby so much, she started eating again and started to grow. I was loving her to death."

✔ When John's son saw the snake in the pet store window, John knew he was in trouble. However, he knew his wife would not allow the boy to have a snake, so John convinced his son that a turtle would make a better pet. They bought a small turtle, a 10-gallon aquarium, some feeder goldfish, and a few aquatic plants. However, neither John nor his son knew how to care for the turtle, and within a few weeks, the turtle was ill, the tank was filthy, and both were disillusioned about turtle ownership.

John said, "It is all my fault, and I'm sorry the turtle is the one suffering. I bought the turtle on the spur of the moment and knew nothing about caring for it. I know now we didn't get a big enough tank and, in fact, didn't get any type of filter at all. Next time we get a pet, we're going to research it first, and I'm going to make sure my son understands that."

✔ Joyce admits that she made her husband buy the small tortoise. They lived in an apartment and couldn't have a dog or cat, so the tortoise would fulfill her pet ownership needs. However, by the tortoise's second summer, it was not eating well and its shell seemed soft. A trip to the veterinarian showed Joyce where she had gone wrong.

> "I had spoiled this little guy and let him eat what he wanted to eat, which was mostly lettuce. Now I know that lettuce is the worst food in the world to feed a tortoise, but I didn't know that at the time. Also, I didn't know there were different kinds of lights to use over reptiles; I assumed a light was a light. So now my pet has metabolic bone disease caused by my not taking care of him properly. But my vet is working with me and hopefully we can fix this."

In Parts III and IV, I talk about turtle care and how you can avoid making these and other mistakes.

Chapter 3

Choosing the Right Turtle or Tortoise for You

. . . .

In This Chapter

▶ Settling on an aquatic, semi-aquatic, or terrestrial chelonian

▶ Determining which characteristics are best suited to your lifestyle

▶ Deciding whether more than one chelonian will fit into your household

. . . .

*W*ith over 250 different species of turtles and tortoises, anyone who wishes to own a chelonian can find a suitable one. Some are plain and blend into the background; others are brightly colored and very attractive. Some have features that can't be considered anything but bizarre, while others are exactly as you would think a turtle should be. Some species are known for being shy and withdrawn; others are outgoing and friendly; still others are outright aggressive.

Some turtles are entirely aquatic, rarely leaving the water. Others spend more or less time in the water. Many tortoises drink water once or twice a day, never willingly entering it; in fact, if these tortoises ever enter the water, they sink like stones! Other differences abound: Many turtles are carnivores, while most tortoises are herbivores; some turtles never get any bigger than the palm of your hand, while others are big enough to ride.

The variety to be found is amazing. Choosing what type of turtle or tortoise is right for you isn't always easy. Knowing something about the various differences in turtles and tortoises — aquatic, semi-aquatic, or terrestrial — may help you decide which turtle or tortoise is best for you. In addition, you may need a few more details. For example, did you know that pancake tortoises *(Malacochersus tornieri)* need rocks or similar hiding places in their cages? They love to climb rocks and, when threatened, cram themselves into crevasses between rocks. If they don't have rocks to climb or someplace else to hide, these cute little tortoises become extremely stressed. This chapter shares some of these sorts of details that can help you choose the right turtle or tortoise for you.

Aquatic, Terrestrial, or Something in Between?

Successful keepers of turtles and tortoises try to provide a captive environment that mimics the turtles' or tortoises' natural conditions as much as possible. By doing so, you place less stress on the chelonians, which increase their chances for long-term survival. This means, though, that before you bring home a turtle or tortoise, you need to know where that turtle or tortoise came from, what it needs to survive, and the conditions you need to provide. Other factors should also influence your decision as to what turtle or tortoise to get, including the species' personality, size, and tendency to thrive (or not thrive) in captivity.

Aquatic and semi-aquatic turtles

In the wild, aquatic and semi-aquatic turtles live wherever there is a constant source of water, coming out to forage, bask in the sun, or lay eggs. Quick-running rivers, slow, meandering streams, and tiny creeks all support turtles. Swamps, ponds, lakes, and even *brackish* (salty) marshes have chelonian residents.

Aquatic and semi-aquatic turtles are relatively intelligent and remarkably adaptive, able to cope with many changes in their environment. Habitat loss, however, is something that these remarkable turtles can't deal with. As a result, turtles are becoming quite rare in some areas.

In captivity, however, several species of aquatic and semi-aquatic turtles make interesting and rewarding pets. Red-eared sliders *(Trachemys scripta elegans)* are colorful, hardy, long-lived turtles. The wood turtle *(Clemmys insculpta),* although not as colorful or striking as the red-eared slider, is, in turtle terms, intelligent and fairly easy to care for. The painted turtle *(Chrysemys picta)* is an attractive North American turtle that likes to bask in the sun or under a heat lamp. The matamata *(Chelus fimbriatus)* is an odd-looking side-necked aquatic turtle. This turtle's head looks like a leaf. When startled, instead of pulling its head into its shell, its neck folds sideways, hence the description *side-necked* turtle.

Some aquatic turtles should be kept only by careful, experienced keepers. The various soft-shelled turtles are very different in appearance; instead of a hard, bony shell, these turtles have a leathery shell. This different look attracts many potential owners, but beware! Some soft-shelled turtles, like the Florida softshell *(Trionyx ferox),* are known for their aggressive nature. These carnivorous turtles bite anything that moves in their tank, including the hands or fingers of their keepers!

Most aquatic and semi-aquatic turtles are *carnivorous* (meat eaters) or *omnivorous* (eating whatever is available, meat or plants), although not all are as aggressive as the soft-shelled turtles. Most of these turtles eagerly catch and eat fish, scavenge, and eat berries, ripe fruits, and some water plants. As pets, these turtles need fish to catch, commercial turtle food, occasional canned meat, and some berries or fruits. Some species have very particular nutritional needs, which I discuss in more detail in Part II.

Aquatic and semi-aquatic turtles need an aquarium (or other waterproof enclosure) that provides plenty of room for swimming as well as room for the turtle to climb out of the water, dry off, and bask under a heat lamp. One or two small turtles could live in a 20-gallon aquarium sectioned off to provide both environments (water and land). Figure, as a general rule, an 8-inch aquatic or semi-aquatic turtle needs at the smallest a 20-gallon (low and long rather than tall) aquarium. Each added turtle should have an additional 10 gallons. So if you have three 8-inch turtles, the smallest the tank should be is 40 gallons.

Most adult turtles eventually need a bigger tank than 20 gallons. Before getting a turtle, prepare for this eventuality.

Aquatic turtles defecate in their swimming water. Because they are carnivores, the water gets dirty quickly. To keep the aquarium clean, keep smells to a minimum, and prevent disease, the water portion of the enclosure or aquarium must be circulated and filtered unless you're prepared to change the water daily. Because few people have that kind of time, a heavy-duty filtration system is a good investment.

After you set up the aquarium or enclosure, aquatic turtles don't require a great deal of your time until it's time to clean the aquarium. This may happen every two, three, or four weeks, depending on the size of the tank, how many turtles you have, the size of the turtles, and the efficiency of the filtration system.

Aquatic turtles rarely enjoy being handled; in fact, most have a well-developed flight instinct. For these turtles, anything that moves is a potential predator, and they view your hand reaching into the aquarium as a predator attacking. Therefore, aquatic turtles should be viewed as decorative pets, much like tropical fish.

Some aquatic turtles aren't good pets. Common snapping turtles *(Chelydra serpentina)*, alligator snapping turtles *(Macroclemys temmincki)*, and bigheaded turtles *(Platysternon megacephalus)* are all unsuitable pets because they bite — and bite hard! The big-headed turtle is also quite an escape artist and an accomplished climber. And alligator snapping turtles can get quite large, making it difficult for even experienced keepers to maintain a clean environment.

Setting up an aquatic turtle tank can be somewhat costly, depending on the size of tank you choose. A simple glass aquarium — 20 to 30 gallons in size — runs from $60 to $100, depending on the brand name and whether it has a cover and a light. Because you need a cover and a light, go ahead and get them all when you buy the aquarium. Then you know that they'll fit.

For semi-aquatic turtles, most major pet stores carry a kit that enables you to divide the aquarium into two sections: part for water and part for land. One brand is called Viquarium. If you can't find a kit at your local pet store, the Pet Warehouse catalog (800-443-1160) carries one.

A filtration system can be expensive. Tell the salesperson what you will be using the system for and how much water (in gallons) you anticipate filtering, and then get the best system you can afford. A cheaper filtration system requires you to clean and change the water more often.

As is true with many reptiles, the turtles will probably be much less expensive than their enclosure. You can usually purchase a red-eared slider for $10 to $30, depending on the size of the turtle. The rarer a species of turtle, the more expensive it is.

Terrestrial turtles

Terrestrial turtles live on land and rarely venture into water. Many, in fact, don't swim well and venture into shallow water only to drink or bathe.

The various box turtles (see Chapters 7 and 8) are the most well-known terrestrial turtles. All the various species of box turtles are alert, responsive turtles who often learn to recognize their owners; some may even eat from your hand. My Gulf Coast box turtle, Onyx, chases me around her outdoor enclosure, following me, stepping on my feet, and watching me intently. When I find a snail or an earthworm, she takes it from my fingers or, if I drop it to the ground, she runs and pounces on it, moving much faster than you would think a turtle could run.

Terrestrial turtles are, as a general rule, not as skittish as most aquatic turtles are. Whereas aquatic turtles often flee at movement in their enclosure, many terrestrial turtles adapt well to captivity and learn to accept touching. Too much handling is, of course, stressful, so approach each turtle as an individual.

Some box turtles are more difficult to keep. The Malayan box turtle *(Cuora amboinensis)* is more aquatic than the American box turtles and needs care more like the semi-aquatic turtles. Ornate box turtles *(Terrapene ornata ornata)* are notoriously difficult to keep healthy and happy in captivity. I have had two long-term captives who are happy only when allowed to roam freely over my entire turtle yard. If confined indoors, they pace and bang into the walls or glass of the enclosure.

All the box turtles have a common characteristic: the ability to completely close the shell, protecting the head and all four legs. When closed, the turtle can close its shell so tightly that not even a knife blade can enter.

The eastern box turtle *(Terrapene carolina carolina)* is a golden-colored, high-domed turtle. The Florida box turtle *(Terrapene carolina bauri)* is often a brightly colored turtle with gold or yellow markings on a darker shell. The ornate box turtle *(Terrapene ornata ornata)* is also known for its brightly colored markings — again, gold or yellow markings on a darker shell. Skin markings also vary in color; some are dark and plain, and others have bright yellow, gold, or red markings. Chinese box turtles *(Cuora flavomarginata)* are from China, Taiwan, and the Ryukyu Islands. The Chinese box turtle has a dark-colored carapace and lighter-colored skin on the head, often with a bright yellow splash of color on the head behind the eyes. This attractive turtle can be kept under the same conditions as the North American box turtles (see Chapter 8).

Although box turtles have been common in the pet trade for many years, some subspecies are easier to find than others. The Mexican box turtle *(Terrapene carolina mexicana)* is rarely, if ever, available for sale. The desert box turtle *(Terrapene ornata luteola)* is also difficult to find. Overcollection for the pet trade and habitat destruction have led to all the *Terrapene* species being placed on the CITES II list (see Chapter 4) as threatened in their natural environment. This list legally regulates the exportation of box turtles. However, many people are breeding these personable turtles. Within a few years, the box turtles available for the pet trade should all be captive-bred rather than wild-caught.

Most terrestrial turtles are omnivores with carnivorous tendencies. Most eat a variety of insects, including earthworms, snails, slugs, beetles, crickets, and sowbugs. They also eat some greens, fruits, and berries, low-fat canned dog food, and water-soaked commercial turtle food. As with most omnivores, a variety of foods is best.

Terrestrial turtles can be great escape artists, so the enclosure must be well-planned and escape-proofed. In the house, a large glass aquarium makes a safe enclosure. A small or hatchling box turtle (or other terrestrial turtle) can live in a 10- to 15-gallon aquarium; however, an adult needs a 20- to 30-gallon-long (or low) tank. A small child's plastic wading pool also makes a great terrestrial turtle enclosure.

Unlike aquatic and semi-aquatic turtles, terrestrial turtles don't need a lot of water or a filtration system. Instead, a shallow bowl (the saucer under your potted plants works well) that can be cleaned daily is all you need.

Many terrestrial turtles, including the various box turtles and the Central and South American wood turtles *(Rhinoclemmys punctularia* and *pulcherrima,* as well as others), thrive in an enclosure furnished with shredded bark, potted plants, hiding places (such as a clay pot lying on its side), and a plant saucer of water. This setup is easy to clean and maintain.

The setup inside your house for a terrestrial turtle isn't nearly as expensive as that for an aquatic turtle, primarily because there's no need for an expensive filtration system. A 20- to 30-gallon aquarium works for most terrestrial turtles, although a wooden box of approximately the same size (or bigger) also suffices. A child's small plastic wading pool, used indoors, works very well and costs only a few dollars. The difference, of course, is that an aquarium can be an attractive centerpiece in your house. If you use a wooden box or a wading pool, where will you put it?

Tortoises

Tortoises are land-based chelonians, entering the water only to drink or bathe. Many tortoises, including the desert tortoise *(Gopherus agassizii),* live in desert areas. These tortoises may drink from rain puddles in the spring, but for the rest of the year they derive all their water needs from the plants they eat.

Not all tortoises are desert animals, however. Tortoises are found all over the world in a variety of habitats. The marginated tortoise *(Testudo marginata)* lives in Greece and forages in dry scrub hillsides, but is also found in cultivated olive groves. The Hermann's tortoise *(Testudo hermanni)* is a European tortoise that prefers meadows, hillsides, and woodlands, avoiding moist places.

In the wild all over the world, the populations of many tortoises are decreasing. Some are used as food sources, some are facing habitat loss, and some are dying because of human warfare. In California, land has been set aside for the California desert tortoise, but many experts feel that this measure is too little, too late. The tortoise is already battling habitat loss, predators, off-road recreational vehicles, and disease. Captive breeding may be the only way to preserve the species.

Many tortoises adapt quite well to captivity, seeming to have a slightly lessened flight instinct as compared to many aquatic turtles. Whereas aquatic turtles seem to feel that anything reaching into their tank could be a predator, most tortoises are more relaxed. Perhaps their increased size and the protection of their armored skin and harder, domed shells make them more secure.

A few tortoise species can be good pets, but only for people who are prepared to deal with their very large size. The Aldabran tortoise (*Geochelone gigantea* or *Aldabrachelys gigantea*) is the largest tortoise species — some individuals weigh 700 pounds! The Galapagos tortoises are the second-largest tortoises in the world, sometimes weighing more than 600 pounds. The third-largest species of tortoise, the African spur-thigh tortoise *(Geochelone sulcata),* often referred to as a sulcata, may surpass 200 pounds. These gigantic tortoises require a lot of food, need room to roam and forage, and produce vast quantities of feces.

The hingeback tortoise is one of the few tortoises with a hinged carapace. These tortoises can't enclose their entire body like box turtles can, but they can protect themselves by closing the back of their carapace. Unfortunately, these beautiful tortoises are very delicate and don't do well in captivity. They need a very large outdoor enclosure and high humidity.

However, many smaller tortoises make excellent pets if you can fulfill their needs. One of their primary needs is room to roam and graze. As herbivores, tortoises are used to foraging for food, so in a confined space, many tortoises feel stressed. I have leopard tortoises and Russian tortoises and enjoy them very much as pets. However, to thrive, both species need outdoor enclosures. I have found that in southern California, Russian tortoises flourish outside all year long, hibernating in the winter as they would in their native habitat. I simply supply a lot of hiding places and bedding material. If I bring them inside, they pace, bang up against the walls of their enclosure, and suffer severely from stress. Although the leopard tortoises can winter well inside for a few months, they're happier outside.

Make your outdoor tortoise enclosure large enough for your tortoise to roam and graze. Figure on about 3 square yards of space for each foot of tortoise length. If you have young, actively growing tortoises, give them enough room to grow.

If your tortoises don't hibernate (see Chapter 22) and you must bring them inside during the winter, their winter enclosure can be smaller, but not by much. Make it as large as possible so that you reduce the stress of being inside. A child's plastic wading pool works for many small tortoises. For bigger tortoises, you may need to build a large wooden box.

Outdoor tortoises need shelter from the weather. I have found that the plastic doghouses available from most pet stores make great tortoise houses. Inside, I suspend a heat lamp that can be turned on and off as needed. The tortoises readily learn to go in the doghouse when the weather cools. These plastic doghouses run from $60 and up, depending on the brand name and size. An outside tortoise in a secure yard with room to graze and a doghouse (tortoise house) needs minimal care from you. *Supplement feed* them — that is, offer foods, vitamins, and calcium in addition to the grass they graze on — every other day or so, make sure that they have water, and check them routinely for illnesses or injuries. You will need to pick up feces daily, too.

If you're keeping tortoises inside, they need the same care that outside tortoises need, and you also must clean their enclosure on a regular basis.

Diurnal or Nocturnal?

Diurnal animals are active during the day, and *nocturnal* animals are active at night. Probably the most famous nocturnal animals are bats. I recently saw a documentary on an educational television channel showing a tremendous flock of bats flying out of a cave at sunset.

The vast majority of turtles and tortoises are diurnal: active during the day. This makes sense because turtles and tortoises are cold-blooded and must warm their bodies with heat from the earth or the sun. However, a few turtles are known to be up foraging at night, especially after a rain. I have often seen my box turtles hunting snails, slugs, or other insects when it's raining, even in the dark of night.

Being diurnal doesn't mean that the turtle or tortoise is active all day, every day. During the heat of summer or in hot climates, many turtles and tortoises forage in the morning and late afternoon, hiding in the shade of a bush during the heat of the day (see Figure 3-1). This prevents overheating in the hot sun.

Figure 3-1: This Gulf Coast box turtle *(Terrapene carolina major)* hides under a bush.

© Liz Palika

So what does this cycle mean to you? First, if your turtles and tortoises are in outdoor enclosures and you supplement feed them, feed them at the right time of day. If they normally eat in the morning before the heat of the day, feed them then. If they're in an indoor cage or enclosure, feed diurnal chelonians in the morning after you turn on the lights over the cage; feed nocturnal chelonians in the evening as you turn lights off. Mist your box turtles a few minutes before you feed them. Turn the tortoises' lights on in the morning, give them time to wake up and warm up, and then feed them. This timing will be more natural and will cause less stress on your pets.

In addition, don't disturb your pets during their natural rest times. If your turtles are diurnal and are normally active during the day, but you're a night owl, don't plan on feeding and touching them at midnight. This, too, causes stress, and stress can kill your chelonians.

Introvert or Extrovert?

When you're planning your turtle's or tortoise's habitat, you need to take into consideration the species' normal temperament and habits.

Something as simple as a hiding place can make all the difference in the world for a captive turtle or tortoise. Pancake tortoises *(Malacocherus tornieri)* need rocks to climb on and hide under. If they don't have those rock piles, they become stressed and will fail to thrive. Box turtles like hiding places, too. A clay plant pot on its side, partially buried in dirt or cage substrate, makes a nice hiding place. A curved piece of cork bark makes another good hiding spot. A securely anchored piece of board that can't fall and trap the turtle also works.

For groups of animals or individual larger tortoises, a doghouse can work well as a shelter. A wooden doghouse or a plastic commercial doghouse can protect from the weather and the sun and be a place of security. Most turtles and tortoises will quickly learn to use a doghouse.

Plants also make good hiding places. In an outside enclosure, any nontoxic, low-growing bush can provide cover. In an indoor cage, small potted plants work, and in an aquarium for aquatic turtles, water plants serve the same purpose. Keep in mind that in the wild, a turtle or tortoise out in the open, especially a smaller or younger chelonian, is more vulnerable to predators. Most tortoises forage in the open but look for cover when they want to rest.

Plants and hiding places also provide shade and protection from the sun or weather. Turtles and tortoises need to control their body temperature and go back and forth from the sun to the shade.

When you first put together your new turtle's or tortoise's cage or enclosure, you may find that your turtle or tortoise hides when it sees movement. It may run to its hiding spot, jump into the water, or pull its head and legs into its shell. Don't worry about this; as your turtle or tortoise adapts to its new enclosure, you will see it out and about more often, especially after it figures out that you're the source of its food! However, make sure that it has lots of hiding places anyway; they will help its adjustment and its sense of safety and, by doing so, will lessen stress.

Younger or Older?

What age should a turtle or tortoise be? Does it make any difference? Yes, it does. If you buy an older adult wild-caught turtle or tortoise, you may find that the animal has major adjustment problems. Very few wild animals ask to be taken into captivity!

On the flip side of the coin, if you're a first-time turtle or tortoise keeper, don't buy a young hatchling. Hatchlings are very fragile and sometimes die even in the care of experienced keepers. In the wild, many eggs are laid so that a few may survive. In captivity, owners want all the eggs and hatchlings to survive, but often that simply won't happen.

Buy a captive-bred turtle or tortoise that is past the hatchling stage, preferably a juvenile or young adult. These chelonians adapt better to changes in their environment.

In addition, federal laws require that all turtles and tortoises be at least 4 inches long (measuring the bottom shell in a straight line) to be offered for sale. The only exceptions are turtles and tortoises being used for research and/or educational purposes. It's not unusual to see turtles and tortoises for sale with signs coaching people to say that their baby turtle will be used for educational purposes to make the sale legal!

When newly hatched, most turtles and tortoises are between the size of a quarter and a silver dollar; the size depends on the species. By the time the turtle or tortoise is 4 inches long, it is eating well, is probably very healthy, and, with continued good care, will survive.

Male or Female?

What sex should you choose? Does it matter? In most cases, sex really doesn't make a difference. In some of bigger tortoise species, males can be aggressive toward other males, and can be quite rough with females, too. Females lay eggs after they reach sexual maturity, even if no male is with them — the eggs will simply be infertile. As pets, both males and females make great pets.

One Turtle or Two?

Turtles and tortoises can be very addicting. To paraphrase a certain brand of potato chips, nobody can have just one! My husband and I started out many years ago with two desert tortoises and now have more than 30 turtles and tortoises, not including hatchlings and eggs incubating.

You need to decide how many turtles or tortoises you plan to have before you set up a cage or enclosure. If you build an enclosure big enough for one tortoise, it may be entirely too small for two or three. Deciding to keep more than one turtle or tortoise should take some consideration. Two turtles or tortoises mean twice the food bill and, potentially, twice the veterinary care bills. However, more than one turtle or tortoise can also be twice the fun!

Most female turtles and tortoises can be kept alone quite well. They aren't usually escape artists, and as long as their cage or enclosure is appropriate to their needs, they will settle in and live comfortably.

Males, however, are a different story. Come mating season (usually spring), a male living without a female becomes agitated. He explores his cage or enclosure, looking for any possible escape route. A male looking for a mate can be quite determined! I have been doing turtle and tortoise rescue work for a number of years, and in the spring, the vast majority of turtles and tortoises found roaming around neighborhoods are males. Therefore, I don't recommend keeping a male by himself unless you're absolutely sure that his cage or enclosure is escape-proof. Even then, he'll be happier with a companion of the opposite sex!

Female turtles and tortoises also do well in groups. They're usually not aggressive and often get along with each other quite well. In fact, they often seem to congregate. Box turtles and pancake tortoises do especially well in groups. Females sometimes battle for a good nesting spot, and although this behavior doesn't happen often, it does happen once in a while, especially if the females are crowded. In nature, this behavior would ensure that populations spread out, aiding in species survival. Other aggressive behavior may occur during competition for food, although these episodes are usually mild and short-lived.

The most common aggressive behavior is the battling of males of the same species for the right to breed a female. This ritualistic fighting usually continues until one male gives way to the other. Although sometimes a male can be hurt — bitten by the other or flipped over — more damage is usually done to the loser's ego than to his body. However, injuries can occur.

African spur-thigh or sulcata tortoises *(Geochelone sulcata)* are big tortoises — up to 200 pounds — and the males are quite aggressive with each other. During combat, a dominant male may flip the subordinate male over, causing stress, injuries, and sometimes even death.

Unfortunately, in some species, battling is necessary for successful breeding. Box turtle breeding success rates increase dramatically when two or more males can compete for breeding rights. Leopard tortoises *(Geochelone pardalis)* also do better when males can compete for the females.

If you're going to keep more than one turtle or tortoise and you don't plan on breeding them, you're better off keeping females. If you do plan on breeding at some point, make sure that you have as many cages or enclosures as you do turtles or tortoises so that you can house each animal (especially each male) separately if need be.

Same Species or Different?

With a few exceptions, it's not a good idea to house different species of turtles and tortoises together. It's not that they won't get along; often they do. However, the different species often carry parasites or diseases (native to their particular species or geographical area) that a species from a different area has no resistance to, making them ill or causing death.

For example, many people in southern California have captive desert tortoises *(Gopherus agassizii).* Many of these long-lived tortoises have been in captivity for many years and have been handed down from one family member to another. Unfortunately, many of these captive tortoises have an upper respiratory disease that's extremely contagious to other tortoises. This disease is treatable with antibiotics but is not curable. Many desert tortoises have lived long and relatively healthy lives with the disease, with outbreaks appearing only in times of stress. However, if someone who enjoys the tortoise happens to bring home a tortoise of another species, that tortoise, too, will get the disease, often with fatal results.

Don't keep breeding-age male and female turtles and tortoises of different species together, either. Often a male doesn't consider the species of the female he attempts to breed; he just knows that she's female! Cross-breeding is rarely successful, and in the rare instances when it is successful, the offspring are usually sterile. With so many populations and species of turtles and tortoises in jeopardy, mixing or cross-breeding different species is unethical.

A large extended family

Seventy-six species of turtles belong to the family *Emydidae.* This is the largest and most diverse family of chelonians and includes turtles on all continents except Australia and Antarctica. These turtles share several characteristics, including a relatively small skull, much like a tortoise. The carapace and plastron are joined by a strong bridge on each side. In addition, all these turtles are aquatic or semi-aquatic.

Size is another factor you must keep in mind when you consider keeping tortoises of different species together. A large adult male sulcata weighing 200 pounds is a formidable animal. If he wants to go somewhere, he's going to go there, and he's not going to care what's in his path. A smaller turtle or tortoise could be severely injured by this behemoth!

If you want to keep turtles and tortoises of different species, for their safety, you must be able to house them separately. I have outdoor enclosures for almost all of my turtles and tortoises and have separate enclosures for the Russian tortoises, the leopards, the sulcatas, and the box turtles.

Chapter 4

Finding Your Turtle or Tortoise

In This Chapter

▶ Deciding between wild-caught and captive-bred

▶ Finding a trustworthy seller

▶ Evaluating the health of your future pet

*S*uppose you've decided that you want a turtle or tortoise as a pet (see Chapter 2), and you've narrowed your choice to a specific type — an aquatic, semi-aquatic, or terrestrial turtle or a tortoise — with specific characteristics (flip to Chapter 3). This chapter helps you locate a prospective turtle and evaluate its health before making the purchase.

Choosing Between Wild-Caught and Captive-Bred Chelonians

When I first began keeping turtles and tortoises some 20 years ago, very few people were breeding turtles and tortoises. If I wanted a particular species, my choices were to buy or adopt a long-term captive or a wild-caught individual. Today, many people are breeding turtles and tortoises, even protected species. Captive-bred turtles and tortoises (as compared to wild-caught ones) are a much better choice as pets and as potential breeding stock.

When you buy a captive-bred chelonian, you're not removing a turtle or tortoise from the wild and thereby removing that individual's potential as a breeding animal. Rather, captive-bred chelonians are well adapted to their captive environment and don't suffer the stress that a wild-caught individual does when suddenly faced with captivity. Captive-bred chelonians are easier to care for and less likely to suffer from the health problems that stress can cause in wild-caught individuals. The benefits of buying or adopting a captive-bred individual are overwhelming compared to the detriments of buying a wild-caught one.

Wild-caught turtles and tortoises

Until recently, if you wanted a turtle or tortoise as a pet, you could be assured that the turtle or tortoise began its life in the wild. The numbers of turtles and tortoises in the wild seemed almost limitless; they were an unending resource to be used as people wished for pets, food, or artifacts.

However, that is no longer so. The Galapagos tortoises (*Geochelone* or *Chelonoidis elephantopus*) were one of the first to suffer. Sailors, whalers, and explorers would stop by the Galapagos Islands and load their ships with giant tortoises. Because the tortoises could go for months without food or water, they became a transportable food source. Very shortly, the numbers of giant tortoises plummeted, so much so that several species are extinct and several others were driven to the brink of extinction.

The populations of sea turtles have plummeted, too. Sea turtles have been used as food much like the Galapagos tortoises, plus their eggs have been harvested by the millions. Today, poachers still steal sea turtle eggs even from protected beaches.

Not all turtles and tortoises caught in the wild were used as food; those captured for sale in the pet trade suffered — and still suffer. Hard statistics are impossible to verify, but some experts believe that it would be a miracle if 1 to 5 out of 100 wild-caught turtles or tortoises survive the first year of captivity.

These animals die for many reasons. Many times they're handled poorly during and after capture. One recently confiscated shipment of eastern box turtles (being shipped from the United States to Europe) had thousands of turtles piled one on top of the other, layer upon layer, in one box. The turtles couldn't move except to flail against each other and urinate and defecate on each other. They had no food or water. Needless to say, when found, the majority of turtles were already dead. Until recently, not much was known about the needs of many turtle and tortoise species, which led to many deaths. Some species need high humidity and high temperatures; those same environmental conditions kill other species.

Some wild-caught chelonians have trouble adapting to a captive lifestyle. To survive to adulthood, a wild turtle or tortoise must be alert, cautious, and aware of its surroundings. In a normal busy household, a turtle or tortoise may become stressed by all the activity. When it discovers that it can't escape all the noise, movement, and confusion, the stress increases. In addition, rarely does a captive turtle or tortoise eat the same foods in captivity that it would eat in the wild. This, too, causes stress. When too much stress builds up, the turtle's or tortoise's immune system suffers, the animal quits eating, and shortly after, it dies.

For a new pet owner, wild-caught turtles and tortoises pose health concerns, too. The majority of wild-caught chelonians are infested with internal parasites, including roundworms, hookworms, whipworms, tapeworms, flukes, and protozoans. Many also harbor mites and ticks. If you acquire a wild-caught turtle or tortoise, have it examined by a veterinarian who specializes in reptile medicine right away. If you have other reptiles at home, quarantine this one away from your pets for at least a month.

Captive-bred turtles and tortoises

While the subject of wild-caught chelonians brings up a number of warnings and dangers, captive-bred turtles and tortoises are just the opposite.

Turtles and tortoises conceived, hatched, and reared in captivity grow up adapted to their lifestyle. They know nothing else and, as a result, have no adaptability problems as long as their environmental needs are met. In addition, these chelonians are (or should be) healthy, well-fed, and free from parasites.

The Galapagos tortoises illustrate the role that captive breeding plays in conservation. Search parties in 1906 counted only three individual Galapagos Hood Island tortoises *(Geochelone elephantopus hoodensis).* However, in the 1960s, additional individuals were found and relocated to the Charles Darwin Research Station, and by 1971, the first eggs were being incubated. These tortoises, as well as other Galapagos subspecies from other islands, are now breeding regularly and successfully.

Similar projects all over the world are saving turtles and tortoises from possible extinction and, in addition, are making turtles and tortoises available to pet owners. Captive breeding is a challenging endeavor; however, the rewards are great for those who persevere. By choosing and buying a captive-bred turtle or tortoise, you help that breeder come closer to making ends meet. No one has gotten rich by breeding turtles and tortoises — most of the rewards are emotional — however, every check helps! Also, when you buy a captive-bred turtle or tortoise, you add a healthy, well-adapted pet to your household: a pet that will be with you for many years to come.

Locating a Seller of Chelonians

Many species of chelonians are being bred in captivity. However, finding someone who breeds the species you're looking for can be tough. Many breeders advertise in regional and national reptile magazines, and some advertise in their local newspapers. Ads may vary from a small classified ad to a larger, full-page, color advertisement. Many others have Web sites or post classified ads on a larger chelonian-oriented Web site, such as www.turtletimes.com. If you have access to the Internet, search under the name of the species you're looking for and see what pops up. You can also refine your search by adding the phrase "breeder of" to the name of the species.

Turtles, tortoises, and the law

Early in the history of capturing turtles and tortoises (for food, artifacts, or the pet trade), few laws governed their capture. However, the disappearance and severely reduced populations of many species motivated environmentalists and conservationists to propose regulations governing the capture, sale, or possession of many threatened species.

The most important law passed for the protection of threatened species is the Convention on the International Trade in Endangered Species (CITES). More than 120 nations have signed this international agreement. The goal of CITES is to protect threatened species from poaching and international smuggling. Under CITES, animals are divided into three groups:

✓ **CITES I are those animals in immediate danger of extinction.** It is illegal to capture, collect, import, or export any of these animals except under special permit, such as those obtained by zoos with breeding programs.

Some turtles and tortoises protected under CITES I are bog turtles *(Clemmys muhlenbergi)*, radiated tortoises *(Geochelone asterochelys radiata)*, angulated tortoises *(Chersina angulata)*, and spotted pond turtles *(Geoclemys hamiltonii)*.

✓ **Under CITES II, animals are listed that aren't in immediate danger of extinction but are threatened and declining in population.** These animals may be captured by special permit but otherwise are protected from capture, import, export, and sale.

Turtles and tortoises protected under CITES II include speckled tortoises *(Homopus signatus)*, yellow-headed tortoises *(Indotestudo elongata)*, sulcata tortoises *(Geochelone sulcata)*, and yellow-spotted Amazon turtles *(Podocnemis unifilis)*.

✓ **Under CITES III, member nations can control specific, native species.** These animals may be traded when the country of origin issues a special permit.

For a complete listing of the turtles and tortoises protected by CITES, contact the local branch of the U.S. Department of Fish and Wildlife.

In addition to CITES, the United States passed the Endangered Species Act in 1973. This federal law was designed to protect threatened and endangered species, protect the habitats those species require to live, and provide a program for the conservation of those species.

A federal regulation that applies specifically to turtle owners bans the sale of any turtle under 4 inches in length. This regulation was adopted in the 1970s after an outbreak of salmonella was attributed to improperly-cared-for baby red-eared sliders *(Trachemys scripta elegans)*.

Many states also have laws that apply to turtles and tortoises. In some cases, the state laws follow the guidelines established by the federal Endangered Species Act; however, most states have also instituted laws protecting native wildlife. To research the laws of your state and the laws concerning the species of turtle or tortoise you would like to own, ask for help from the reference librarian at your local community library. He or she can point you to the publications you need.

After you have the names of two or three people who breed the species you're looking for, ask a few questions. Many things can affect the health of the offspring, including the health of the parents and the care the offspring have received since hatching. So ask the breeder how long he or she has been breeding this species. How is the health of the parents? Have they suffered from any diseases, especially upper-respiratory diseases that could be passed to the offspring? When were the parents last checked for internal parasites? Have the hatchlings been checked for internal parasites? In what conditions are the chelonians kept? How would the breeder describe the cage or enclosure?

If the breeder lives relatively close to you, ask if you can see the parents, the offspring, and the enclosure or cage. When you visit, check whether the parents are active, healthy, and alert. If the breeder offers something to eat, do the chelonians have a good appetite? Are the offspring active and alert? Are the cages and enclosures clean?

If the breeder doesn't live nearby, ask if he or she will send photographs of the parents, the offspring, and their cages and enclosures. Be sure to offer to pay for the photos and postage. Photos don't serve the same purpose as a real visit, but you can still see whether the parents appear to be healthy, the offspring look well cared for, and the cages are clean (at least at the time the photos were taken).

Some breeders, especially those overwhelmed by several large *clutches* (litters) hatching at the same time, may sell their surplus to pet stores or reptile dealers. Often, these are healthy young animals; unfortunately, if you buy those chelonians, you know nothing about their background, the heath of the parents, and how they were cared for during shipping and at the store or dealer's facility.

My favorite way to find a reputable breeder is by word of mouth. If I start asking for breeders of a particular species at reptile shows, through friends, or on the Internet, I pay attention when several people mention one or two breeders favorably. To me, satisfied customers with healthy animals are the best referrals a breeder can have.

Evaluating a Chelonian's Health

Before deciding to purchase a turtle or tortoise, take a look at the chelonian to determine whether your future pet is healthy. Look specifically at the following:

✔ **Make sure that the animal is bright and alert.** Not all chelonians are active when strange people are watching, but it should be paying attention to its surroundings. If the turtle pulls its head into its shell, just be quiet and wait it out until it extends its head again.

- ✔ **Look at the turtle's or tortoise's eyes.** They should be clear and bright, with no swelling and no matter or crusty material. If you're looking at a tortoise that comes from a desert region, don't be alarmed at slight watering of the eyes; this is a flushing mechanism. However, crusty eyes aren't good and are a sign of a bigger health problem. If the eyes are shut and the turtle obviously doesn't want to open them, avoid that turtle, too.

- ✔ **Focus in on the nose.** The nose and nostrils should be clean, with no bubbling mucus and no runny nose. Avoid any turtle or tortoise that's breathing through its mouth instead of its nose. These are signs of respiratory infection or even pneumonia — serious problems!

- ✔ **Look at the turtle's or tortoise's legs.** You shouldn't see any obvious signs of injury or swelling. If you pull gently on a back leg, the chelonian should pull that leg back from you. If it doesn't, or does so weakly, don't buy it.

- ✔ **Look at the tail area.** Avoid turtles or tortoises that look as if they have had diarrhea, or that have signs of infection or parasites.

- ✔ **Look at the shell.** The shell should be hard (except for softshell turtles, discussed in Chapter 5, and pancake tortoises, covered in Chapter 9). Make sure that you don't see any signs of bleeding under the *scutes* (the keratin layer that covers the bony part of the shell). Minor injuries to the shell are often unavoidable but should be well healed. Avoid turtles and tortoises with severe injuries to the shell, drilled holes in the shell, or cracked shells.

- ✔ **Weigh the chelonian.** When you pick up the turtle, you should be surprised by its weight. A healthy turtle feels heavy for its size, as if the shell were full of water. If the turtle or tortoise feels light, don't choose that one.

If possible, buy your new pet from someone who will give you a health guarantee. Because the seller has no control over how you will care for the turtle or tortoise, most guarantees are for a very short period — even 24 hours. Even a short guarantee works, however, if you take your new pet directly to a veterinarian specializing in reptiles. Have your new pet checked over carefully, and if the vet has any concerns about the turtle's or tortoise's health, contact the seller.

Part II
The Who's Who of Turtles and Tortoises

The 5th Wave   By Rich Tennant

"Pssst - box turtle? Genuine Coahuilans,
real clean..."

In this part . . .

Turtles come in different shapes, sizes, and colors. Some have smooth shells, and some have rough. Some are designed to blend into the background, while others are brightly colored. Some are aquatic, others are semi-aquatic, and still others are semi-terrestrial or terrestrial.

Tortoises come in a variety of sizes and colors as well. Some are brightly patterned, and others are camouflaged. Some have armored skin with spikes and spurs, and others look less formidable. Some tortoises weigh upward of hundreds of pounds, while others weigh less than a pound, full-grown.

The chapters in this part tell you all about some of the more popular pet turtles and tortoises so that you can decide which one is right for you.

Chapter 5

Aquatic Turtles

● ●

In This Chapter

▶ Understanding aquatic turtles

▶ Providing the proper environment for your new pet

▶ Knowing what to feed your aquatic turtle

● ●

*Y*ou can find aquatic turtles in a variety of shapes, sizes, and markings. Some have bright, attractive markings, and others have earth-tone colors that blend into the background. Some are herbivores, some carnivores, and some omnivores (see Chapter 1 for definitions), but all need a constant source of water.

The variety among some of the different species is amazing — this chapter introduces you to 18 of the most popular. For reference, keep the following terminology in mind:

✔ **Basking site or basking area:** An area for a turtle to absorb warmth from sunshine or another heat source

✔ **Brackish water:** Salty water

✔ **Carapace:** The top shell covering the back

✔ **Carrion:** Decaying flesh that's used for food

✔ **Clutch:** A nest of eggs

✔ **Feral turtles:** Those turtles released and returned to the wild

✔ **Hatchlings:** Baby turtles

✔ **Keel:** A ridge in the carapace, usually from front to rear, that follows or parallels the spine

✔ **Mollusks:** Shellfish

✔ **Plastron:** The lower shell covering the belly

✔ **Scute:** A single section of the shell; each shell is made up of many scutes

✔ **Vent:** Equivalent to an anal opening; also known as the *cloaca*

Red-Eared Slider (Trachemys scripta elegans)

The red-eared slider has a low, domed shell, ranging in color from albino yellow to green to almost black. Yellow head markings (stripes) are offset by a bright red spot behind the eyes, hence the name *red-eared*. The yellow stripes and markings are usually outlined in black.

Adult red-eared sliders are normally 5 to 8 inches long. A male has a longer tail than a female, and his vent is farther down the tail (about halfway), whereas a female's opening is closer to her body. Males have longer front claws than females do.

- **Geographical origin:** North America, from Indiana south to the Gulf of Mexico and west to New Mexico. Feral red-eared sliders settled in a variety of locations scattered all over the world.

- **Native habitat:** These turtles thrive in a variety of freshwater habitats and are quite adaptable.

- **Captive environment:** Use an aquarium that's no smaller than 20 gallons long (or low), with an additional 10 gallons for each additional adult turtle. Use a good filtration system. These turtles like to bask, so provide a fair-sized warm basking place. A submersible (underwater) heater with the temperature adjusted to 75 to 80 degrees keeps the water warm enough for activity. (See Chapter 18 for the lowdown on aquariums.)

- **Diet:** Red-eared sliders are omnivorous, eating aquatic plants, fish, insects, and carrion, although adult females are largely herbivorous and young and adult males are more carnivorous. In captivity, you can use small feeder fish as well as commercially bred insects such as mealworms, waxworms, and crickets. Soaked dry dog food, commercial turtle food, and chopped vegetables round out a nutritionally complete diet.

- **Breeding:** Red-eared sliders reproduce quite easily in captivity. Two to twenty eggs are laid per clutch, after which you need to incubate at 83 degrees with high humidity. The eggs will begin hatching at about 65 to 75 days.

Painted Turtle (Chrysemys picta)

Painted turtles grow to about 10 inches in length. The carapace is dark green to black with yellow or red markings. The painted turtle's head has yellow stripes.

✔ **Geographical origin:** North America from coast to coast, and from Canada to Mexico, provided that the turtles find the conditions they prefer.

✔ **Native habitat:** This turtle lives in shallow ponds, swamps, and slow-moving streams. It hibernates under the ice in winter.

✔ **Captive environment:** The smallest allowable aquarium size is 20 gallons long (or low) for an adult. Add 10 gallons per additional turtle. Provide a basking area and a good filtration system. Use an underwater heater, adjusted to 75 degrees, to keep the water warm enough for activity.

This species thrives better in outside ponds than it does indoors.

✔ **Diet:** Painted turtles are omnivorous, eating fish, insects, aquatic plants, fruits, berries, and carrion. In captivity, you can supplement their diet with commercial turtle food, soaked dry dog food, insects, and small feeder fish, with chopped vegetables and occasional berries or chopped fruit. Hatchlings are more carnivorous than adults.

✔ **Breeding:** Breeding begins after hibernation. Incubate the five or so eggs laid at 82 degrees, 90 percent humidity, and they will begin hatching between 55 and 80 days later.

Common Map Turtle (Graptemys geographica)

These turtles get their name from the pattern of lines on their skin and, in some cases, on their carapace. The lines often seem to copy the lines on a map. You may notice a big difference in size between males and females; males grow to only 6 inches, while females may be twice that size. This turtle has strong, wide jaws that are adapted to crushing mollusks.

✔ **Geographical origin:** North America, from the Great Lakes south through Alabama.

✔ **Native habitat:** These are river turtles rather than pond turtles. They appreciate moving water, but they avoid fast-moving rivers.

✔ **Captive environment:** Use a larger aquarium or set up a good-sized outdoor pond. The common map turtle is shy and requires hiding places; too much activity or too few hiding places can result in stress, which can, in turn, lead to a lowered immune system response. Establish basking areas as well.

- ✔ **Diet:** Common map turtles are carnivorous — eating small fish, insects, and carrion — with omnivorous tendencies. In captivity, they readily eat small feeder fish, insects, and earthworms; they may accept commercial turtle foods, too.

- ✔ **Breeding:** Common map turtles lay their eggs in sandy soil, laying ten or so eggs per clutch. Incubate the eggs at 82 degrees, with hatching due in 55 to 65 days.

Mississippi Map Turtle (Graptemys pseudogeographica)

The Mississippi map turtle is an attractive 8- to 11-inch turtle. In both sexes, the carapace is ridged with a pronounced keel running from front to back. The plastron is greenish yellow, with double dark lines along the seams. The skin is olive green to brown, with yellow stripes. The stripes curve around the eyes, making a big circle that emphasizes each eye. Males are about half the size of females, which reach just under 1 foot in length. Males also have longer front claws than females and have long, thick tails.

- ✔ **Geographical origin:** South central North America, primarily the Mississippi basin area.

- ✔ **Native habitat:** This turtle favors fresh water that has a thick, muddy bottom.

- ✔ **Captive environment:** The Mississippi map turtle likes to bask, so a large basking area is a necessity. It also enjoys aquatic plants. A 20-gallon tank setup is the minimum size; this turtle likes to swim.

- ✔ **Diet:** In the wild, Mississippi map turtles eat small fish, insects, larvae, and some shellfish. In captivity, small feeder fish, insects, earthworms, and commercial turtle food will suffice.

- ✔ **Breeding:** Reproduction is basically the same as for the common map turtle (see the preceding section), although the range of eggs per clutch is from 1 to 22, and the eggs are slower to hatch (around 90 days at 78 degrees).

Eastern Mud Turtle (Kinosternon subrubrum)

The eastern mud turtle is small with a smooth oval carapace. Hatchlings have three keels, which they lose as they age. Colors range from yellowish brown to black. The plastron has two hinges that close to protect the turtle. The skin is usually brown with some yellow blotches or spots. Males have longer, thicker tails.

- ✔ **Geographical origin:** This turtle is found from or almost to southern New England south to the Gulf Coast, west to southern Illinois, and southwest to Texas.

- ✔ **Native habitat:** The common mud turtle prefers quiet waters, including slow-moving rivers, marshes, swamps, ponds, and drainage ditches. It's sometimes found in brackish water.

- ✔ **Captive environment:** Good filtration is needed for cleanliness, but avoid a strong current. A basking area is necessary, although your turtle may not use it.

- ✔ **Diet:** This omnivorous species eats mollusks, aquatic plants, algae, insects, and small fish. In captivity, vary your turtle's diet and include small feeder fish, insects, commercial turtle food, and chopped dark green vegetables.

- ✔ **Breeding:** Three to five eggs are laid and should be incubated at 78 degrees and 90 to 95 percent humidity. Hatching starts between 90 and 130 days later. Three clutches may be laid each summer.

The hatchlings are keeled, with a small ridge running down the backbone of the carapace. A hatchling's carapace is dark brown to black with light spots, and the plastron has orange or red blotches.

Striped Mud Turtle (*Kinosternon baurii*)

This small turtle, reaching 5 inches or less in length, has a broad, smooth carapace. It ranges in color from tan to black and sometimes has stripes. The plastron has two hinges to close the shell. Males have longer, thicker tails.

- ✔ **Geographical origin:** North America, from southeastern Virginia south through Florida.

- ✔ **Native habitat:** This turtle likes quiet waters, such as swamps, bogs, and ponds. It is sometimes found in brackish water.

- ✔ **Captive environment:** Provide good filtration for cleanliness, but avoid a strong water flow. Provide a basking area as well.

- ✔ **Diet:** This omnivorous species eats mollusks, aquatic plants, algae, insects, and small fish. A varied diet, including small feeder fish, insects, commercial turtle foods, and chopped dark green vegetables, is good for captives, too.

Reeve's Turtle (Chinemys reevesi)

This small turtle (up to 9⅓ inches) is understated in coloring, tending to blend into the background. The carapace is usually brown, sometimes black, and has three well-defined median keels. The plastron is yellow with brown blotches on each scute. The skin is brown to black with broken stripes and spots of yellow. Males become quite dark as they age and may lose all their yellow markings. Females are larger than males; males have longer, thicker tails and slightly concave plastrons.

These turtles make undemanding pets when their environmental needs are met. They have amusing personalities and become quite tame, although males sometimes fight with one another. Most learn to eat from your hand and readily come to the side of the tank when approached.

- ✔ **Geographical origin:** Korea, Hong Kong, mainland China, and Japan.

- ✔ **Native habitat:** This turtle enjoys fresh water in a variety of habitats.

- ✔ **Captive environment:** Consider using a 20-gallon-long (or low) aquarium, although one turtle may exist in a smaller tank. A good filtration system is needed. The aquarium needs some land mass as well; a vivarium with both land mass and water is best (see Chapter 13). These turtles are fond of basking, so provide a dry land area with a hot lamp.

- ✔ **Diet:** Reeve's turtles are omnivorous, eating aquatic plants, insects, and small fish. In captivity, provide a diet of small feeder fish and commercially produced insects (such as crickets, mealworms, and waxworms), supplemented with commercial turtle food, soaked dry dog food, and chopped dark green vegetables. This small turtle has a voracious appetite; be careful not to overfeed yours!

- ✔ **Breeding:** Breeding takes place after hibernation. After the four to nine eggs are laid, incubate them at 78 degrees with 90 percent humidity. Hatching takes place in about 99 days.

European Pond Terrapin (Emys orbicularis)

The European pond terrapin is a personable turtle that responds to its feeder. This medium-sized turtle reaches about 8 inches in length. The carapace varies from olive green to dark brown to black with small spots. The spots are yellow to white and very small, looking almost like flecks. The plastron is also dark brown or black and is hinged, although the hinge doesn't always close in adults. Males have reddish eyes, while females have yellow eyes. The tails of males are longer. This species is protected in many areas but is being bred in captivity.

- **Geographical origin:** This turtle has had a wide geographical distribution across North Africa and Europe, but pollution is threatening its existence in many areas.

- **Native habitat:** Primarily a river turtle.

- **Captive environment:** An adult needs a minimum of 20 gallons, with another 20 gallons per additional adult. Provide a good filtration system and a basking area. This species will thrive in an outdoor pond.

- **Diet:** This carnivorous species eats small fish, insects, amphibians, and snails. Commercial turtle foods aren't always accepted by the European pond terrapin. Earthworms, mealworms, waxworms, and crickets are acceptable.

- **Breeding:** Courtship takes place in the water, where it begins with the male trying to grab the female, often scratching at her carapace in the process. Three to sixteen eggs are laid per clutch — most often about eight. The eggs are leathery and oval-shaped and should be incubated at 82 to 84 degrees.

Smooth Softshell Turtle (*Trionyx muticus*)

The shell of the smooth softshell turtle isn't a hard keratin-like material but instead is leathery and smooth. These turtles range from tan to dark brown or olive, some with spots or blotches on the back toward the tail. These turtles have a narrow, pointed noses and range in size from 7 to 14 inches.

The smooth softshell turtle bites! It's known for having a vicious temper, so only experienced turtle keepers should keep it. Always cover the aquarium with a secure lid, and never let children poke their fingers into the aquarium. Because of their aggressive nature, these turtles should be housed alone.

- **Geographical origin:** Texas north to North Dakota and east to Ohio.

- **Native habitat:** Rivers.

- **Captive environment:** A good filtration system in a 20-gallon tank with a basking area suits these turtles well.

- **Diet:** These turtles are carnivorous, with a natural diet of fish, snails, insects, worms, and amphibians. In captivity, they eat small feeder fish, insects, and earthworms. In addition, many learn to eat commercial turtle foods and soaked dry dog food.

- **Breeding:** Twenty to thirty eggs are laid per clutch. The eggs should be incubated at 82 degrees and 90 percent humidity for 55 to 60 days.

Spiny Softshell Turtle (Trionyx spinifera)

The sweet-looking spiny softshell turtle is attractive but quite aggressive: It bites! Small black spots dot the carapace (see Figure 5-1), which is small, leathery, and often a coffee color. These turtles have long, thin noses. They range in size from 8½ to 21 inches.

Figure 5-1:
The spiny softshell turtle (*Trionyx spinifera*).

- ✔ **Geographical origin:** Eastern North America, Montana, and the Colorado River.
- ✔ **Native habitat:** These turtles are found in a variety of habitats, from fast-moving streams to slow, quiet lakes and ponds. They are normally found in bodies of water with soft, muddy bottoms.
- ✔ **Captive environment:** Use a standard 20-gallon aquatic setup with a tight-fitting cover to keep the turtle in and fingers out. (Remember, these turtles bite!)
- ✔ **Diet:** In captivity, these turtles eat small feeder fish, insects, and earthworms. Some may be taught to eat commercial turtle foods.
- ✔ **Breeding:** Fifteen eggs are generally laid per clutch, although four to thirty have been recorded. Incubate the eggs in high humidity at 86 degrees, and they will hatch in 55 to 60 days.

Matamata (Chelus fimbriatus)

The matamata is an odd-looking turtle: Its shell is small, and its head looks like a leaf (see Figure 5-2). This camouflage enables the turtle to disappear in its environment and makes it an effective predator. When the matamata retracts its head, its neck folds to the side, as do those of other side-necked turtles. The carapace is light to dark brown and oblong; the back of the carapace is serrated. The plastron is yellow and rather small, leaving more of the turtle's legs, neck, and head exposed than in most other turtle species. The head is large and triangular in shape, and the skin is grayish brown. Males have concave plastrons and longer, thicker tails than females do. This turtle can reach up to 18 inches in length.

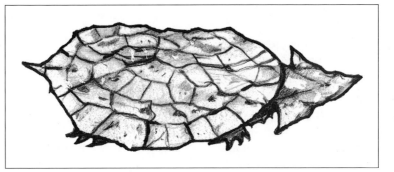

Figure 5-2:
The
matamata
*(Chelus
fimbriatus).*

The matamata has been known to bite and should be kept with caution. This turtle is also one of the few to have nocturnal tendencies.

- **Geographical origin:** Northern South America.

- **Native habitat:** This turtle inhabits slow-moving waters, especially streams, marshes, and pools. It rarely leaves the water.

- **Captive environment:** A 20-gallon long (or low) aquarium with water about 6 inches deep serves this turtle well. Amazingly enough, the matamata isn't a good swimmer, even though it's an aquatic turtle. It can't tolerate alkaline water conditions, so make sure that your matamata's water has a pH of 6.5 to 6.8 or lower. (See Chapter 18 for more information on water conditions.)

- **Diet:** This carnivorous turtle eats fish and other animals. In captivity, it accepts small feeder fish, as well as insects and earthworms. You may have difficulty getting this turtle to eat anything other than live foods.

- **Breeding:** Ten to thirty eggs are laid per clutch. They should be incubated at 82 degrees with 80 percent humidity. Some peat should be part of the incubation medium, because a pH level of 6 or below is necessary. Eggs hatch after approximately 200 days.

Big-Headed Turtle (Platysternon megacephalum)

This turtle, around 7 inches long with an extremely long tail and powerful jaws, has a disproportionately large head, hence its name. The head is often half as wide as the carapace and is not retractable. Colors range from yellow to brown, some with spots and some without.

These turtles are known to bite! Handle with care.

- **Geographical origin:** Widely distributed throughout southern China and southeast Asia.
- **Native habitat:** This turtle lives in cool mountain streams and small rivers.
- **Captive environment:** The big-headed turtle needs cooler water; water in the 60s is fine. Provide a basking area even though this species rarely basks. The cage or aquarium needs a secure cover — this turtle can climb!
- **Diet:** This turtle is carnivorous, feeding on worms, fish, carrion, and mollusks. In captivity, offer small feeder fish, insects, and canned dog food. Some big-headed turtles may learn to accept commercial turtle food.
- **Breeding:** One to two eggs are laid per clutch and should be incubated at 78 degrees with 90 percent humidity. Hatching times are varied.

Hatchlings are more brightly colored than adults, with a keel running down the backbone of the carapace. Hatchlings are quite aggressive.

Florida Cooter (Pseudemys floridana)

The Florida cooter is a good-sized freshwater turtle, reaching 16 inches in length. The carapace is brown, sometimes with yellow markings, and the plastron is yellow without other markings. The skin is brown or black with yellow stripes. Males have long front claws and long, thick tails. Females are usually larger than males.

- **Geographical origin:** North America, in the Atlantic coastal plains from the Carolinas through Florida.
- **Native habitat:** This turtle is found in fresh water, from slow-moving streams to ponds to marshes. It requires a soft bottom and adequate basking sites.

- ✓ **Captive environment:** A 20-gallon aquarium will do for a turtle up to 6 inches long, although this turtle prefers to be in an outdoor pond. Inside or out, basking areas are a necessity.

- ✓ **Diet:** This herbivorous turtle eats primarily aquatic vegetation. In captivity, a varied herbivore diet (see Chapter 19) will do just fine. Hatchlings eat insects and small fish.

- ✓ **Breeding:** Courtship is elaborate, with the male using his long front claws to stroke the female's head. He swims above her as he strokes her. Ten to twenty eggs are laid per clutch and need to be incubated at 80 degrees with 80 percent humidity. Hatching takes place between 70 and 100 days.

  Hatchlings are as wide as they are long and are more brightly colored than adults. They are also more omnivorous than adults and will accept insects, especially worms, as well as plant foods.

Yellow-Headed Temple Turtle (Hieremys annandalei)

The name *temple turtle* comes from the native custom of placing these turtles in the pools and canals surrounding Buddhist temples. Buddhists believe that saving a life (even the life of a turtle) gains favor for the saver in the hereafter.

This is a big freshwater turtle, reaching 24 inches in length. The plastron and bridge are yellow, and the carapace is dark. Males have concave plastrons and thicker tails.

- ✓ **Geographical origin:** Asia, from Thailand through Vietnam and northern Malaya.

- ✓ **Native habitat:** This turtle lives in flooded fields, swamps, and slow-moving rivers.

- ✓ **Captive environment:** A 20-gallon aquarium with a large basking area does quite nicely for one 6-inch specimen.

- ✓ **Diet:** This herbivore eats green plants in the wild, including rice in the fields, aquatic vegetation, and algae. In captivity, a varied herbivore diet (see Chapter 19) will suffice.

- ✓ **Breeding:** Very little is known about the breeding habits of this species. Future keepers will have to let you know.

New Guinea Side-Necked Turtle (Chelodina parkeri)

This strange-looking turtle, which grows 14 to 16 inches in length, has a smooth, fairly flat shell. The carapace is dark brown, and the plastron is cream to yellow. The distinguishing feature of this turtle (and other side-necked turtles) is its extremely long neck. To retract its neck, this turtle must fold it so that the head faces sideways. Males have longer, thicker tails and flatter carapaces than females.

- ✔ **Geographical origin:** New Guinea.

- ✔ **Native habitat:** This turtle lives in swamps as well as at the edges of lakes and rivers.

- ✔ **Captive environment:** A standard aquatic turtle setup in a 20-gallon tank with a basking area suits this turtle quite well.

- ✔ **Diet:** Little is known of this species' eating habits in the wild; in captivity, the New Guinea side-necked turtle eats small feeder fish and insects.

- ✔ **Breeding:** Very little is known about the breeding habits of these turtles. Future keepers will have to let you know.

Twist-Necked Turtle (Platemys platycephala)

Like the New Guinea side-necked turtle (see the preceding section), the twist-necked turtle is a side-necked turtle. It varies in color from tan to grayish brown, often with brown to yellow borders of the scutes. The plastron is yellow, and the upper side of the head is reddish brown. The average length is about 5 inches.

- ✔ **Geographical origin:** Argentina, Paraguay, and Bolivia.

- ✔ **Native habitat:** This turtle lives in slow-moving streams, shallow lakes, and lagoons. It rarely comes out of the water.

- ✔ **Captive environment:** A standard 20-gallon aquatic turtle setup with good filtration serves this turtle well. Provide a basking area even though these turtles rarely leave the water.

The twist-necked turtle is shy and needs quiet, privacy, and hiding places, so provide aquatic plants in its aquarium.

- **Diet:** In the wild, this turtle is carnivorous. In captivity, provide small feeder fish, snails, insects, and earthworms. Some twist-necked turtles learn to accept commercial turtle foods.

- **Breeding:** This species is difficult to breed in captivity. The females prefer to lay their eggs in wet sand or mud. Incubate the eggs in very high humidity at 84 degrees.

Chicken Turtle (Deirochelys reticularia)

This small to medium-sized aquatic turtle, averaging about 10 inches in length, has an oval, olive-colored carapace with radiating yellow lines. Females are larger than males. The plastron is yellow; some turtles have a dark edging on the plastron. The head is long and narrow with a long snout and a very, very long neck. The skin is olive to brown. Males have long, thick tails.

- **Geographic origin:** From Virginia south through North Carolina into southern Florida and west to the Gulf of Mexico.

- **Native habitat:** Still waters, swamps, and marshes.

- **Captive environment:** This turtle is fairly large for an indoor aquarium, although young turtles thrive inside. Keep adults in an outdoor pond and enclosure (see Chapter 15). Filtration should be gentle; these turtles don't like fast-moving water. Because this turtle is prone to shell problems in captivity, make sure that all surfaces around the turtle are clean and soft.

- **Diet:** Chicken turtles are omnivorous and readily eat snails, slugs, insects, tadpoles, and plants. Hatchlings are more carnivorous than adults.

- **Breeding:** Breeding takes place in the spring, with five to fifteen eggs laid per clutch, and several clutches laid each year. Incubate the eggs at 90 percent humidity, 84 degrees; hatching will occur in 70 to 100 days.

Delayed development is not unusual in this species; the eggs may hatch days or even weeks apart. So if one or two eggs hatch and the others don't, don't throw away the unhatched eggs. They may yet hatch!

Florida Red-Bellied Turtle (Pseudemys nelsoni)

This aquatic turtle has a high, domed carapace, and the back portion over the back legs is serrated. Young turtles have a dorsal keel that's lost or worn down in adults. The carapace is black with red and yellow markings. The plastron is reddish orange, and the skin is black with yellow stripes. Males have long, curved front claws and long, thick tails. Florida red-bellied turtles grow to about 15 inches, with females larger than males.

- ✔ **Geographic origin:** Southern Georgia south through Florida.

- ✔ **Native habitat:** Swamps, lakes, and most other waters.

- ✔ **Captive environment:** These turtles are best kept outside in a pond enclosure (see Chapter 15). They prefer still waters with lots of aquatic vegetation. This species loves to bask, so provide a basking area.

- ✔ **Diet:** Although the young are quite carnivorous, the adults are herbivorous. Treat all ages as omnivorous and offer both plant and animal foods.

- ✔ **Breeding:** Courtship is an elaborate affair, with the male gently stroking the female's face with quivering foreclaws. Five to twenty clutches may be laid each year, with eight to ten eggs laid per clutch. During incubation, keep the humidity high (90 to 95 percent) at a temperature of 84 degrees.

Chapter 6

Semi-Aquatic Turtles

● ●

In This Chapter

▶ Getting the scoop on semi-aquatic turtles

▶ Furnishing your pet's apartment

▶ Understanding what semi-aquatic turtles eat

● ●

Semi-aquatic turtles are primarily water-loving turtles that also spend time out on land. They come in a variety of sizes, shapes, and personalities, and they vary in their need and desire for habitats. Some wood turtles, for example, spend most of their time in the water, while others enjoy more time on land. (Chapter 13 shows you how to set up a home for a semi-aquatic turtle.)

This chapter gives you details on 17 of the most popular semi-aquatic turtles. But first, here's a quick vocabulary lesson to help you with the terminology in this chapter:

✔ **Basking site or basking area:** An area for a turtle to absorb warmth from sunshine or another heat source

✔ **Brackish water:** Salty water

✔ **Carapace:** The top shell covering the back

✔ **Carnivore:** A meat eater

✔ **Carrion:** Decaying flesh that's used for food

✔ **Clutch:** A nest of eggs

✔ **Estivates:** Hibernates in summer

✔ **Hatchlings:** Baby turtles

✔ **Herbivore:** A plant eater

✔ **Keel:** A ridge in the carapace, usually from front to rear, that follows or parallels the spine

✔ **Omnivore:** Eats both meat and plants

✔ **Plastron:** The lower shell covering the belly

- ✔ **Scute:** A single section of the shell; each shell is made up of many scutes
- ✔ **Side-necked turtle:** A type of turtle that folds its neck to the side when it retracts its head
- ✔ **Vivarium:** An aquarium divided into two sections — one for water and one for land mass

Bog Turtle (Clemmys muhlenbergii)

The bog turtle is quite small, never growing larger than 5 inches in length. It has a brown shell with dark brown skin and a distinctive patch of bright yellow or orange skin right behind its eyes and jaw. A small dorsal keel is present. The plastron is dark brown to black with a few irregular, lighter markings.

- ✔ **Geographical origin:** Isolated areas in eastern North America: southern New York state, Massachusetts, Connecticut, New Jersey, and Pennsylvania.
- ✔ **Native habitat:** This turtle likes quiet, slow-moving waters and flooded meadows.

The attractive little bog turtle is rapidly disappearing from its range due to habitat destruction. It's protected by law from collection in the wild; however, it's being bred in captivity. Because this species is protected, don't acquire a bog turtle unless you know that it's captive-bred, you have the proper permits, and you're sure that you can care for it properly.

- ✔ **Captive environment:** A shallow vivarium split half and half water and land area will do fine. The water should be fairly shallow (4 inches or so), and the land area should be made of soft potting soil. A reptile heat light can create a basking site at one spot over the land area.
- ✔ **Diet:** The bog turtle is an omnivore with carnivorous tendencies. In captivity, it can eat snails, earthworms, commercially produced insects (crickets, mealworms, and waxworms), and commercial turtle food. Also offer berries and chopped fruits.
- ✔ **Breeding:** Breeding takes place in water and can be quite lengthy. Two to six eggs (typically three) are laid and should be incubated at 78 to 84 degrees with 100 percent humidity. Eggs hatch 42 to 80 days later.

Hatchlings must be maintained in a high-humidity environment. A vivarium, with the water level reaching no higher than the hatchlings' nose, works well. A basking light should heat a basking spot to at least 85 degrees.

Spotted Turtle (Clemmys guttata)

This very attractive little turtle reaches a maximum length of 5 inches. Females are larger than males. The carapace is dark brown to black with yellow spots all over it, and the skin is patterned after the carapace. The young have few spots, but as the turtles mature, more spots appear.

The species is also sexually dichromatic; females have yellow chins and orange eyes, while males have light brown chins and brown eyes.

- ✔ **Geographical origin:** Eastern North America, from Maine to Florida and from the Atlantic coast inland to Illinois.

- ✔ **Native habitat:** These turtles like small ponds, especially beaver ponds. Quiet marshes, swamps, and flooded fields are all possible homes.

- ✔ **Captive environment:** A vivarium divided into half water and half land mass will do nicely. The water should be shallow — 3 to 4 inches deep. Have a basking light over one corner of the land area.

- ✔ **Diet:** This species is carnivorous. It will accept small feeder fish, insects, earthworms, and sometimes commercial turtle foods. Plant matter is rarely accepted but should be offered.

- ✔ **Breeding:** The spotted turtle has been bred successfully in captivity. Because populations are decreasing in the wild, please consider breeding your spotted turtle. Four eggs are laid per clutch; incubate them at 78 to 86 degrees with 100 percent humidity, and they'll start hatching between 44 and 70 days later.

  Hatchlings can swim almost right away, so the terrarium setup for the hatchlings should have a shallow swimming area and easy access to land. Over one corner of the land area, provide a basking spot that's heated to 85 degrees. Hatchlings are almost entirely carnivorous and eat almost anything that moves and is small enough to be eaten.

Blanding's Turtle (Emydoidea blandingii)

This is a hardy, friendly, and attractive little turtle. (See Figure 6-1 for an example of this turtle.) Adult size is normally 7 to 8 inches long. The carapace is dark brown, marked with lighter-colored teardrop-shaped spots. The head is dark, while the jaw, chin, and throat are bright yellow. The plastron is pale yellow with dark blotches. Males have dark upper jaws, while those of females are yellow. In addition, females have longer plastrons than carapaces and broader bodies than males have.

Figure 6-1:
The
Blanding's
turtle
(*Emydoidea
blandingii*).

- ✔ **Geographical origin:** This turtle is found around the Great Lakes and New England. Populations have been disrupted and isolated due to habitat destruction and glacial activity.

- ✔ **Native habitat:** This turtle prefers shallow lakes, ponds, and slow-moving streams.

- ✔ **Captive environment:** A vivarium divided half and half between water and land serves nicely. The water should be well filtered but quiet. A submersible underwater heater should keep the water temperature at about 70 degrees. If the water is colder than this, the turtle will continue to move about but may not eat. Provide a basking spot over one corner of the land area.

- ✔ **Diet:** These turtles are good eaters. They accept small live fish, insects, and commercial turtle food and are especially fond of live crustaceans. Supplement that with soaked dry dog food.

- ✔ **Breeding:** Ten to fourteen eggs are laid per clutch. Incubation temperature should be 80 degrees with 90 percent humidity. Eggs start hatching between 55 and 70 days later.

Malayan Box Turtle (Cuora amboinensis)

These attractive little turtles have dark brown carapaces without markings. They grow to 8 inches in length as adults. The hinged plastron is lighter, sometimes yellow to brown, and can completely enclose the turtle inside. The head has yellow stripes on a brown background, and the lower jaw and chin are yellow.

Look for a captive-bred Malayan box turtle if you decide to adopt one. Most wild-caught Malayan box turtles are infested with protozoans and, in many cases, salmonella.

- ✔ **Geographical origin:** All over southeast Asia, including Java, Indonesia, India, and Bangladesh, as well as the Philippines.

- ✔ **Native habitat:** These semi-aquatic turtles are found in shallow waters, especially flooded fields and slow-moving streams.

- ✔ **Captive environment:** A 20-gallon-long (or low) tank is the smallest you want to use. It needs to be divided into a vivarium that's at least half water. Provide a basking area, and keep the humidity high.

- ✔ **Diet:** Malayan box turtles are omnivorous, eating insects, worms, snails, slugs, and plants, both aquatic and terrestrial. Some also eat canned dog food, soaked dry dog food, and commercial turtle food.

- ✔ **Breeding:** This species is shy and gentle; however, if you keep more than one male in the same enclosure, fighting will occur during breeding season. The males can be quite aggressive during these fights, often inflicting serious injuries on each other. In addition, courtship can be dangerous, with the males often biting the females on the neck.

  Two to four eggs are laid per clutch, and they should be incubated at 82 degrees with 90 to 100 percent humidity. Hatching occurs between 70 and 85 days later.

Red-Bellied Side-Necked Turtle (Emydura subglobosa)

The red-bellied side-necked turtle, which reaches about 10 inches in length, has a gray or brown carapace with a yellow plastron bordered in pink to red. The skin on the head is gray with a yellow stripe. This turtle has a red stripe on its jaw.

- ✔ **Geographical origin:** Australia and New Guinea.

  Exporting this turtle from Australia is unlawful, but it is often exported from New Guinea and is being bred in captivity in increasing numbers for the pet trade.

- ✔ **Native habitat:** This attractive turtle primarily inhabits rivers, lakes, and lagoons. It seems to be susceptible to water pollution, developing both skin and shell infections in polluted waters.

- ✔ **Captive environment:** This turtle needs both water and land areas. It is an enthusiastic basker and spends quite a bit of time soaking up heat. A submersible heater should keep the water temperature at 75 to 78 degrees. These turtles are prone to skin and shell infections if the quality of their water is not maintained, so a good filtration system is important.

- ✔ **Diet:** This omnivorous turtle feeds on small fish and aquatic plants. In captivity, the red-bellied short-necked turtle eats small feeder fish as well as a variety of insects. It also quickly learns to eat commercial turtle food, canned dog food, and soaked dry dog food.

- ✔ **Breeding:** Ten eggs constitute an average clutch. Incubation should be at 82 degrees with 100 percent humidity, and hatching should start 70 to 85 days later.

Spiny Turtle (Heosemys spinosa)

This unique-looking turtle, which reaches about 9 inches in length, has spines on the marginal scutes of the carapace and the keel. The marginal scutes are also covered in an attractive pattern of fine brown-black lines. The carapace is dark brown, and the plastron is yellow. The spiny turtle, when small, has very sharp spines all around the margins of its nearly circular carapace. As it ages, it becomes more elongated and gradually loses its spines at about 5 inches.

- ✔ **Geographical origin:** Asia, from Thailand through Burma and Malaysia.

- ✔ **Native habitat:** This walking pincushion lives near quiet, clear streams in forests. This turtle is quiet and secretive, and little is known about where it lives and reproduces.

- ✔ **Captive environment:** This little turtle needs at least a 20-gallon-long (or low) vivarium. Create a basking area on one side of the land area, and keep a pile of shredded bark where the turtle can burrow and hide on the other side. Mist often to increase the humidity. This turtle likes low light and has even been seen feeding at night, so if you use incandescent bulbs over the tank for heat, make sure that they're red or black. (Don't use white light!) Maintain a water temperature of 75 to 80 degrees; add an underwater heater if necessary.

- ✔ **Diet:** This omnivorous species leans toward being an herbivore. It eats earthworms, mealworms, and waxworms as well as tomatoes, strawberries, aquatic plants, and chopped green vegetables. Some individuals like commercial box turtle foods that have a fruity smell and taste.

- ✔ **Breeding:** One or two eggs are laid per clutch. They should be incubated at 78 degrees for 90 to 100 days.

Indian Snail-Eating Turtle (Melanochelys trijuga)

The carapace of this turtle, elongated and with three keels, is black. The plastron is much paler. The skin on the head and legs is gray, and the toes are webbed. Males have concave plastrons and longer, thicker tails than females. Although the Indian snail-eating turtle can reach 8 inches in length, it's usually much smaller.

- **Geographical origin:** India, Sri Lanka, and Bangladesh.
- **Native habitat:** This freshwater turtle likes quick-moving streams and the damp areas near those waters.
- **Captive environment:** A standard vivarium works well for these turtles, as long as you provide hiding places. Use a good filtration system because this species has a low tolerance for water pollution.

  These turtles can be very delicate and difficult to keep. Before buying one, make sure that you can meet all of its needs.

- **Diet:** Judging by this turtle's name, you've probably figured out that snails can be a big part of this turtle's diet. It also eats small fish, some aquatic plants, canned dog food, and commercial turtle food. This omnivorous species leans toward being carnivorous.
- **Breeding:** Males can be quite aggressive and should be separated from each other during breeding. Females should be checked often for injuries. Four to six eggs are laid and should be incubated at 76 degrees with 100 percent humidity. Hatching starts between 65 and 75 days later.

African Helmeted Turtle (Pelomedusa subrufa)

This side-necked turtle is medium-sized, more than 8 inches long, with a brown or gray carapace and a yellow plastron. Males have concave plastrons and long, thick tails. The carapace of a female is broader than that of a male.

- **Geographical origin:** Africa and Madagascar.
- **Native habitat:** This turtle lives in and around lakes, ponds, and watering holes. It's very tolerant of water conditions: When small water holes dry up, this turtle either estivates under the drying mud or travels cross-country in search of water.
- **Captive environment:** This turtle does better in an outside enclosure than indoors. An outdoor pool or pond with land area around it (see Chapter 15) suits this turtle quite well. Also, because this species thrives in a group, set up an outside enclosure that's large enough for several turtles.

✔ **Diet:** In the wild, this carnivorous species has been known to hunt in packs. Several turtles gang up to pull down larger prey, such as water birds, large fish, or large amphibians. In captivity, this turtle eats just about anything, including soaked dry dog food, commercial turtle food, and canned dog food. To maintain a balanced diet, also feed some fruit and chopped green vegetables.

✔ **Breeding:** Breeding often takes place in water. Six to fifteen eggs are laid per clutch and should be incubated at 82 degrees, 90 percent humidity, for 75 to 90 days.

South American and Central American Wood Turtle (*Rhinoclemmys pulcherrima* and *Rhinoclemmys punctularia*)

These semi-aquatic turtles have a keeled carapace. The plastron is yellowish in color. Males are smaller than females and have longer tails. *Rhinoclemmys pulcherrima* reaches about 10 inches in length; *Rhinoclemmys punctularia*, 8 inches.

✔ **Geographical origin:** South and Central America.

✔ **Native habitat:** Both species are semi-aquatic and semi-terrestrial and are found in forested and rainforest regions.

✔ **Captive environment:** A standard vivarium that's half water and half land area suits both species. The land area should have some shredded bark where the turtle can hide. Potted plants can also provide hiding places. Provide a basking area and slightly acidic water (with a pH of less than 6.8 — see Chapter 18). Some of these turtles tend to be nocturnal; if you notice this tendency, make sure to install a red or black basking light, not a white one.

✔ **Diet:** These turtles are herbivores that also eat insects. A variety of chopped green vegetables, fruits, earthworms, snails, and other insects suits them just fine.

✔ **Breeding:** Courtship is enthusiastic, with the male circling the female, biting at her head. Copulation may occur in water or on land. Eggs should be incubated at 82 degrees and 90 percent humidity for 65 to 90 or more days.

All color photos © Bill Love

This diamondback terrapin hatchling shows off its unusual coloration against a leaf.

This spiny turtle hatchling has unusual spikes around the edges of its carapace. These spikes will wear down and become smoother as it ages.

Bright markings, such as those on this Florida box turtle hatchling, serve as camouflage in the wild.

This leopard tortoise hatchling is tiny now but will not remain so for very long.

Most turtle hatchlings are carnivorous and will bite anything that moves, such as this meal-worm. (spotted turtle)

This hatchling, a red-bellied slider, has pulled in its head and legs as a defensive measure.

Marine turtles, such as this green sea turtle, do not make good pets but can be admired from afar.

This yellow-spotted Amazon side-necked turtle hatchling has unusual light coloring. These turtles are popular pets, but this aberration probably wouldn't survive in the wild.

Most aquatic and semi-aquatic turtles, like this black-knobbed map turtle, can swim quite well even as hatchlings.

Most aquatic turtles enjoy getting out of the water to bask in the sun. (red-eared slider)

This Vietnamese box turtle hatchling shows the prominent ridged keels down its carapace.

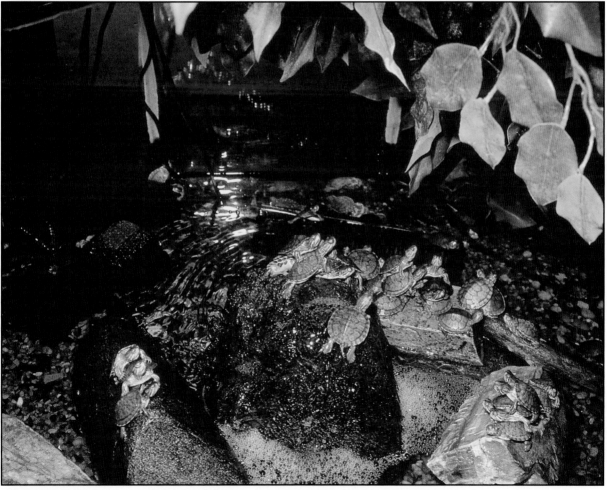

This great enclosure supplies the turtles with plenty of fresh, clean water, basking spots, and some land area.

Scuba divers often follow green sea turtles, enjoying their grace in the water.

All marine turtles, including this Fly River turtle, are legally protected, and many are severely endangered.

This northern Australian snake-necked turtle shows the species' elongated neck.

This toad-headed turtle is a handsome adult and can be a good pet when its needs are met.

The eastern painted turtle needs either a large indoor vivarium with plenty of swimming room, land area, and a basking spot or, even better, an outdoor pond.

This three-toed box turtle will do better in an outside enclosure. If possible, only hatchling box turtles should be kept inside.

If you like the Blanding's turtle, make sure that the one you get is captive-bred and that you have the proper permits to keep it. Do not pick up one in the wild, as they are protected throughout most of their range.

This turtle, a ringed map turtle, has an attractive color pattern on both its shell and skin.

The Chinese yellow-marginated box turtle can be a good pet if you give it the proper care.

The diamondback terrapin is uniquely marked and colored.

The alligator snapper turtle can cause tremendous harm when it bites.

The red-footed tortoise, like many other tortoises, will hold food under one foot so that it can take a bite.

The pancake tortoise is uniquely shaped and has a flexible carapace, unlike other tortoises.

The Madagascar bowsprit tortoise is a very popular pet and is being bred in captivity, so well-adjusted, captive-bred hatchlings are becoming available.

The radiated tortoise is a very attractively marked tortoise.

The Asian softshell turtle has a soft shell but a hard bite, so be careful!

The matamata in a nice enclosure.

With legs outstretched, this chelonian looks comfortable and relaxed.

Black Marsh Terrapin (Siebenrockiella crassicollis)

This small turtle, which reaches at least 8 inches in length, has a black carapace and a black and cream plastron. A medial keel divides the carapace, and the rear of the carapace is serrated. The skin ranges from gray on the head to black on the legs. The feet are webbed.

This turtle has a strong odor — so much so that the people of Thailand, Java, and Malaya call it the "bad-smelling turtle."

- **Geographical origin:** Thailand, Java, Borneo, and Malaya.
- **Native habitat:** This turtle lives in and around marshes and swamps.
- **Captive environment:** A standard vivarium works nicely, although this turtle does better outside in a larger enclosure. Provide a basking area.
- **Diet:** This carnivorous species readily accepts earthworms, commercially available insects, snails, shrimp, frogs, and commercial turtle foods.
- **Breeding:** Three to four eggs are laid per clutch and should be incubated at 82 degrees and 90 percent humidity. Hatching begins 60 to 80 days later.

African Forest Turtle (Pelusios gabonensis)

The carapace of this turtle, which darkens with age, is buff to gray with a distinct black stripe. The plastron and bridge are black with yellow seams, and the head is buff-colored with dark stripes. Males have slightly concave plastrons and longer, thicker tails. The female's carapace is broader than that of the male. This turtle reaches about 5 inches in length.

- **Geographical origin:** West Africa, from Zaire north toward Liberia.
- **Native habitat:** This is a tropical rainforest turtle, where it lives in and close to marshes, swamps, and quiet streams.
- **Captive environment:** A standard vivarium (with half water and half land area) is fine for this turtle. Make sure that there's plenty of swimming room, and also provide a basking area. Keep the water temperature between 70 and 75 degrees and use a good filtration system, because these turtles like to eat in their water and can be very messy eaters.

- ✔ **Diet:** This carnivorous species eats insects, worms, snails, and fish. The diet should be the same in captivity.

- ✔ **Breeding:** Up to 25 eggs are laid per clutch. They should be incubated at 82 degrees and 95 percent humidity for 60 to 70 days.

Western Pond Turtle (Clemmys marmorata)

This turtle is small to medium-sized, up to 8 inches long, with a low, somewhat flat carapace that's dark olive to black. A pattern of small spots or lines may radiate from the center of each scute, although this pattern is absent in some populations. The plastron is yellow. The skin of the head is dark, while the jaws and chin are lighter in color. Males have concave plastrons and longer tails.

- ✔ **Geographical origin:** Western North America, from extreme southern mainland British Columbia south through Baja California.

- ✔ **Native habitat:** This semi-aquatic species lives in a variety of habitats, from brackish coastal waters to swift-moving, freshwater streams.

- ✔ **Captive environment:** This turtle does much better in an outdoor enclosure than it does inside, so consider providing a small pond or pool with access to land area (see Chapter 15). Provide hiding places in the land area.

  This species is an escape artist, so outdoor enclosures must be very secure.

- ✔ **Diet:** This omnivorous species leans toward being carnivorous. It eats insects, worms, snails, slugs, and carrion as well as fruits and aquatic plants. In captivity, it also eats chopped meats, canned dog food, soaked dry dog food, and commercial turtle foods.

- ✔ **Breeding:** Three to eleven eggs are laid per clutch and should be incubated at 82 degrees and 90 percent humidity. Hatching starts between 70 and 80 days later.

Spotted Pond Turtle (Geoclemys hamiltonii)

This relatively large (up to 14 inches), very attractive aquatic turtle spends time basking on logs or rocks near water. It has a domed carapace with three keels. The color of the carapace, the rear of which is serrated, is black, as is the skin. The carapace and skin are covered with lighter-colored spots of white or yellow. Older turtles lose their spots and may be entirely black. The plastron is yellow with dark spots or dark lines. Males have concave plastrons and longer, thicker tails than females.

- ✔ **Geographical origin:** Northern India, southern Pakistan, Assam, and the Bangladesh, India, and Ganges Rivers.

- ✔ **Native habitat:** This quiet species lives in rivers and wells.

- ✔ **Captive environment:** A standard vivarium (half water and half land area) suits this species just fine. Provide a basking area and plenty of places to hide.

- ✔ **Diet:** This species is entirely carnivorous. In captivity, provide small fish, snails, slugs, earthworms, and other insects. Some will accept canned dog food.

- ✔ **Breeding:** Very little is known about breeding these turtles in captivity. Future keepers will have to let you know the details. In the wild, breeding occurs twice a year.

Malayan Snail-Eating Turtle (Malayemys subtrijuga)

This small to medium-sized turtle (up to 8 inches in length) has a dark brown to mahogany carapace, with a yellow to cream-colored border. The oval carapace has three ridges. The plastron, which is flat, is lighter-colored with a brown pattern. The Malayan snail-eating turtle has dark skin, and its head has several yellow stripes. Males have longer, thicker tails.

This turtle can be difficult to keep in captivity. Before getting one, make sure that you can care for it properly.

- ✔ **Geographical origin:** Southern Vietnam, Burma, Malaya, and Java.

- ✔ **Native habitat:** This turtle likes quiet, slow-moving waters, especially ponds, marshes, drainage ditches, and flooded fields.

- ✔ **Captive environment:** A standard vivarium will work as long as the filtration system is effective but with a slower water current. Provide a basking area as well.

- ✔ **Diet:** As you may have guessed from its name, this turtle is primarily a snail eater, but in captivity, it also eats worms, insects, and small feeder fish. It doesn't respond well to non-live foods.

- ✔ **Breeding:** Future keepers will have to share their knowledge about this species' breeding needs, as very little is known.

Japanese Turtle (Mauremys japonica)

This small (5 to 7 inches long) semi-aquatic turtle has a brown and black carapace with a low medial keel. The plastron is also dark, usually matching the carapace. The head is relatively small and is lighter in color than the shell, usually with small dots or spots on it. The plastron of the male is only slightly concave; however, the male's tail is longer and thicker that the female's.

- **Geographical origin:** The Japanese islands of Shikoku, Kyoshu, and Honshu.

- **Native habitat:** This dark turtle is found in flooded fields, marshes, canals, and drainage ditches.

- **Captive environment:** This turtle thrives outside in a semi-aquatic environment. It likes water with a muddy bottom, but it also like to wander about on land. Provide a basking light.

- **Diet:** This omnivorous turtle has carnivorous tendencies. It eats small feeder fish and insects. It has also been seen eating aquatic plants. In captivity, offer your Japanese turtle a variety of foods, including commercial turtle foods.

- **Breeding:** Five to eight eggs are laid per clutch and should be incubated at 78 to 82 degrees, 80 percent humidity. They will begin hatching in about 70 days.

Asian Yellow Pond Turtle (Mauremys nigricans)

This medium-sized turtle (almost 8 inches long) has a dark gray to dark brown carapace and a lighter-colored plastron. The scutes of the plastron have a darkened spot or splotch, while the skin of the head and neck is gray to olive with a broad yellow stripe. The oval carapace has three low, poorly developed keels. Males have slightly concave plastrons and longer, thicker tails than females have.

- **Geographical origin:** Southern China, northern Vietnam, and Taiwan.

- **Native habitat:** This turtle is found in slow-moving waters, including flooded fields, marshes, and swamps.

✔ **Captive environment:** A standard vivarium will do well. These turtles are relatively tolerant of water conditions, although the water should be maintained at about 75 degrees. A basking light is needed, because these turtles do like to bask. Provide a good-sized land area.

✔ **Diet:** This omnivorous turtle shows a decided preference for fish. In captivity, it eats small feeder fish eagerly. Also offer earthworms, insects, aquatic plants, chopped dark green vegetables, commercial turtle foods, and soaked dry dog food.

✔ **Breeding:** Incubate eggs at 85 to 86 degrees, 90 percent humidity, for 60 to 75 days.

Mediterranean Turtle (Mauremys leprosa)

This brown, medium-sized (up to 9 inches long) turtle has a slightly keeled carapace. The plastron is yellow. Young turtles have yellow or orange markings on the carapace, but these marks fade with age. The skin is gray to tan with yellow stripes. Males are smaller than females, have slightly concave plastrons, and have longer, thicker tails.

✔ **Geographical origin:** Western Spain and Portugal to northern Africa.

✔ **Native habitat:** This turtle is found in and around freshwater sources, including ponds, lakes, rivers, streams, and drainage ditches.

✔ **Captive environment:** A standard vivarium serves these turtles well. They tolerate a variety of water conditions. Supply a basking light, because these turtles like to bask and do so often.

Keep a close watch on the scute seams on the carapaces of these turtles. Sometimes bacteria invades the seams, causing infected spots. Wash infected spots with a disinfectant such as Betadine daily.

✔ **Diet:** These omnivorous turtles readily eat just about anything. Supply small feeder fish, insects, earthworms, soaked dry dog food, and commercial turtle food.

✔ **Breeding:** Courtship begins underwater, but copulation can occur underwater or on land. Males may battle and, when they do, can hurt each other. The males occasionally bite the females, too, so examine females closely after breeding attempts.

Five to ten eggs are laid per clutch, with three clutches possible during a breeding season. Eggs incubated at 84 degrees usually hatch in about 70 days or fewer (probably 45).

Chapter 7

Semi-Terrestrial and Terrestrial Turtles

In This Chapter

▶ Getting acquainted with semi-terrestrial and terrestrial turtles

▶ Understanding the sort of environment these turtles need

▶ Feeding your turtle a high-performance diet

*S*emi-terrestrial turtles live primarily on land but occasionally go into the water, sometimes to feed, sometimes to breed, and sometimes to escape predators. *Terrestrial* turtles go into water only to drink or bathe, and one species can't swim at all even though it does go into shallow water. Keep in mind, however, that each turtle is an individual. As with semi-aquatic turtles (see Chapter 6), some turtles make up their minds about how much time to spend in or out of the water. (Chapter 14 illustrates how to set up an indoor cage or enclosure for a semi-terrestrial or terrestrial turtle, and Chapter 15 shows you how to build an outdoor enclosure.)

This chapter uncovers 14 of the most popular semi-terrestrial and terrestrial turtles. Note that some of the turtles in this chapter are box turtles from around the world; see Chapter 8 for a listing of box turtles that originate specifically in North America.

Some of the turtle vocabulary used in this chapter can be a bit tricky. Here's the lowdown on the more common terms:

- **Basking site or basking area:** An area for a turtle to absorb warmth from sunshine or another heat source

- **Brackish water:** Salty water

- **Carapace:** The top shell covering the back

- **Carnivore:** A meat eater

- ✔ **Carrion:** Decaying flesh that's used for food
- ✔ **Clutch:** A nest of eggs
- ✔ **Estivates:** Hibernates in summer
- ✔ **Hatchlings:** Baby turtles
- ✔ **Herbivore:** A plant eater
- ✔ **Keel:** A ridge in the carapace, usually from front to rear, that follows or parallels the spine
- ✔ **Plastron:** The lower shell covering the belly
- ✔ **Omnivore:** Eats both meat and plants
- ✔ **Scute:** A single section of the shell; each shell is made up of many scutes
- ✔ **Terrarium:** An aquarium or cage that contains live plants, higher humidity, and no swimming water

Wood Turtle (Clemmys insculpta)

This semi-terrestrial turtle, which grows up to 10 inches in length, has a brown, rough-textured carapace. This rough texture looks like carved wood, hence the turtle's name. The plastron is yellow with dark markings. The head and neck may have orange spots or colorings. (See Figure 7-1.)

Figure 7-1:
The wood turtle (*Clemmys insculpta*).

✔ **Geographical origin:** South from eastern Canada to northern Virginia, and west to Michigan and northern Iowa.

Buy only captive-bred wood turtles — don't pick one up in the wild and take it home with you. These attractive turtles are protected in almost all their native states. Check the laws in your area regarding wood turtle ownership.

✔ **Native habitat:** Deciduous woodlands, fields, and meadows.

The wood turtle is a good example of the variety of behaviors found within one species. In some parts of its geographic range, the wood turtle is almost totally terrestrial, hence its inclusion in this category. However, in other parts of its range, this species spends quite a bit of time in or near water. To satisfy both of these needs (terrestrial and semi-aquatic) when keeping wood turtles, keep them in a terrestrial habitat but provide water in the cage at all times — even if it's just enough to wade through or soak in.

✔ **Captive environment:** This active turtle needs a large indoor cage or a secure outdoor enclosure. Provide hiding places such as potted plants. Provide water in a large plant saucer and a basking light.

The cage or enclosure must be very secure; this species is known for its climbing ability.

✔ **Diet:** You can feed this omnivorous species a variety of foods in captivity. Commercially grown insects (crickets, mealworms, and waxworms) are acceptable, as are snails, slugs, sowbugs, pillbugs, and earthworms. Canned dog food, soaked dry dog food, commercial turtle food, and chopped green vegetables are also good. Every once in a while, offer a tomato or strawberry.

✔ **Breeding:** Rain can trigger breeding, which takes place after hibernation. In an outside enclosure, you can stimulate this instinct by turning on the sprinklers. Males can be quite aggressive, and often only one can be kept in each cage or enclosure. Eight to ten eggs are laid and should be incubated at 80 to 84 degrees and 90 percent humidity. Eggs hatch in about 40 days.

Pay a visit to some turtle friends

The Columbus Zoo is home to one of the largest reptile collections in the United States. This zoo specializes in turtles and has bred more than 40 different species, including the rare yellow-spotted Amazon turtle.

Stompin' at the Savoy

Many people believe that the wood turtle is one of the most intelligent of the chelonian family. These turtles have even been taught to run mazes for behavior experts. In the wild, this species has been seen *worm stomping:* The turtle lifts its front legs off the ground and thumps them back down very hard. Earthworms respond to the vibration by coming out of the soil. It takes a smart turtle to figure that out!

Brown Wood Turtle (Rhinoclemmys annulata)

This medium-sized (6 to 8 inches in length) terrestrial turtle is brown to black. It has a relatively high carapace. The carapace may be entirely brown or black or may have orange or tan spots or blotches. The plastron is dark, too, but it may have yellow seams or borders. Males have more concave plastrons, thicker tails, and narrower shells.

- **Geographical origin:** Central America, from Panama south through Costa Rica, Ecuador, Columbia, and Nicaragua.

- **Native habitat:** This turtle is found in tropical rainforests and lowland forests up to 1,500 feet in elevation.

- **Captive environment:** A standard terrarium suits this species. Use leaf litter or shredded bark to create hiding places. Supply a basking area. Make sure that these turtles have some water; they like to soak and use water for mating.

- **Diet:** This herbivorous species feeds primarily on seedlings, shrubs, and fruits. A diet composed of a variety of vegetables, fruits, and commercial iguana (an herbivorous lizard) works well. Some brown wood turtles also eat insects, so you may want to offer mealworms or crickets and see what response you get. If you do feed insects, especially to a breeding female turtle, make sure that you feed the insects first, before any plant food, so that she gets the added nutrition.

- **Breeding:** These little turtles lay only one or two eggs at a time — unusual for the chelonian world. Breeding usually occurs after a rain and may happen in the water. Males can be somewhat aggressive, so keep only one male in each cage or enclosure. Incubate the eggs at 84 degrees and high (90 percent) humidity. Incubation times vary widely, from 65 to 90 days. Hatchlings can be carnivorous in the beginning, eating more plant matter as they grow up.

Furrowed Wood Turtle (Rhinoclemmys areolata)

This terrestrial turtle has a relatively high-domed, keeled carapace that's dark brown in color, often with yellow blotches. It grows up to 8 inches in length. The plastron is yellow with dark blotches. The skin is dark with yellow or red stripes or red circles.

- ✔ **Geographical origin:** Mexico south through Guatemala.

- ✔ **Native habitat:** This grasslands turtle is especially attracted to damp grasslands bordering on marshy areas. It has also been found in wooded areas.

- ✔ **Captive environment:** A standard terrarium is fine as long as you provide hiding places. Provide water and a basking area. This wood turtle likes higher humidity than many other wood turtles do. Using shredded bark as a base can help increase the humidity without creating a sour or smelly cage.

- ✔ **Diet:** This omnivorous species eats insects, vegetables, and fruits, as well as crickets, earthworms, and waxworms.

- ✔ **Breeding:** As with many wood turtles, breeding usually begins after a rainfall. Only one male should be kept in each cage, as males can battle quite ferociously, sometimes hurting each other. Males sometimes bite the female, too, so after breeding sessions, check her for injuries, especially to the head and neck. A clutch is usually just one or two eggs; incubated at 84 degrees in high (90 percent) humidity, they generally hatch in 65 to 70 days.

If the eggs don't hatch at 70 days, don't toss them out. Some wood turtles have delayed development and may hatch as late as 90 days after laying.

Mexican Red Wood Turtle (Rhinoclemmys rubida)

This medium-sized (up to 6 inches) turtle has a brown carapace that's rough in texture, with a medial keel and posterior serrated scutes. The plastron is yellow with brown blotches. A yellow horseshoe-shaped spot is on the top of the head. Other yellow stripes mark the sides of the head.

- ✓ **Geographical origin:** The west coast of Mexico, particularly rocky hillsides.

- ✓ **Native habitat:** This species lives in low scrublands and woodlands.

- ✓ **Captive environment:** A standard terrarium works well. This turtle likes to dig, so shredded bark makes the perfect base for its terrarium. Supply water in a shallow plant saucer. Also provide a basking area.

- ✓ **Diet:** Mexican spotted wood turtles are omnivores, eating just about anything. In captivity, feed a varied diet of insects, meats, vegetables, fruits, and commercial turtle foods.

- ✓ **Breeding:** As with most wood turtles, a rainfall often stimulates breeding. A clutch is usually one or two eggs; incubated at 84 degrees, the eggs usually hatch in 65 to 70 days.

  Hatchlings can be quite carnivorous and may not take plant foods for the first few months, but offer them anyway. Favorite foods for hatchlings include small mealworms, earthworms, waxworms, and small crickets.

Diamondback Terrapin (Malaclemys terrapin)

This small to medium-sized turtle has a gray, brown, or black carapace. Some individuals have concentric growth rings on each scute. Some also have knobs or keels on the carapace, as shown in Figure 7-2. The skin is light with dark flecks or spots. The eyes are black. Females grow up to 9½ inches long, and males to between 4 and 5 inches.

Figure 7-2:
The diamond-back terrapin (Mala-clemys terrapin).

These turtles are attractive and appeal to many people. Some experts feel that captive breeding may be needed to help save them from future extinction. However, they do require specialized care (such as the brackish water mentioned later in this section). Don't attempt to keep these turtles unless you can meet their needs.

- ✔ **Geographical origin:** Eastern North America, from Cape Cod south to the Florida Keys and west to Texas.

- ✔ **Native habitat:** This is truly a brackish water turtle that's rarely found in fresh water. It thrives in tidal flats, coastal marshes, coves, and lagoons.

During the 19th century, the diamondback terrapin was hunted extensively for food. It was considered the most desirable and tastiest turtle for eating. Thousands upon thousands were shipped to markets and restaurants in New York and other large cities. By the early 1900s, diamondbacks had become rare or nonexistent in many parts of their geographic range, especially in the north. Legal protection has helped the turtles recover somewhat, but unfortunately, some ethnic groups still demand turtle meat.

- ✔ **Captive environment:** Special care is needed to provide brackish water conditions in captivity. A tropical fish store specializing in saltwater fish can sell you the tools you need to set up and maintain a saltwater environment. In addition, this turtle needs hiding places and land area with a basking lamp.

- ✔ **Diet:** In captivity, these turtles readily eat snails, earthworms, and other insects. In addition, offer chopped green vegetables, commercial turtle food, and soaked dry dog food.

- ✔ **Breeding:** Mating takes place in the spring, usually underwater. Four to eighteen eggs, with six being the typical clutch, are laid and should be incubated at 86 degrees with high humidity. Hatching takes place in about 65 days.

Giant Asian Pond Turtle (Heosemys grandis)

This fairly large (up to 19 inches in length) semi-terrestrial turtle has a brown to black carapace, the rear of which is serrated. The yellow plastron may have fine line markings, usually in brown, which show up clearly on a yellow background.

✔ **Geographical origin:** Thailand, Burma, Malaysia, Cambodia, Vietnam, and Laos.

✔ **Native habitat:** Although this turtle does go into the water frequently, it also spends a lot of time on land. It lives in and near rivers, ponds, swamps, and marshes.

✔ **Captive environment:** In captivity, these turtles seem to spend most of their time out of the water, so a standard terrarium works fine. Supply water in a large plant saucer. Hiding places and potted plants are needed, as is a basking spot.

✔ **Diet:** This omnivorous turtle eats insects and plants. In captivity, these turtles are attracted to tomatoes and strawberries. Feed a balanced diet of vegetables, fruits, insects, dog food, and commercial turtle food.

✔ **Breeding:** A typical clutch is one to eight eggs. The eggs should be incubated at 80 degrees with 90 percent humidity for 99 to 113 days. Hatchlings are primarily carnivorous, becoming omnivorous as adults. Feed a vitamin/mineral supplement twice a week.

Black-Breasted Leaf Turtle or Vietnam Wood Turtle (Geoemyda spengleri)

This small (up to 5 inches in length) brown turtle has three keels on its carapace, which is serrated. Its skin color is olive-brown with a yellow stripe on the head. Males have slightly concave plastrons and longer, thicker tails.

✔ **Geographical origin:** Southern China through Vietnam, as well as the island of Okinawa.

✔ **Native habitat:** This terrestrial turtle rarely enters the water, and then only to drink. It lives in forests and wooded areas, where it likes to hide in leaf litter.

✔ **Captive environment:** A standard terrarium works well as long as you use shredded bark as a base and supply plenty of hiding places. Offer water in a small, shallow plant saucer.

✔ **Diet:** This omnivorous species readily accepts snails and other insects as well as a variety of fruits. In captivity, it also eats commercial turtle foods.

✔ **Breeding:** Eggs should be incubated at 78 degrees and 90 percent humidity for about 70 days.

Asian Leaf Turtle (Cyclemys dentata)

This turtle has a well-camouflaged carapace that resembles the leaves it hides in. The dark brown carapace has flaring, pointed marginal scutes that blend in with fallen leaves. The plastron is lighter in color with darker, thin stripes. Males have longer, thicker tails. Adult turtles reach 10 inches in length and are more terrestrial; juveniles are very aquatic.

- **Geographical origin:** Northern India south through Burma, Thailand, Vietnam, Burma, and Malaysia.

- **Native habitat:** This secretive species has been hard to study in the wild. As a result, expert opinions differ. Some experts claim that this species is semi-aquatic, while others claim that it's semi-terrestrial. To simplify matters, these turtles spend some time in the water but also spend a considerable amount of time on land. For the most part, they are found near hilly or mountainous streams and are quite active at dawn and dusk.

- **Captive environment:** Provide a land area with lots of hiding places. Shredded bark makes a good base. This species needs more water than just a shallow plant saucer, so you may want to use a small plastic pan (such as a dishpan or kitty litter box). The water must be either filtered or changed daily. Provide a basking area, too.

Although these turtles are shy in the wild, in captivity they're known to be hardy pets, easy to keep healthy and well fed. Many owners say that they're also quite responsive, learning to recognize their owners (feeders).

- **Diet:** Hatchlings are quite carnivorous, eating just about any moving thing that they can fit in their mouths. Adults are more omnivorous and eat insects, fruits, and vegetables. Some have learned to accept commercial turtle foods and soaked dry dog food.

- **Breeding:** The two to four eggs laid should be incubated at 82 degrees with 80 percent humidity for 75 to 90 days. Several clutches per year may be laid.

Stripe-Neck Leaf Turtle (Cyclemys tcheponensis)

The carapace of this 9-inch turtle is dark brown with a medial keel. The plastron is light brown. Dark brown radiations mark the shell. The head is dark, with four stripes along the head and neck. Males have longer, thicker tails. In both sexes, the rear of the carapace is serrated.

When possible, buy a captive-bred stripe-neck leaf turtle, because many wild-caught specimens are infested with parasites.

- **Geographical origin:** Vietnam, Laos, and Thailand.

- **Native habitat:** This turtle always lives near water but spends part of its time on land.

- **Captive environment:** A standard well-planted terrarium works well. Supply water in a shallow plant saucer. This species needs high humidity, so mist the terrarium daily.

  This alert and active turtle, not at all shy, rapidly becomes tame in captivity. It can make a very responsive pet and quickly learns to eat from the hand.

- **Diet:** This omnivorous species eagerly eats a variety of foods. Offer insects, fruits, and commercial turtle foods.

- **Breeding:** The ten to fifteen eggs laid should be incubated at 82 degrees with 80 percent humidity for 75 to 90 days.

Vietnamese or Jagged-Shelled Turtle (Pyxidea mouhotii)

This small turtle, 8 inches or less in length, has a brown and somewhat flat (rather than domed) carapace. The plastron is yellow with brown blotches. The head is relatively large with a hooked upper jaw. The skin is dark gray. Males have brown skin on the head with red stripes, while females are yellowish with yellow stripes. The irises of males' eyes are also reddish, while females' eyes are yellowish. Both sexes have serrated rear carapaces and three well-developed keels running lengthwise down the carapace.

- **Geographical origin:** Cambodia, Vietnam, Laos, northeast India, and Thailand.

- **Native habitat:** This turtle lives in tropical forests where it hides in leaf litter. It's not an aquatic turtle but does like to live near water. If its environment is too dry, it will estivate until the next rain.

- **Captive environment:** A standard terrarium works well, as long as you provide a shallow water bowl (plant saucer). Leaf litter, shredded bark, and potted plants can provide hiding places. This turtle enjoys basking and being sprinkled.

✔ **Diet:** This species is omnivorous, eating insects and fallen fruit. In captivity, feed a variety of foods, including earthworms, commercial insects, fruit, commercial turtle foods, canned dog food, and soaked dry dog food.

✔ **Breeding:** The one to three eggs laid should be incubated at 80 degrees and 90 to 100 percent humidity for 75 to 90 days.

This turtle has not often been successfully bred in captivity. However, provided the right environment, captive breeding can be done. Humidity in the environment seems to be one key. The species likes humidity, so mist your turtle a couple of times a day. If she lays eggs, incubate them in damp vermiculite (90 to 100 percent humidity) at 80 degrees until they hatch. Hatchlings are primarily carnivorous.

Indochinese Box Turtle or Flowered Box Turtle (Cuora galbinifrons)

This small turtle, about 8 inches in length, has a high-domed carapace that's dark brown to black in color with lighter-colored blotches. Juveniles have a keel, but it disappears in adults. Yellow to cream stripes may be present on the carapace. The plastron is brown to black but may have some yellow markings. The head is dark also, again with lighter stripes or blotches. The plastron can close completely, enclosing the turtle inside.

✔ **Geographical origin:** Southern China south through Vietnam.

✔ **Native habitat:** This terrestrial species is usually found in bushy habitats at high altitudes, as well as in forests.

✔ **Captive environment:** A standard terrestrial setup works well. You can supply water in a shallow plant saucer. Potted plants, shredded bark, and leaf litter make excellent hiding places.

This turtle can be very shy; when disturbed, it closes itself in its shell and doesn't open up for quite a long time. If there is too much activity, this turtle will suffer from stress. Hiding places can give the turtle some security, but resist handling the turtle until it adjusts to captivity. Better yet, buy only captive-bred turtles.

✔ **Diet:** In captivity, this turtle eats insects, earthworms, chopped meat, canned dog food, some fruits, and commercial turtle food.

Breeding: Most Indochinese box turtles share similarities regarding breeding. The males can be quite aggressive breeders. Three to four eggs are laid per clutch. The eggs should be incubated at 82 degrees with 95 to 100 percent humidity for 70 to 85 days.

Chinese Box Turtle (Cuora flavomarginata)

Also called the yellow-margined box turtle, this is an attractive little turtle. It has a dark brown carapace (up to 7 inches in length) with a yellow dorsal keel. The plastron is brown in the center with yellow along the border. The skin is lighter in color with a yellow stripe on the head. A vertebral keel runs down the carapace, as do two broken, disrupted keels on either side. The male's plastron is rounded in the rear, while the female's is bent upward slightly. The male also has a longer, thicker tail.

- ✔ **Geographical origin:** China, Taiwan, and the Ryukyu islands.

- ✔ **Native habitat:** This shallow water turtle is found in and around flooded rice fields and marshes. It spends most of its time on land and, when disturbed, pulls into its shell, closing the plastron.

- ✔ **Captive environment:** A standard terrarium works well, with water in a plant saucer and potted plants for hiding. Also offer a basking area.

- ✔ **Diet:** This omnivorous species eats fruits, fish, insects, and commercial turtle food. As with most omnivores, providing a varied diet is important.

- ✔ **Breeding:** Breeding usually takes place in the rainy season or after a rain. Males can be quite aggressive, so check females for injuries after breeding attempts. Single egg clutches aren't unusual in this species. Eggs should be incubated at 82 degrees, 90 to 95 percent humidity, for 70 to 85 days.

Chinese Three-Striped Box Turtle (Cuora trifasciata)

This handsome turtle, about 8 inches long, has a medium-brown carapace highlighted by three black stripes running from head to tail. The plastron is dark brown also and has a hinge. The skin is gray with black and white stripes on the head.

- ✔ **Geographical origin:** Southern China through northern Vietnam, Hainan Island, and Hong Kong.

- ✔ **Native habitat:** This turtle lives near water, primarily streams, but spends most of its time on land.

✔ **Captive environment:** A standard terrarium suits this species. Supply water in a shallow plant saucer. This species is not quite as shy as some of the other *Cuora* box turtles, and they like to bask, so include a basking light and area in the cage or enclosure.

✔ **Diet:** This species is entirely carnivorous, eating snails, earthworms, and other insects, as well as small fish. In captivity, you can offer small feeder fish and commercially available insects, as well as insects from your backyard.

✔ **Breeding:** Breeding usually takes place after a rain. Males can be quite aggressive, so only one male should be kept in each cage or enclosure. Check females for injuries after breeding attempts. Single egg clutches are not unusual in this species, although two eggs are typical. Eggs should be incubated at 82 to 86 degrees, 90 to 95 percent humidity, for 60 to 85 days.

Indian Black Turtle (Melanochelys trijuga)

This plain-colored semi-terrestrial turtle has an elongated carapace with three slightly elevated dorsal keels. The carapace is dark brown, as is the plastron. The head is also brown, although usually lighter in color than the shell. A male's tail is longer and thicker than a female's. The Indian black turtle generally grows to a little over 15 inches in length.

✔ **Geographical origin:** India, Nepal, Burma, Sri Lanka, and Bangladesh.

✔ **Native habitat:** The Indian black turtle always lives near water. It swims well, but it spends considerable time out of the water basking. In hot, dry weather, it estivates under leaf litter until rains come.

✔ **Captive environment:** A standard terrarium works well, with water supplied in a shallow plant saucer. Leaf litter and other hiding places are necessary. It's unknown whether a basking light is needed; to be safe, supply one and see whether your turtle uses it.

✔ **Diet:** This herbivorous species has omnivorous tendencies, eating aquatic plants, vegetation, and occasionally carrion. As with all herbivores and omnivores, a varied diet is best.

✔ **Breeding:** Males can be quite aggressive during breeding. Keep only one male per enclosure, and check females for injuries. Eggs should be incubated at 76 to 78 degrees with 100 percent humidity for 70 days.

Chapter 8

North American Box Turtles

· ·

In This Chapter

▶ Finding out about North American box turtles

▶ Setting up the proper environment

▶ Knowing how and what to feed a box turtle

· ·

Orth American box turtles have long been among the most popular pet turtles. Most of the species adapt quite well to captivity and, when provided with the right environment, breed readily in captivity. These medium-sized turtles are attractive, amusing, personable, and intelligent. With proper care, it's not unusual for these turtles to live for 75 to 100 years.

In this chapter, I list the North American box turtles separately because they can be such special pets. The other box turtle species listed in Chapters 6 and 7 are unrelated to the North American box turtles.

Keep the following in mind when selecting or living with a box turtle:

✔ A box turtle can close its shell so tightly that even a knife blade can't be inserted. (Don't try this at home, please!) It can remain that way for up to an hour, breathing very little, until it senses that the danger has moved on.

Because of habitat destruction and overcollection for the pet trade, some box turtle species are now protected. If you want a box turtle as a pet, make sure that it's captive-bred, not wild-caught. Also check the local and state laws to make sure that it's legal for you to have a particular species.

✔ Because box turtles like to bask in the sun, especially in the early morning, situate your outside enclosure so that it gets early-morning sun. In fact, as long as box turtles have hiding places and shady spots where they can cool off, the enclosure can get sun all day. (Chapter 15 tells you how to build an outdoor enclosure.)

- ✔ Most box turtles hibernate in the winter, and healthy adults should be allowed to do so. If you have an outside enclosure, a pile of straw or shredded bark over some soft sand or dirt will suffice as a hibernation spot. After the turtles dig in, place a waterproof board over the pile to keep out some of the weather. Indoor turtles can hibernate in a small box placed in a cool, dark place in the house.

- ✔ Breeding box turtles is relatively easy. Breeding behavior starts in the spring after hibernation and is an active, drawn-out affair. Four to eight eggs are laid per clutch and should be incubated at or above 83 degrees to produce females and below that temperature to produce males, both at 90 to 100 percent humidity. Eggs begin hatching after 57 to 136 days.

As you go through some of the information in this chapter, watch for the following terminology:

- ✔ **Basking site or basking area:** An area for a turtle to absorb warmth from sunshine or another heat source

- ✔ **Carapace:** The top shell covering the back

- ✔ **Carnivore:** A meat eater

- ✔ **Carrion:** Decaying flesh that's used for food

- ✔ **Clutch:** A nest of eggs

- ✔ **Hatchlings:** Baby turtles

- ✔ **Plastron:** The lower shell covering the belly

- ✔ **Omnivore:** Eats both meat and plants

- ✔ **Scute:** A single section of the shell covering, like a fingernail; each shell is made up of many scutes

- ✔ **Terrarium:** An aquarium or cage that contains live plants, a higher humidity, and no swimming water

A long, long time ago

Terra means "land" or "earth," and *terrapen* means "land turtle": The Latin family name for box turtles is *Terrapene.* One and a half million years ago, a box turtle known as *Terrapene* *carolina putnami* lived throughout the southern United States. It was larger than today's box turtles, with a carapace of over 10 inches in length.

Toxic turtle

Whereas the diamondback terrapin (see Chapter 7) was nearly driven to extinction because of its use as a gourmet food item, the box turtle never had to worry. Native Americans warned the early white settlers that the little golden box turtle was poisonous, and those who didn't believe the Native Americans soon learned to trust them. Apparently, box turtles in the wild consume wild fungi (mushrooms and toadstools) that can make their flesh toxic.

Eastern Box Turtle (Terrapene carolina carolina)

This medium-sized box turtle measures about 4 to 6 inches from nose to tail along the carapace. The carapace is high-domed, usually golden brown in color with brightly colored markings (see Figure 8-1). The plastron is concave in males and flat in females, and it can close completely, enclosing the turtle inside. The dark skin may have bright red or yellow spots, splashes, or blotches of color. This turtle has four toes on each hind foot. The claws of a male's hind feet are short and curved, while on females the rear claws are longer and straighter. Males also have longer, thicker tails and bright red eyes.

Figure 8-1:
The eastern box turtle (*Terrapene carolina carolina*).

- ✔ **Geographical origin:** From Maine south to northern Florida and west to Michigan and Tennessee.
- ✔ **Native habitat:** This turtle particularly likes open woodlands, shrubs, and fields. It drinks water and sometimes soaks in shallow water, but it's not an aquatic turtle.

✔ **Captive environment:** Hatchlings and juveniles can be maintained in a standard terrarium with hiding places and a basking spot. Adults, however, do much better outside. Indoors, adults tend to get lethargic or just the opposite, too active, beating up against the sides of their terrarium.

In an outdoor setup, provide hiding places and water in a shallow plant saucer. Although these turtles are not aquatic — or really even semi-aquatic — by nature, water is important. A cage or enclosure that's too dry can lead to significant health problems, including those of the eyes and ears. Make sure that there is always water in the shallow saucer, and either mist the indoor cage or turn the sprinklers on in the outdoor enclosure on a regular basis.

The outside enclosure must be escape-proof; these little turtles are great climbers and enthusiastic escape artists.

✔ **Diet:** The eastern box turtle is an omnivore as an adult. This turtle will try just about any food placed in front of it, making it easy to feed. A balanced captive diet should include insects, earthworms, canned dog food, soaked dry dog food, chopped fruit (including strawberries and bananas), and tomatoes. Your eastern box turtle will even appreciate a little tofu once in a while. Hatchlings are carnivores and become more omnivorous as they grow up.

✔ **Breeding:** Breeding behavior starts in the spring after hibernation and is an active, drawn-out affair. Four to eight eggs are laid per clutch and should be incubated at 78 to 83 degrees at 90 to 100 percent humidity. Eggs begin hatching after 70 to 85 days.

Three-Toed Box Turtle (Terrapene carolina triunguis)

The most obvious difference between this turtle and the eastern box turtle is the number of toes on the back feet. The eastern box turtle has four toes, and the three-toed box turtle has — guess? — yes, three toes. Otherwise, the two species look very much alike. Males often have red on their heads. Males also have thicker, longer tails and slightly concave plastrons. This turtle grows to about 5 inches in length.

✔ **Geographical origin:** Central and southern North America, from Missouri south through Texas and east to Alabama and the Florida panhandle.

✔ **Native habitat:** This turtle is terrestrial but goes into the water more willingly than the eastern box turtle does. The three-toed box turtle has even been found foraging in the water. Otherwise, this turtle inhabits a wide variety of terrain, usually staying close to water and food.

✔ **Captive environment:** This box turtle does well inside as a hatchling and as a juvenile but should be kept outside as an adult. Like the eastern box turtle, it will struggle to escape if kept inside too long. Indoor enclosures should include a basking spot and hiding places.

Three-toed box turtles enjoy humidity. A cage or enclosure that's too dry can lead to significant health problems, including those of the eyes and ears. Make sure that water is always present in a shallow saucer, and either mist the indoor cage or turn the sprinklers on in the outdoor enclosure on a regular basis.

Outside, a standard terrestrial turtle enclosure works well. Make sure to provide plenty of hiding spots. Because this turtle likes water, you can provide a slightly larger water bowl, but make sure that the turtle can get in and out easily without tipping over.

✔ **Diet:** This box turtle is an omnivore and will eat just about anything. When it forages in the water, it eats small fish, amphibians, and aquatic plants. On land, it eats earthworms, snails, slugs, and fallen fruits. In captivity, a varied and balanced omnivore diet suits it quite well. Hatchlings are carnivorous, often refusing food that's not alive. Juveniles become more omnivorous as they grow up.

✔ **Breeding:** Breeding behavior is apt to occur during or after a rain, especially a thunderstorm. Some researchers, noting the tendency for this behavior to be stimulated by a thunderstorm, wonder whether the electrical charges in the air from these storms have anything to do with the turtles' behavior. The research will be interesting!

Florida Box Turtle (Terrapene carolina bauri)

The carapace of this species of box turtle is much thinner and higher than those of other box turtles are; it is high-domed and golden to dark brown in color, often with bright yellow radiating markings. The head also has yellow stripes or spots. Males have slightly concave plastrons, shorter rear claws, and longer, thicker tails than females. Males may also have red irises, but both sexes usually have dark eyes and heads with a blue-black cast. These turtles range in size from 6 to 9 inches.

✔ **Geographical origin:** Central Florida south through the Keys.

The Florida box turtle is protected in its native state; if you see one, don't pick it up to carry it home. However, this attractive subspecies is becoming more readily available from breeders.

✔ **Native habitat:** These box turtles, like three-toed box turtles, willingly go into water more often than other species. Some even forage in the water, although they spend most of their time on land.

✔ **Captive environment:** Hatchlings and juveniles can be housed inside, but adults should be kept in an outdoor enclosure. Provide lots of hiding places, as well as potted plants. A pile of shredded bark gives the turtles something to burrow into. They also need a basking spot.

Because these turtles like water, provide something a little bigger than a plant saucer for water. Just make sure that the turtles can climb in and out safely without flipping over.

✔ **Diet:** Hatchlings and juveniles are carnivorous (usually exclusively so), and adults are omnivorous. Feed a good, balanced omnivore diet with an emphasis on variety. Include insects, earthworms, snails, fruits, and tomatoes in the diet.

✔ **Breeding:** Breeding behavior is most apt to occur during or after a rain, especially a thunderstorm. You may occasionally see females laying their eggs during a thunderstorm.

Gulf Coast Box Turtle (Terrapene carolina major)

Gulf Coast box turtles, which grow up to 9 inches in length, are the largest North American box turtles. The carapace is very dark, often black, and sometimes has radiating light stripes on the scutes. An all-black turtle is not unusual. The carapace may have radiating yellow or light marks or lines on it, especially on a young turtle, but these markings often disappear as the turtle ages. This turtle also has webbed feet — more so than the other box turtles — and swims quite well.

✔ **Geographical origin:** Southwestern Georgia and northwestern Florida west to eastern Texas, along the coastal plain.

✔ **Native habitat:** This turtle is terrestrial but goes into the water occasionally to feed on insects or amphibian larvae. Otherwise, it's found in a variety of habitats throughout its geographic range.

Gulf Coast box turtles, depending on where they live (in the wild and as pets), may or may not hibernate. If they don't hibernate, they can stay amazingly active through the winter. You'll have to watch your turtles; if they don't hibernate, make sure that they have enough warmth to continue eating throughout the winter.

✔ **Captive environment:** A standard terrestrial setup outside is fine for adults; you can use a standard terrarium inside for hatchlings and juveniles. Don't attempt to keep adults indoors for a long period; they won't thrive.

Supply water in a shallow plant saucer. Clean it often, because this turtle often defecates in its water. In an indoor terrarium, provide a basking light and a soaking pad.

These turtles are very curious and explore their surroundings more than they hide. They appreciate having things to crawl in, on, and under. Make sure that the enclosure is escape-proof, too!

✔ **Diet:** This omnivorous species leans toward being carnivorous. Although all box turtle hatchlings are carnivorous, Gulf Coast box turtles seem to retain more of an appetite for live foods than most other box turtle species do. Although you should continue to offer insects and earthworms, make sure to supply a good, balanced, omnivore diet, too. Earthworms and snails are favorites, as are insects, strawberries, tomatoes, canned dog food, and soaked dry dog food. Tofu is a special treat.

✔ **Breeding:** Most box turtles breed after coming out of winter hibernation, but the Gulf Coast box turtle has a short hibernation period or doesn't hibernate at all. Many stay active and eating all winter long, and breeding occurs in the spring as the weather warms up and the days get longer. Typically, six eggs are laid in each clutch, and as many as four to five clutches can be produced in a breeding season.

Mexican Box Turtle (Terrapene carolina mexicana)

This three-toed turtle (on the rear feet) has a high-domed shell that's golden brown in color. Sometimes the carapace has yellow markings or spots; sometimes it's plain. Skin coloring can be quite bright, with red and/or yellow scales on a dark background. The Mexican box turtle grows to about 6 inches in length.

✔ **Geographical origin:** Eastern Mexico, from Nuevo Leon south to Vera Cruz.

✔ **Native habitat:** This turtle inhabits scrub forests and brushy grasslands. It's usually within walking distance of water but rarely goes in other than to drink.

This species is protected in the wild; if you're given one, make sure that it's captive-bred. As well as being illegal, wild-caught Mexican box turtles don't do well in captivity.

✔ **Captive environment:** As with most other box turtles, hatchlings and juveniles can be housed inside, but adults should be kept outside. A standard terrestrial turtle setup is fine. Water can be supplied in a shallow plant saucer. Provide a basking light for an indoor terrarium.

✔ **Diet:** Hatchlings are carnivorous but fairly quickly become omnivorous. This turtle is an opportunist, eating anything that appears in front of it. Supply a good, balanced, omnivore diet with plenty of variety. The Mexican box turtle likes insects, earthworms, and fruits especially well.

✔ **Breeding:** Breeding behavior for this species is very much like that for the other box turtles and usually occurs after a rain.

Yucatan Box Turtle (Terrapene carolina yucatana)

This four-toed species has a somewhat elongated, high-domed carapace that's brown with dark markings. The skin tends to be lighter than that of many other box turtles — sometimes even tan or beige. Males are about 6 inches in length; females are smaller.

✔ **Geographical origin:** Southeastern Mexico on the Yucatan Peninsula.

✔ **Captive environment:** Hatchlings can be kept inside in a terrarium, and adults can be kept outside in a terrestrial turtle enclosure. Provide hiding places as well as a basking light for an indoor terrarium. Offer water in a shallow plant saucer.

These turtles are rare and endangered. If you want to keep them, make sure that they are captive-bred and legally obtained. Other than hatchlings, prepare to keep them outside. Adults will not adapt to an indoor cage.

✔ **Diet:** This species is omnivorous, and although it's assumed that hatchlings are carnivores because of their preferences in captivity, little is known about hatchlings in the wild. Feed a varied, balanced, omnivore diet, including earthworms, commercially available insects, soaked dry dog food, canned dog food, chopped vegetables, and fruits.

✔ **Breeding:** Breeding behavior starts in the spring after hibernation, generally during or after a rain. Four to eight eggs are laid per clutch and should be incubated at 78 to 83 degrees at 90 to 100 percent humidity. Eggs begin hatching after 70 to 85 days.

Coahuila Aquatic Box Turtle (Terrapene coahuila)

This isolated species is golden brown in color, usually without markings on the shell. The carapace is high-domed, as it is on other box turtles. The plastron is yellow to olive with dark seams, and the skin is grayish brown to olive. This turtle has four toes on the hind feet. The male's plastron is concave, and he has a longer, thicker tail than a female. The male's eyes are brown flecked with yellow, and the female's are yellow flecked with brown. This turtle grows to about 6½ inches in length.

- **Geographical origin:** A pocket of box turtles became isolated in an oasis in Cuatro Cienegas, Mexico, surrounded by the desert.

- **Native habitat:** These box turtles began living in and around the oasis, not able to leave because of the desert. They are now living in and around small spring-fed marshes surrounded by desert.

- **Captive environment:** An outside terrestrial turtle enclosure works for these turtles as long as you provide a small pond or pool for them to soak, swim, and forage in.

- **Diet:** This species is omnivorous and, due to its circumstances in the wild, will even eat aquatic vegetation. In captivity, feed a varied omnivore diet that includes chopped dark green vegetables.

- **Breeding:** Mating usually occurs in the fall or winter when rains occur. The male pursues the female and bites at her head until she withdraws it into her shell. Several clutches of three to six eggs may be laid throughout the season. Hatchlings are brightly colored with yellow and black markings and are quite carnivorous, becoming more omnivorous as they grow up.

Ornate Box Turtle (Terrapene ornata ornata)

This turtle is high-domed, although higher above the hinge and more flat-topped than the *Terrapene carolina* turtles. The carapace is usually brown or gold with a pattern of yellow lines radiating across each scute. The plastron has dark brown lines across each yellow scute. The ornate box turtle grows to about 6 inches in length.

- **Geographical origin:** Texas (except in the Trans-Pecos region) north to Nebraska and southern South Dakota and east to Illinois.

- **Native habitat:** This species has adapted to arid grasslands and prairies, often living far from water.

  Living in deserts and arid grasslands, ornate box turtles are experts at finding water. It's not unusual to find them soaking in and drinking from puddles after a thunderstorm. They're most active at night and in the early morning.

- **Captive environment:** A standard (but larger than normal) terrestrial outdoor enclosure serves these turtles well; they don't thrive indoors. They also do better when they have plenty of room to roam. Provide hiding places, as well as some shredded bark or leaf litter to hide in. Also supply water in a shallow plant saucer.

  The walls of the enclosure should be higher than normal, because these turtles are escape artists and can climb quite well, especially in corners, where they brace their legs against each side and shimmy on up and over the walls.

- **Diet:** These turtles, like other box turtles, are carnivorous when young and omnivorous as adults. However, many ornate box turtles retain a tendency toward carnivorous eating habits even as adults. It's not unusual to see ornate box turtles eating carrion.

- **Breeding:** Breeding behavior starts in the spring after hibernation and usually occurs during or after a rain. Four to eight eggs are laid per clutch and should be incubated at 78 to 83 degrees at 90 to 100 percent humidity. Eggs begin hatching after 70 to 85 days.

Desert Box Turtle (Terrapene ornata luteola)

This turtle is though to be the descendent of the Pliestocene era box turtle *Terrapene carolina putnami*. It resembles the other box turtle species in many ways, with a high-domed shell and sometimes colorful skin or shell patterns, with one exception: It has a very dark plastron with no markings. This turtle grows to about 6 inches in length.

Most male box turtles have red irises; however, in these turtles, males may have red irises or bright yellow-green heads. Males do have longer, thicker tails than females, and the rear sections of their plastrons may be slightly concave.

- ✔ **Geographical origin:** Extreme western Texas, northern Mexico, southern New Mexico, and Arizona.

- ✔ **Native habitat:** This species lives in arid grasslands, prairies, and deserts with low brush being the dominant vegetation.

- ✔ **Captive environment:** A standard terrestrial outside enclosure works well for these turtles. As for the other ornate box turtles, the enclosure should be larger than normal and escape-proof. These turtles, especially the males, are inquisitive and active and will escape when they can. This turtle also likes to bask. Providing water in a shallow plant saucer is fine.

- ✔ **Diet:** As with other box turtles, the young of this subspecies are carnivorous. The adults are omnivorous with carnivorous tendencies, eating carrion, insects, fallen fruits, and vegetation. A varied omnivore diet that relies heavily on insects suits this turtle well.

- ✔ **Breeding:** Breeding behavior starts in the spring after hibernation. Two to four eggs are laid per clutch and should be incubated at 78 to 83 degrees at 90 to 100 percent humidity. Eggs begin hatching after 70 to 85 days.

Nayarit Box Turtle or Spotted Box Turtle (Terrapene nelsoni nelsoni)

This rather small (6-inch), narrow-bodied box turtle has coffee-colored spots on the carapace and plastron. The background color of the carapace is usually yellow to tan but may be darker. The plastron is dark brown, often with yellow borders, spots, and streaks. The skin of the head, legs, and tail is yellowish brown. The hind feet have four toes. Males have slightly concave plastrons and longer, thicker tails than females.

- ✔ **Geographical origin:** A very small area in Pedro Pablo in western Mexico, although other locations are suspected.

- ✔ **Native habitat:** This turtle lives in grass savannas, oak woodlands, and dry scrub forests, usually over 2,000 feet in elevation.

- ✔ **Captive environment:** A standard terrestrial outside enclosure works well for this turtle. A basking area is needed, either in the sun or artificially lit. Offer water in a shallow plant saucer. The Nayarit box turtle needs hiding places as well.

- ✔ **Diet:** Captives do well on a standard omnivore diet that includes animal protein, insects, fruits, and some vegetables. Some captives have learned to eat commercial turtle food.

- ✔ **Breeding:** Breeding behavior starts in the spring after hibernation. Two to four eggs are laid per clutch and should be incubated at 78 to 83 degrees at 90 to 100 percent humidity. The eggs begin hatching after 70 to 85 days.

Klauber's Box Turtle (Terrapene nelsoni klauberi)

Klauber's box turtle has a tan to dark brown carapace with numerous small spots. It has four toes on the hind feet and grows to 6 inches (or smaller) in length.

- **Geographical origin:** The southwestern Sonora and Terreros, Sinaloa areas of Mexico.

- **Native habitat:** Grasslands, hilly forests, and scrublands, usually under 1,000 feet in elevation.

- **Captive environment:** A standard terrestrial outside enclosure is fine. Provide hiding places, a basking spot, and water in a shallow plant saucer.

- **Diet:** This opportunistic omnivore eats many insects and some plant matter. In captivity, these turtles learn to accept a variety of foods, including insects, soaked dry dog food, commercial turtle food, and some fruits.

- **Breeding:** Breeding behavior starts in the spring after hibernation. Four to eight eggs are laid per clutch and should be incubated at 78 to 83 degrees at 90 to 100 percent humidity. The eggs begin hatching after 70 to 85 days.

Chapter 9

Small Tortoises

This chapter introduces you to ten of the most popular small tortoises, which are fun because they combine the traits of their bigger relatives with the more convenient size of smaller pets. Small tortoises are found on a few different continents, but most are from Europe, Asia, and Africa.

As you go through this chapter, you may see some unfamiliar terms. For reference, keep the following tortoise jargon in mind:

✔ **Basking site or basking area:** An area for a tortoise to absorb warmth from sunshine or another heat source

✔ **Carapace:** The top shell covering the back

✔ **Carrion:** Decaying flesh that's used for food

✔ **Carnivore:** A meat eater

✔ **Clutch:** A nest of eggs

✔ **Estivates:** Hibernates in summer

✔ **Hatchlings:** Baby tortoises

✔ **Herbivore:** A plant eater

✔ **Omnivore:** Eats both meat and plants

✔ **Plastron:** The lower shell covering the belly

✔ **Scute:** A single section of the shell; each shell is made up of many scutes

✔ **Terrarium:** An aquarium or cage that contains live plants, higher humidity, and no swimming water (Chapter 14 shows you how to build an indoor terrestrial tortoise habitat; Chapter 15 tells you how to build an outdoor enclosure)

Angulated Tortoise or Bowsprit Tortoise (Chersina angulata)

The carapace of this tortoise is red-tinted (with a reddish brown background color) and elongated. Males are typically larger than the females, reaching 10½ inches in length, while females rarely exceed 6½ inches.

- ✔ **Geographical origin:** South Africa.

- ✔ **Native habitat:** Dry grasslands and savannas.

- ✔ **Captive environment:** These tortoises do well outside during the summer months in warmer climates. Use a standard terrestrial tortoise setup. During the winter months, angulated tortoises don't hibernate and need a spacious indoor enclosure. These tortoises prefer a somewhat dry environment. Preferred temperatures range from 80 to 90 degrees.

- ✔ **Diet:** The angulated tortoise is an herbivorous species, so feed a varied herbivore diet (see Chapter 19). Alfalfa hay is usually accepted quite well. Tortoises in the wild have been seen to eat carrion and carnivores' feces, but because of the uncertainties of both items as food sources, I don't recommend either as part of a captive tortoise's diet.

- ✔ **Breeding:** Males battle quite strenuously during breeding and often flip each other over. Single eggs are laid several times during the summer. Incubate the eggs at 86 degrees and 60 to 70 percent humidity (or drier) for a little less than 3 months to 14 months. Females can lay several clutches each summer (up to seven have been reported) or can go a year between clutches. The normal interval between clutches is four to six weeks.

When a hatchling initially opens the egg, it breathes, and then it may remain in the egg for several days while absorbing the remaining nutrition from the egg sac. Don't try to take the hatchling from the egg, although you can gently mist the edges of the open egg to keep the hatchling from dehydrating and sticking to the egg. When you mist the egg and hatchling, you may dampen the hatchling, but don't drown it!

Pancake Tortoise (Malacochersus tornieri)

The pancake tortoise, which grows to 7 inches in length, is one of the most unique tortoises in the world: Because its carapace is flattened, the tortoise looks like it has been squashed! (See Figure 9-1.) The shell is flexible (to a certain extent) and is tan to golden-brown in color, sometimes with a lighter radiating pattern on the scutes. The plastron is yellow to tan with blotches of brown.

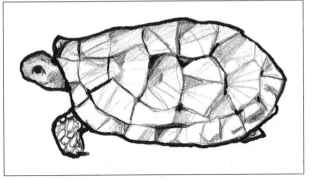

Figure 9-1:
The
pancake
tortoise
(Malaco-
chersus
tornieri).

- **Geographical origin:** East Africa along the Kenya-Tanzania border.

- **Native habitat:** This tortoise lives in arid scrub and grasslands that have a lot of rocks and boulders.

- **Captive environment:** Captive breeding of the pancake tortoise is increasing, and soon all pancake tortoises offered for sale will be captive-bred. These tortoises can be kept indoors if they have a fairly large cage. They do well outside in a dry, somewhat arid climate. (High humidity isn't conducive to good health for a pancake tortoise.) They do prefer a dry, rocky environment much like they would have in the wild.

  When threatened, this little tortoise runs quickly to rock piles and wedges itself into crevices. If something or someone tries to pull the tortoise from the rocks, it inflates its lungs and braces itself against the rocks. Hiding places, therefore, are absolutely necessary. These tortoises are great climbers and escape artists, so make sure that the sides of the cage or enclosure are high with a screen across the top or an inverted (to the inside of the cage or enclosure) board around the edges. Supply water in a shallow bowl. Keep daytime temperatures between 75 and 85 degrees, with a basking spot at about 90 degrees. Overnight temperatures should be cooler.

  These are fairly active tortoises, especially in the morning and afternoon. Being social in nature, they do well in a group.

- **Diet:** These tortoises are herbivores with a preference for grasses. If they live outside, give them grass to graze on. A bale of alfalfa hay also provides good nutrition. An herbivore diet of chopped dark green vegetables, with a vitamin/mineral supplement with a calcium:phosphorus ratio of 2:1 (or higher in calcium), is sufficient. A pancake tortoise might accept fruits as well.

- **Breeding:** Males battle during breeding season, often flipping each other over. Eggs are laid singly and should be incubated at 86 degrees at 50 to 70 percent humidity. Hatching generally occurs at about 140 days.

The owner of a California pet store was recently charged with violating the Endangered Species Act when he illegally imported 80 pancake tortoises from Tanzania. If convicted, the man faces up to ten years in prison and a maximum fine of $500,000. If you plan to own a pancake tortoise, make sure that the tortoise you buy is captive-bred!

Russian or Horsfield's Tortoise (Testudo or Geochelone horsfieldi)

This small tortoise (9 inches or less in length) has a golden-brown shell that isn't high-domed, but instead is just slightly rounded. Sometimes the plastron has some darker markings. The skin color is often very similar to the shell color, making the tortoise almost entirely a golden-brown color.

I've found Russian tortoises to be friendly, outgoing tortoises. When I step into their enclosure, they dash at my feet, nibbling at my toes (not hard) while I rub their heads. They literally beg for flowers and eat them from my hand.

- **Geographical origin:** Southeastern Russia from the Caspian Sea south through Iran, Afghanistan, and Pakistan.

- **Native habitat:** This little tortoise is found in dry and arid to semi-arid grasslands, through deserts and rocky hillsides. Because of its extended range, the Russian tortoise is often also called the *central Asian tortoise,* the *Afghan tortoise,* or the *steppe tortoise.* These various common names often lead to confusion, hence the reliance on the scientific name.

- **Captive environment:** This tortoise doesn't do well in an indoor enclosure; therefore, keep only hatchlings inside. Outside, a standard terrestrial turtle or small tortoise enclosure serves quite well. Make sure to set it up in a dry location, because these tortoises don't tolerate high humidity or dampness. Dig up a small area and mix the dirt with shredded bark to create a place where the tortoises can burrow and hide. Russian tortoises are eager, enthusiastic diggers, so make sure that the tortoises can dig burrows but can't dig under the walls of their enclosure. You can provide water in a shallow plant saucer, although these tortoises often don't use it. They do well in a small group in a large outdoor pen.

Russian tortoises have a reputation for being difficult to keep in captivity. I find them extremely easy to keep as long as they're outside and the enclosure is in a dry section of the yard.

Russians hibernate in the winter and estivate in the heat of summer. If adequate digging material and shelter are available, they can do both in their outdoor enclosure.

✔ **Diet:** This species is herbivorous but isn't much for grazing. Instead, these tortoises enjoy fleshy vegetables, some fruits, tomatoes, and flowers. Nasturtiums are particular favorites — a Russian tortoise will eat the flowers and the leaves.

✔ **Breeding:** Breeding behavior starts in late spring or early summer. Males kept together will battle; they also will court females of a different species and even challenge males of a different species. These little tortoises are so bold that a male of mine challenged a male sulcata (many times larger — see Chapter 11) and courted a female sulcata weighing over 130 pounds!

When courting a female, the male bobs his head up and down quite vigorously, much like iguanas and bearded dragons do. During breeding, the males are vocal, producing high-pitched squeaks. Breeding itself is quite aggressive. Three to five eggs are laid at a time, and up to four clutches per year can be laid. The eggs should be incubated at 82½ degrees, 70 to 80 percent humidity, and should hatch between three and ten months later.

Hermann's Tortoise (Testudo hermanni)

This tortoise is golden-brown in color with two dark stripes on the plastron. The marginal scutes of the carapace that extend over the rear legs flare out somewhat. Males have longer, thicker tails. Females are often larger than males, with females reaching 10 inches in length and males averaging about 5 inches and occasionally reaching 6 inches in length.

✔ **Geographical origin:** Europe, from France south through Italy, Greece, Yugoslavia, and Turkey.

Le Village des Tortugas is a turtle and tortoise conservation facility located outside Gonfaron, France. A number of different turtle and tortoise species find refuge there, but the facility specializes in breeding the Hermann's tortoise, France's only native tortoise.

✔ **Native habitat:** This tortoise lives in Mediterranean forests, arid grasslands, and scrub hillsides. Much of its natural habitat has been lost to development.

✔ **Captive environment:** This tortoise is hardy and resilient, but it does require a somewhat dry and sunny outdoor enclosure. It is more tolerant of dampness than the Russian tortoise but still doesn't thrive in a damp enclosure. This tortoise likes plants to hide under rather than burrows, so provide lots of hiding places.

These tortoises hibernate in the winter and may estivate during the extreme heat of summer, depending on their location.

✔ **Diet:** Like the Russian tortoise, this tortoise likes fleshy vegetables. (In the wild, it can be an agricultural pest.) A varied herbivore diet will do quite nicely. These little tortoises have also been known to eat insects, including snails and slugs, caught in their outside enclosure — behavior that isn't altogether unusual for herbivorous tortoise species. They are still considered herbivores, however, rather than true omnivores.

✔ **Breeding:** The males don't battle as many other species do, and they aren't quite as rough on the females, either. Eggs are laid in clutches of three to five, which should be incubated at 91 degrees, 80 percent humidity. They will hatch between 60 and 70 days later.

North African Tortoise or Moorish Tortoise (Testudo graeca)

You can find many subspecies of this tortoise, with males averaging about 6 inches in length and females averaging 7 to 8 inches. Although colors vary, this tortoise is often golden-brown with black flecks, spots, and markings. The skin is yellowish to tan, with small thigh *tubercles* (spurs) on the hind legs.

This species has been called a spur-thigh tortoise because of the spurs on its rear thighs. However, another tortoise is also called a spur-thigh: *Geochelone sulcata,* a much larger tortoise that's covered in Chapter 11, also has spurs. To prevent confusion, most experts are now calling *Geochelone sulcata* the sulcata tortoise and the *Testudo graeca* the North African tortoise.

✔ **Geographical origin:** Southern Spain to northern Africa to Israel, Syria, western Greece, Romania, and Bulgaria, and from Turkey east to Russia and Iran.

✔ **Native habitat:** Dry, open grasslands and arid hillsides.

✔ **Captive environment:** These tortoises don't do well inside. Their outdoor enclosure must be as large as possible and fairly dry with open sunny spots. Provide hiding places, too.

North African tortoises seem to have little resistance to some of the diseases, especially the upper respiratory diseases, that other tortoises carry. As a result, always keep these tortoises by themselves and not in mixed "herds" with other species.

✔ **Diet:** This tortoise really enjoys flowers, especially nasturtiums, hibiscus, and roses. Provide a varied herbivore diet that includes commercial tortoise food and a vitamin/mineral supplement with a calcium:phosphorus ratio of 2:1. Like the Hermann's tortoise, this tortoise has been known to eat insects, especially slugs and snails, but these seem to be opportunist situations rather than a true dietary trend.

✔ **Breeding:** A typical clutch is four to five eggs, which should be incubated at 91 degrees, 70 to 80 percent humidity; they may hatch between 70 and 85 days later, or even months later. After an egg is *pipped* (a tooth breaks the shell and the hatchling tortoise takes its first breath), the hatchling may remain in the egg for as long as two to three days while absorbing the egg sac. Don't try to pull the hatchling from the egg. You can, however, keep the hatchling and the egg damp by misting them gently to help prevent the hatchling from sticking to the egg's membranes or edges. Be careful not to drown the hatchling while misting it! Hatchlings usually begin eating within two days of coming out of the egg.

Greek Tortoise (Testudo graeca ibera)

This tortoise is a subspecies of *Testudo graeca* and is also known as the Turkish tortoise or Turkish spur-thigh tortoise. It's greenish brown with dark brown to black markings on the carapace (see Figure 9-2). Males average about 7 inches in length; females, about 8 inches.

Figure 9-2: The Greek tortoise *(Testudo graeca ibera)*.

✔ **Geographical origin:** Turkey, Greece, Romania, western Iran, Jordan, Iraq, and southern Russia.

✔ **Native habitat:** Grasslands, hillsides, and dry forests.

- **Captive environment:** This tortoise is hardy, robust, and very adaptable. Provide a standard outside terrestrial enclosure. Supply plenty of hiding places and open basking spots. These active tortoises often try to climb, so keep the sides of the enclosure relatively high. You can provide water in a shallow bowl or saucer.

- **Diet:** A standard herbivore diet (see Chapter 19) with a variety of foods will satisfy this tortoise's needs.

- **Breeding:** Males are quite active when courting and bump or ram the female while trying to make her stop walking away. If kept in a mixed-species enclosure, the males will battle with males of other species, although courtship is limited to their own species. Usually six to ten eggs are laid: Incubate them at 84 degrees and 80 to 90 percent humidity for 60 to 80 days.

Egyptian Tortoise (Testudo kleinmanni)

This tortoise is very small. Males are usually smaller than females; males average just under 4 inches in length, and females may reach 4½ inches. (The largest known female was just over 7 inches long.) The carapace is yellow to golden-brown in color, and the plastron is pale yellow.

- **Geographical origin:** Egypt, Libya, Israel, and the deserts of the Nile delta.

- **Native habitat:** The Egyptian tortoise prefers dry woodlands, dry scrublands, and deserts where vegetation exists.

Habitat loss and warfare are severely threatening this species' survival. In addition, collection for the pet trade has reduced those populations remaining. Captive breeding is increasing, however, and may be the future for this species. Verify local and federal laws prior to purchasing an Egyptian tortoise.

- **Captive environment:** These tortoises can be kept inside or outside in a secure, roomy terrestrial enclosure. Provide hiding places and basking areas. Keep daytime temperatures between 78 to 84 degrees. When the temperature is too high, these tortoises cease all activity and hide.

- **Diet:** Provide a standard herbivore diet with an emphasis on vegetables and other plant matter and a few fruits. You can also offer commercial tortoise food. Feed a vitamin/mineral supplement as well.

- **Breeding:** Breeding is an interesting time with these tortoises because they can be quite vocal. Males make a very untortoiselike sound. One or two eggs are laid at a time and should be incubated at 91 degrees and 70 to 80 percent humidity. Eggs hatch between two and three months later.

Chaco Tortoise (Geochelone or Chelondoidis chilensis)

The oval carapace is light to dark brown, and the *marginals* (the carapace rim of small scutes) are serrated in young tortoises. The plastron is light brown, sometimes with dark markings. Males are often larger than females. The average length of this species is about 10 inches.

- ✔ **Geographical description:** Southwestern Bolivia, western Paraguay, and Argentina.
- ✔ **Native habitat:** Dry grasslands, savannas, and thorn and scrub brush.
- ✔ **Captive environment:** Provide a standard terrestrial turtle habitat. Offer water in a shallow plant saucer and provide a basking area. These tortoises may or may not hibernate, depending on the climate. In colder regions, keep them inside through the winter, with temperatures ranging from 75 to 85 degrees and a basking hot spot at 90 degrees. Nighttime temperatures can be cooler.
- ✔ **Diet:** A good herbivore diet suits these tortoises. Feed lots of dark green plants, grasses, and a few fruits.
- ✔ **Breeding:** One to six eggs are laid and should be incubated at 86 degrees and 70 percent humidity for three to five months.

Bell's Hingeback Tortoise (Kinixys belliana)

While you can find several subspecies of hingeback tortoises, all have a hinged carapace that can close to protect the hind legs. (Hatchlings don't show their hinges.) The Bell's hingeback has a brown carapace with yellow to red markings, although markings vary. The plastron is yellow with darker markings. Both males and females average about 8½ inches in length.

- ✔ **Geographical origin:** Somalia south through Zaire and west through Senegal; East Africa south of the Sahara and Madagascar.
- ✔ **Native habitat:** Dry grasslands.
- ✔ **Captive environment:** Small tortoises can be kept inside, but adults do better in outdoor enclosures. This species needs a drier environment than many of the other hingeback tortoises do. Provide water in a shallow plant saucer.

✔ **Diet:** Hingeback tortoises are omnivores — unusual in tortoises, most of whom are herbivores. These tortoises eat snails, slugs, insects, earthworms, fruits, and green plants. Provide a standard omnivore diet with an emphasis on variety. In an outside enclosure, keep a small compost heap where the tortoises can dig for worms and sowbugs.

✔ **Breeding:** Even though males kept together often fight — sometimes very roughly — a male kept with at least one other male will breed better. Because of the potential for harm when they do fight, supervise them closely and watch for wounds and other injuries. Four to eight eggs are laid at a time and should be incubated at 86 degrees and 80 percent humidity. Eggs hatch about three months later. Several clutches may be laid each summer in intervals of four to six weeks.

Serrated Hingeback Tortoise (Kinixys erosa)

This tortoise has a hinged carapace, which is dark brown, sometimes with yellow markings. The plastron is also dark, again sometimes with yellow markings. The marginal scutes have a jagged appearance, hence the name *serrated.* This species is the largest of the hingeback tortoises, with males reaching 12 inches in length and females reaches 10 inches.

✔ **Geographical origin:** West Africa east toward Gabon, Congo, and Uganda.

✔ **Native habitat:** This tortoise lives in forests, including tropical forests, and prefers damper areas. It has even been found in water — very unusual for a tortoise.

✔ **Captive environment:** This tortoise requires high humidity to stay healthy. It actually does well in a greenhouse, which is hot and humid. Use a terrestrial enclosure (inside or outside), but keep the humidity level high, either by keeping the outdoor enclosure wet or by using a plastic sheet to roof part of the enclosure. Placing several plants in the enclosure provides a wooded look and offers hiding places.

✔ **Diet:** This omnivorous species eats a variety of insects, snails, slugs, and worms, as well as plants and fruits. A varied omnivore diet is fine.

✔ **Breeding:** Males are quite aggressive at breeding time and may inflict serious injuries on each other when battling. The male may even cause damage to the female in his excitement, so check females for injuries after all breeding attempts. Two to four eggs are laid at a time and should be incubated at 84 degrees, 80 percent humidity. They hatch after 90 to 100 days.

Texas Tortoise (Gopherus berlandieri)

The Texas tortoise has a light brown to yellowish carapace; the plastron is tan to yellow. Males have longer, narrower carapaces than females and concave plastrons. This species is not as large as its cousins, the desert tortoise and the Florida gopher tortoise. Average length is between 6 and 8 inches.

- **Geographical origin:** Southern Texas south into northeastern Mexico.

- **Native habitat:** Scrub forests in southern Texas, arid grasslands, open woods, and arid deserts.

- **Captive environment:** Provide an outdoor enclosure with sunny basking spots and a few plants for hiding. This small tortoise tolerates humidity better than the desert tortoise does. A doghouse with an incandescent bulb for heat is needed.

Although these tortoises will live together in a group, avoid overcrowding, which creates stress. A group of one male and three females can live comfortably in a 20 foot x 20 foot enclosure.

- **Diet:** This species is herbivorous. Feed a varied diet that includes grasses, alfalfa hay, dark green vegetables, flowers, and a few fruits. Also provide a vitamin/mineral supplement twice a week.

- **Breeding:** Two to four eggs are laid per clutch and should be incubated at 84 degrees with humidity between 70 and 80 percent. The eggs should hatch between 90 and 120 days later.

Chapter 10

Medium-Sized to Large Tortoises

Medium-sized and large tortoises require more room than their smaller cousins (flip to Chapter 9) but not as much room as their giant relatives (see Chapter 11). With a bigger tortoise, you need to take into consideration space requirements, the amount of food needed, and the feces to be cleaned up. You also need to look at the security of your yard or tortoise enclosure. A 50-pound tortoise — or even a 25-pound tortoise — can easily break through a weak fence. The walls of the fence or around your tortoise yard must be solid (not see-through) and strong, and must go into the ground at the base.

A large tortoise and a garden are not compatible. Well, that's not totally true. The tortoise will love your garden! But the garden will not be in the same shape after the tortoise is through with it. Tortoises go through — not around — everything, and that includes gardens, lawn furniture, lawn ornaments, kids' toys, and everything else you normally find in a backyard.

This chapter discusses nine of the most popular medium-sized to large tortoises. For reference, refer to the following tortoise lingo as you progress through the chapter:

- **Basking site or basking area:** An area for a tortoise to absorb warmth from sunshine or another heat source

- **Carapace:** The top shell covering the back

- **Carrion:** Decaying flesh

- **Clutch:** A nest of eggs

- **Hatchlings:** Baby tortoises

- **Herbivore:** A plant eater

- ✔ **Plastron:** The lower shell covering the belly
- ✔ **Scute:** A single section of the shell; each shell is made up of many scutes

Chapter 15 tells you how to build an outdoor enclosure.

Desert Tortoise or California Desert Tortoise (Gopherus agassizii)

The desert tortoise's carapace, which can reach 19 inches in length, is light brown, although it often darkens with age. Some older tortoises have almost black carapaces. The plastron is tan to light brown, sometimes with lighter markings. Males are much larger than females and have concave plastrons.

- ✔ **Geographical origin:** Southwestern United States, including southern Nevada, southwestern Utah, southwestern California, and western Arizona; northwest Mexico.

This tortoise is protected, both federally and by many states. It's illegal to collect this tortoise, the California state reptile, in the wild in California or anywhere in its range. However, this tortoise breeds readily in captivity, and thousands (perhaps even hundreds of thousands) of desert tortoises live in captivity.

- ✔ **Native habitat:** Deserts, arid grasslands, and thorn scrub.

- ✔ **Captive environment:** This tortoise doesn't tolerate humidity well. Because it must live outside due to its size, provide an outdoor enclosure on the dry, sunny side of your house. If you live in a damp, cold, rainy climate, please don't try to keep this tortoise. A doghouse with an incandescent bulb is necessary for a shelter and a hiding place. These tortoises dig tunnels if warm hiding places are not available.

Many captive desert tortoises carry an upper respiratory disease that's extremely contagious. It can be treated with antibiotics but can't be cured. In times of stress, the disease flares up. As a result, don't release captive tortoises into the wild; the danger of transmitting this disease to wild populations is too great. Tortoises with upper respiratory disease shouldn't be allowed to hibernate. Also, keep desert tortoises away from other tortoise species that have no resistance to the disease.

- ✔ **Diet:** The desert tortoise is an herbivorous species. In the wild, it often eats cactus, and in captivity, dethorned cactus is an excellent food. A standard herbivore diet is fine. Allow the tortoise room to graze on grass, too.

- ✔ **Breeding:** Breeding behavior starts in the spring after hibernation. Males often battle, sometimes flipping each other over. Six to twelve eggs are laid per clutch and should be incubated at 91 degrees with 70 to 90 percent humidity. The eggs will hatch between 80 and 120 days later.

Bolson Tortoise (Gopherus flavomarginatus)

The Bolson tortoise is the largest terrestrial chelonian in North America, reaching 14½ inches in length. This tortoise is golden-brown to brown in color, often with darker markings. The plastron is lighter in color, again sometimes with darker markings. Rear marginal scutes (over the back legs) are flared and serrated. Males have concave plastrons and longer, thicker tails.

- **Geographical origin:** Mexico, at the border of Chihuahua, Coahuila, and Durango states.

- **Native habitat:** This desert tortoise thrives in arid grasslands and deserts with vegetation.

- **Captive environment:** This tortoise requires a dry outdoor enclosure, as big as you can make it. It doesn't tolerate high humidity or damp conditions. Erect a doghouse with an incandescent bulb for shelter, heat, and a hiding place.

- **Diet:** This desert species is herbivorous. Offer grazing areas, alfalfa hay, varied vegetables, and a few fruits. Dethorned cactus is always a treat. You also can offer commercial tortoise food once in a while.

- **Breeding:** Breeding populations of this tortoise are needed because fewer than 7,500 are estimated to be alive today. Unfortunately, due to their small number, much is unknown about this species, including breeding requirements and behaviors. What is known is that three to eight eggs are laid at a time and should be incubated at 91 degrees at 70 to 80 percent humidity. The eggs should hatch between 80 to 100 days later.

The vast geographical basin in Mexico where this tortoise lives is gradually becoming more and more arid. Although the tortoise could probably survive this climatic change, other changes are occurring, too. Livestock are now grazing the deserts where this tortoise is trying to survive, and herders routinely kill tortoises found among the livestock. Tortoises also end up in stewpots. However, this tortoise will breed in captivity, and as with so many other tortoises, captive breeding may save this species from extinction.

Gopher Tortoise or Florida Gopher Tortoise (Gopherus polyphemus)

The Florida gopher tortoise has a higher dome than the other gopher tortoises. The carapace is dark brown to black, and the plastron is lighter, sometimes gray. Males have more concave plastrons. The record length is about 10 inches. (Figure 10-1 shows what this tortoise looks like.)

Figure 10-1:
The Florida
gopher
tortoise
(*Gopherus
polyphemus*).

✔ **Geographical origin:** Southeastern United States from southeastern South Carolina through Florida and west to Louisiana.

✔ **Native habitat:** Grasslands, beach margins, and woodlands.

Habitat destruction and the illegal collection for the pet trade and stew-pot are decimating many regional populations. In addition, this tortoise is used as a food in many parts of its geographic range.

✔ **Captive environment:** This tortoise needs a large outdoor enclosure with low-growing shrubs or potted plants for hiding and a sunny spot for basking. Set up a doghouse with an incandescent red bulb for heat, shelter, and a hiding place. This species is much more tolerant of humid conditions than the California and Texas tortoises are.

✔ **Diet:** This herbivorous species sometimes eats carrion and insects. Offer grass for grazing, soaked dry dog food, commercial tortoise food, and a variety of dark green vegetables. Once in a while, offer fruit.

✔ **Breeding:** Four to ten eggs are laid at a time and should be incubated at 91 degrees at 70 to 80 percent humidity. The eggs should hatch between 80 and 120 days later.

Red-Footed Tortoise (Geochelone or Chelonoidis carbonaria)

This tortoise has an elongated, somewhat narrow carapace that's black in color, sometimes with yellow or orange markings. The plastron is yellowish brown with some darker markings. Head scales are sometimes yellow. Scales on the legs and feet are red, hence the tortoise's name. Males sometimes reach up to 20 inches in length.

- ✔ **Geographical origin:** Southeastern Panama; east of the Andes in Columbia, Venezuela, Bolivia, Paraguay, and northern Argentina; Suriname; Guyana; and Brazil.

- ✔ **Native habitat:** This tortoise lives in grasslands, savannas, and humid but not tropical forests. Many Caribbean islands now have populations of red-footed tortoises. The population of tortoises on Trinidad is probably natural; the other island populations are suspected to have been introduced.

  Unfortunately, the native people in this tortoise's range consider red-footed tortoise meat a delicacy. In addition, they use its shell as a musical instrument.

- ✔ **Captive environment:** This tortoise prefers a more humid environment than many other tortoises do. If you live in a warm, humid climate where this tortoise could live outside, this is the tortoise for you. A doghouse with an incandescent bulb can provide heat (if you don't live in Hawaii or the Florida Keys), shelter, and a hiding place.

- ✔ **Diet:** This omnivore enjoys fruits, such as mangoes, melons, grapes, and other sweet fruits, including berries; grasses; alfalfa; and dark green vegetables. In the wild, it has been known to eat carrion; in captivity, offer commercial tortoise food and, once in a while, soaked dry dog food. The red-footed tortoise always eats flowers — favorites include rose blossoms, hibiscus, and nasturtiums.

- ✔ **Breeding:** This tortoise breeds quite readily in captivity. Males put together during breeding season will fight, sometimes causing injury to one another. During courtship, the male circles the female repeatedly. When she stops walking forward, he stops in front of her, extends his head, and then rapidly moves it back and forth, sideways, with a jerking motion. Occasionally, the male bites at the female's head, sometimes causing wounds. The male is quite vocal during copulation.

  Four to five eggs are laid per clutch and should be incubated at 86 degrees with 75 to 80 percent humidity. Eggs take a long time to hatch — they won't do so until 120 to 155 days later. Two to three clutches may be laid each summer.

Yellow-Footed Tortoise or Forest Tortoise (Geochelone or Chelonoidis denticulata)

This tortoise is distinguished from the red-footed tortoise primarily by the bright yellow scales on its legs. The yellow-footed tortoise is also larger and a lighter golden-brown in color. Whereas red-footed tortoises may reach 12 inches in length, yellow-footed tortoises commonly grow to 20 inches, with a length of 28 inches the record in captivity.

- ✔ **Geographical origin:** Southeastern Venezuela to Brazil, throughout the Amazon basin; Guyana, Suriname, Trinidad, and Grenada.

- ✔ **Native habitat:** Tropical rainforests.

- ✔ **Captive environment:** This tortoise likes a heavily planted enclosure with lots of hiding places. Provide a basking spot and high humidity, which is necessary for good health. The yellow-footed tortoise also needs water; provide a shallow plant saucer large enough for drinking and soaking. Keep daytime temperatures in the high 70s to low 80s. Nighttime temperatures can be cooler but not cold (keep them above 55 degrees).

- ✔ **Diet:** This tortoise is an omnivore. In the wild, it eats fallen fruits and some carrion; in captivity, offer a varied herbivore diet with lots of fruit, some soaked dry dog food, commercial tortoise food, and an assortment of vegetables.

- ✔ **Breeding:** Males fight, often severely, so keep only one male in each enclosure. During courtship, the male circles the female, stopping her forward motion, and then, when in front of her, sweeps his head from side to side. Four to ten eggs are laid and should be incubated at 82 degrees and 80 percent humidity. The eggs hatch between 140 and 160 days later.

Burmese Black Tortoise and Burmese Brown Tortoise (Manouria emys phayeri and emys emys)

The Burmese brown tortoise is a rusty brown with occasional gold flecks; the Burmese black is almost black and very round when viewed from above. Both of these tortoises have a single large *tubercle* (an enlarged scale made of the same material as fingernails) on each thigh. The Burmese black tortoise is the larger subspecies, reaching 24 inches in length; the Burmese brown tortoise reaches 19 inches.

- ✔ **Geographical origin:** The Burmese black tortoise is found in high-altitude mainland locations in northeast India, Bangladesh, Burma (Myanmar), and Thailand. The Burmese brown tortoise is found in lower altitudes and warmer areas through the same range and on some Indonesian islands, including Sumatra and Borneo.

- ✔ **Native habitat:** This is a forest tortoise, living in tropical evergreen woodlands. It's one of the most primitive tortoises — one of the most ancient of the existing terrestrial species.

✔ **Captive environment:** These tortoises don't need as much room as you might think because of their size. Three square yards of space per foot of tortoise length is plenty. They do like to hide under low-growing plants and also like to soak in water. They don't require high temperatures as most other tortoises do; in fact, they do well in temperatures averaging in the 60s and low 70s.

✔ **Diet:** This tortoise is an omnivore and likes to graze and nibble on bushes and shrubs. It has also been known to eat carrion. In captivity, feed it a varied herbivore diet supplemented by commercial tortoise food and soaked dry dog food.

✔ **Breeding:** Thirty-five to forty-five eggs are laid at a time. The female actively guards her nest for a few days, sometimes longer. The eggs should be incubated at 86 degrees and 90 percent humidity for 70 to 80 days or until they hatch.

Marginated Tortoise (Testudo marginata)

This attractive tortoise has flared marginal scutes over the rear legs. The carapace is dark brown to black with yellow markings. The plastron is quite dark, as is the skin. Females average slightly less than 10 inches in length, while males are slightly longer, to 12 or even 13½ inches. Females, however, are generally heavier than males. Males have longer tails and much more prominent marginal flares over their back legs.

✔ **Geographical origin:** Greece.

✔ **Native habitat:** Dry scrub woodlands and olive groves.

✔ **Captive environment:** Provide a standard terrestrial tortoise enclosure. This tortoise needs nothing out of the ordinary.

✔ **Diet:** The marginated tortoise is an herbivore. Feed it a varied diet consisting of fruits, vegetables, and commercial tortoise food.

✔ **Breeding:** This species breeds quite readily in captivity. One to twelve eggs are laid; incubate them at 91 degrees and 75 to 80 percent humidity. The eggs should hatch around 90 days later.

Elongated Tortoise (Indotestudo or Geochelone elongata)

The carapace of an elongated tortoise, especially a male, is decidedly elongated — narrower than that of other tortoises. The carapace is greenish yellow or brownish yellow, while the plastron is yellow-tan. The skin on the legs is light brown to olive; the head is more yellow. Males average 12 or 13 inches in length, and females average around 11 inches.

Indotestudo travancorica, or the travancore tortoise, is similar to the elongated tortoise except that it has a flatter and wider carapace that's a darker brown.

- **Geographical origin:** Southeast Asia.

- **Native habitat:** Tropical forests.

- **Captive environment:** Use an outside terrestrial tortoise enclosure and provide several low-growing plants for shade and hiding places. This tortoise needs a fairly good-sized plant saucer for water and enjoys rain showers and yard sprinklers. The elongated tortoise is most active in the early morning and evening hours; midday finds it hiding and asleep.

- **Diet:** This herbivore also eats insects. Snails, slugs, and earthworms are accepted eagerly. Feed a varied herbivore diet with fruits, vegetables, soaked dry dog food, and commercial tortoise food. Alfalfa pellets (rabbit food) soaked in water are usually eaten readily. You can offer dry cat food soaked in water once in a while (not regularly) to provide additional protein.

- **Breeding:** During courtship, the male chases the female, ramming her and biting at her head. One to eight eggs are laid and should be incubated at 86 degrees with 70 to 80 percent humidity. The eggs should hatch about 137 days later.

Hatchlings require an unusually humid environment to survive: Ambient humidity should be at least 90 percent, with temperatures in the mid-80s.

Chapter 11

Really Big Tortoises

. . . .

In This Chapter

▶ Identifying the really large tortoises

▶ Caring for your large tortoise's environment

▶ Feeding your tortoise effectively

. . . .

Ⅰn Chapter 12, I mention that the leopard tortoise *(Geochelone pardalis)* is the fourth largest tortoise in the world, with some adult individuals reaching 100 pounds in weight. A 100-pound tortoise is a big tortoise — and that's just the fourth largest! Who are the other three? This chapter tells you about these huge creatures.

If you need assistance in wading through technical jargon in this chapter, check the list that follows for quick definitions:

✔ **Basking site or basking light:** An area for a tortoise to absorb warmth from sunshine or another heat source

✔ **Carapace:** The top shell covering the back

✔ **Clutch:** A nest of eggs

✔ **Hatchlings:** Baby tortoises

✔ **Herbivore:** A plant eater

Flip to Chapter 15 for tips on building an outdoor enclosure.

Sulcata Tortoise (Geochelone sulcata)

The sulcata is the third largest tortoise species, with adult males often reaching 200 pounds. Lengths routinely reach 30 inches. The carapace is tan in color and has a low, curved shape (not domed like that of the leopard tortoise — see Chapter 12). The back legs have tubercles or spurs. The skin is also tan in color.

The sulcata *(Geochelone sulcata)* has been called the African spur-thigh tortoise. To confuse things, the North Africa tortoise *(Testudo graeca)* has also been called a spur-thigh. Experts are now trying to clarify things, and the sulcata is being referred to as a sulcata, while the *Testudo graeca* is being called the North African tortoise (see Chapter 10 for details).

- ✔ **Geographical origin:** Africa, from Ethiopia and Sudan westward through Chad, Niger, and Mali to Senegal. This tortoise generally ranges along the southern edge of the Sahara Desert.

- ✔ **Native habitat:** Varied, from desert fringes to grasslands and dry savannas.

- ✔ **Captive environment:** This hardy, resilient, and adaptable tortoise requires a lot of room. Keep an adult in a yard no smaller than 10 yards x 10 yards. A doghouse with an incandescent red bulb for heat provides shelter and a hiding place.

  These tortoises will dig if you don't provide adequate hiding places. They can dig tremendous burrows, excavating tremendous volumes of dirt! Many times, you can prevent this behavior by offering a number of different places to hide.

  If you adopt a sulcata, the walls or fence around your yard must be solid, secure, and into the ground. These tortoises are amazingly strong, are very curious, and don't take no for an answer! If a sulcata can see through a fence, it may muscle its way through, taking the fence down in the process. Concrete walls are the best restraint, but the walls must be higher than the tortoise is long. A large female of mine was able to climb up a 16-inch-tall restraining wall, where she got into the flower bed and proceeded to mow down six rose bushes!

- ✔ **Diet:** This tortoise likes to graze and can keep a grass lawn mowed quite nicely. In addition, feed a standard, varied herbivore diet. A bale of alfalfa hay in the tortoise yard is a good source of food and fiber. Because these tortoises grow so rapidly, give a daily vitamin/mineral supplement with a calcium:phosphorus ratio of 2:1. A *cuttlebone,* which is a hard chunk of calcium from a cuttlefish (as pet birds eat), also provides calcium.

- ✔ **Breeding:** Sulcatas are breeding very well in captivity, so much so that you won't have a tough time buying a captive-bred juvenile. One sulcata owner said that breeding sulcatas is something like breeding rabbits; if you aren't careful, you'll be overrun with them!

  Only one male should be kept with one or more females, because the males frequently battle each other viciously. Fifteen to twenty eggs are laid at a time and should be incubated at 87 degrees at 80 percent humidity. The eggs will hatch between 75 and 100 days later. Several clutches — sometimes as many as six — may be laid per year, with an interval of four weeks between clutches.

Adding a sulcata to your family is a decision that you want to make with a great deal of thought. This big tortoise requires a great deal of food and produces vast quantities of feces. Within a few short years, you won't even be able to pick up your pet! Can you handle that?

Galapagos Tortoise (Geochelone or Chelonoidis elephantopus)

This is the second largest species of tortoise in the world today. Actual descriptions of the various subspecies differ, as follows:

- **Abingdon Island tortoise:** This subspecies has a black carapace shaped like a saddle, very narrow and compressed. Only one specimen, Lonesome George, remains alive.

- **Volcan Wolf tortoise:** This tortoise has a gray, saddleback carapace with the rear marginals flared. This subspecies is located on the area around Volcan Wolf at the northern end of Albemarle Island.

- **Chatham Island tortoise:** This tortoise has a wide, black carapace, not a saddleback but not domed, either. The rear marginals are turned down. This species is located on the northeastern part of Chatham (San Cristobal) Island, and the population is severely endangered.

- **James Island tortoise:** This tortoise has a gray to black carapace, not a saddleback and not quite a domed shell, either. The rear marginals are upturned. This tortoise lives on James (San Salvador) Island. A captive-breeding program is doing well at the Charles Darwin Station.

- **Duncan Island tortoise:** This tortoise, one of the smallest Galapagos tortoises, has a gray saddleback carapace with serrated rear marginals. It is restricted to Duncan (Pinzon) Island, and the population is severely endangered.

- **Sierra Negra tortoise:** This subspecies has a gray-brown to black carapace, not a saddleback and not quite a domed shell, either. It's restricted to the Sierra Negra area of southeastern Albemarle (Isabela) Island. The population is severely endangered.

- **Hood Island tortoise:** This is the smallest of the Galapagos tortoises. It has a black saddleback carapace with a deep cervical indentation. It lives on Hood (Espanola) Island. Captive breeding is ongoing at the Charles Darwin Station; only 20 individuals (if that!) are left in the wild.

- **Volcan Darwin tortoise:** This tortoise has a gray, oval carapace that's rather flattened in appearance. This species is found near Volcan Darwin in north central Albemarle (Isabela) Island. The population is endangered.

✔ **Indefatigable Island tortoise:** This tortoise has a black carapace that's oval, domed, and higher in the center than in the front. This tortoise is found on Indefatigable (Santa Cruz) Island. The population is endangered but is larger than most other species. Captive breeding may provide some relief by releasing young tortoises back into the wild.

✔ **Narborough Island tortoise:** This subspecies is extinct.

✔ **Volcan Alcedo tortoise:** This tortoise has an oval, domed black carapace. It's found on the higher slopes on central Albemarle (Isabela) Island. This species has the largest population of any Galapagos species, yet is endangered.

✔ **Iguana Cove tortoise:** This species has a heavy-domed, black carapace. It's found near Cerro Azul on Albemarle (Isabela) Island. Captive breeding has been initiated at the Charles Darwin Station because the population is severely endangered.

Figure 11-1 shows an example of a Galapagos tortoise.

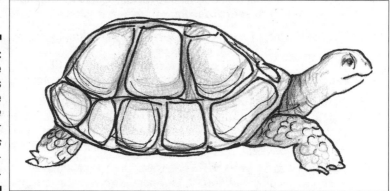

Figure 11-1:
The Galapagos tortoise (*Geochelone* or *Chelonoidis elephantopus*).

Darwin's theories

Charles Robert Darwin (1809–1882) was a British naturalist who, as a young man, traveled around South America to the Galapagos Islands on the *H.M.S. Beagle*. Upon his return to Great Britain, he published his views on evolution based in great part on his observations of the plants and reptiles (including the giant tortoises) on the islands. His theories of evolution conflicted greatly with the prevalent Christian theories of the origins of the world and caused a great deal of controversy that continues even today.

Every once in a while, a classified ad will appear in a reptile magazine for a Galapagos juvenile or two or three. If you can afford the price, should you get one? Do you have the room? Can you afford to make the enclosure secure and safe? Can you afford to feed this tortoise? Are you willing to pick up after it? Do you have someone to leave this tortoise to when you can no longer take care of it? If you can answer yes to all these questions, make sure that you get the necessary permits before you buy your new baby. The seller should be able to help you.

Here's the rest of the lowdown on Galapagos tortoises:

- **Native habitat:** The island terrains differ slightly. Some are more arid than others; some more volcanic. Vegetation also differs by island.

- **Captive environment:** These tortoises need as much room as the Aldabran tortoises (see the following section). A strong fence is a necessity; these are strong tortoises, and if a 500-pound tortoise gets out, you may have trouble getting it back in. A tall, concrete wall set well into the ground makes the best fence.

- **Diet:** In the wild, the tortoises primarily graze on grasses and browse on shrubs, cactus, and anything else edible within reach. In captivity, an herbivore diet in vast amounts is perfect — tomatoes, squash, cabbage, and other vegetables. A bale of alfalfa hay is good food and good fiber. Give iodine supplements to prevent goiter.

- **Breeding:** Galapagos tortoises have been bred in captivity. The San Diego Zoo has bred them, as have a few other zoos and some individuals. Four to twenty-four eggs may be laid per clutch and should be incubated at 86 degrees and 80 percent humidity. The eggs should hatch between 100 and 120 days later.

Aldabran Tortoise (Geochelone or Aldabrachelys gigantea)

The Aldabran tortoise (which can be quite expensive) is the largest tortoise in the world, with some males weighing over 400 pounds — the record Aldabran weighs 700 pounds. Aldabran tortoises have been measured at 42 inches in length. The carapace and skin are uniformly gray in color. Males are larger than females and have longer, thicker tails.

Tortoise keepers who have Aldabran tortoises say that they're personable, friendly tortoises. However, a 400- to 500-pound tortoise is a major commitment. Think about whether you are truly prepared to care for an animal of this size before you buy that cute little hatchling.

Extinction inevitable?

The long-term survival of the Galapagos tortoises on their native islands is in doubt. Some of the species are holding their own, but many others are in grave danger. Researchers, especially those working at the Charles Darwin Station, are trying to make sure that these giant tortoises survive. Unfortunately, hunting, collection, and introduced predators, including dogs, cats, and rats, have already done a lot of damage. However, captive breeding may ensure that at least a few of the subspecies survive.

✔ **Geographical origin:** Aldabra Island in the Indian Ocean.

✔ **Native habitat:** Grasslands, scrub areas, and mangrove swamps.

✔ **Captive environment:** These tortoises need a large area. The tortoise enclosure should be no smaller than 10 yards x 10 yards for a small adult and no smaller than 15 yards x 15 yards for a full-sized adult. The fence around the tortoise yard must be very strong and secure; a concrete block wall is best.

Ideal temperatures range from the high 70s to the high 80s. Basking lights in a large tortoise house can supply supplemental heat. Also, these tortoises do well in a group. If you have the facilities for one, you may as well get two or three!

Captive-bred babies are sometimes available from breeders and reptile suppliers. Check local regulations as to permits that may be required.

✔ **Diet:** These giant tortoises are herbivores and eat a lot of food. Keep a bale of alfalfa hay, which can satisfy their hunger, within reach. In addition, offer whole squash, pumpkins, and other melons. A varied herbivore diet works well. Aldabran tortoises also like to graze.

Hatchlings and juveniles need a lot of calcium in their diet; offer a good vitamin/mineral supplement with a calcium:phosphorus ratio of 2:1 on a daily basis. Also offer a cuttlebone (as for a pet bird) once in a while.

✔ **Breeding:** These tortoises have been breeding quite well in captivity. If you have the room, separate the male from the female for a month or two prior to breeding season. Four to fourteen eggs are laid per clutch and should be incubated at 86 degrees and 70 to 80 percent humidity. The eggs will hatch between 100 and 130 days later.

Hatchlings need warm to hot temperatures; keep a spot under a basking light at 90 to 95 degrees. When the temperature is too cool, hatchlings are prone to respiratory infections.

Chapter 12

Special Tortoises

. . . .

In This Chapter

▶ Getting to know five special tortoises

▶ Knowing how to outfit an enclosure

▶ Feeding your tortoise at the proper time

. . . .

*W*hat makes a tortoise special? Usually it's the tortoise's appearance: The star tortoise, radiated tortoise, geometric tortoise, and leopard tortoise are beautiful tortoises with unique colorings and markings. The leopard tortoise also happens to be a very large tortoise (see Chapter 11 for other large tortoises).

Some of the special tortoises in this chapter are quite rare due to declining populations. Although extinction is awful for any species, it would be even more tragic to lose one of these special species. Captive breeding may save these tortoises from extinction.

Many tortoises are bred in captivity, some quite successfully. The leopard tortoise is being produced in large numbers, and more people are breeding the star, radiated, and geometric tortoises. If you can keep one (or more) of these tortoises, you may decide to breed them. There's a special wonder in breeding a beautiful tortoise, especially one that's declining in number in the wild.

Because all these species are endangered, all have laws restricting their import and trade. Before you buy, make sure to find out whether the tortoise you're about to acquire was obtained legally and is legal to own in your area. Also make sure that you have the proper permits (both federal and state) and that the individual tortoise you're buying was bred in captivity.

As you go through this chapter, you may see some unfamiliar terms. For reference, keep the following tortoise jargon in mind:

- ✔ **Basking site or basking area:** An area for a tortoise to absorb warmth from sunshine or another heat source

- ✔ **Carapace:** The top shell covering the back

- ✔ **Clutch:** A nest of eggs

- ✔ **Hatchlings:** Baby tortoises

- ✔ **Herbivore:** A plant eater

- ✔ **Plastron:** The lower shell covering the belly, chest, and so on

- ✔ **Scute:** A single section of the outer fingernail-like covering shell; each shell is made up of many scutes

- ✔ **Terrarium:** An aquarium or cage that contains live plants, a higher humidity, and no swimming water (Chapter 14 shows you how to build an indoor terrestrial tortoise habitat; Chapter 15 tells you how to build an outdoor enclosure)

Star Tortoise (Geochelone elegans)

This is one of the world's most beautiful tortoises. It has been collected in the wild in large numbers, depleting many populations. The star tortoise averages about 6 inches in length for males, with 15 inches the maximum. The carapace is domed, although it appears lumpy, with each scute having a slightly raised center. The carapace has a dark brown or black background with radiating white or yellow stripes on each scute. The plastron is yellow with black radiating stripes. The head and skin are yellow to tan.

The star tortoise is on the CITES II list, which means that it's protected. Never buy a wild-caught star tortoise; not only may it have been imported illegally, but wild-caught tortoises have a difficult time adjusting to captivity. Star tortoises are now being bred in captivity, and these pets are healthier than their wild cousins and don't have adjustment problems. Buy a captive-bred baby!

- ✔ **Geographical origin:** India and Sri Lanka (Ceylon).

- ✔ **Native habitat:** Deciduous forests, grasslands, and dry savannas. Habitat destruction is endangering many wild star tortoises. Overcollection for the pet trade has also been a problem.

- ✔ **Captive environment:** Provide a standard terrestrial tortoise enclosure, and keep the enclosure on the dry side, watering the grass while the tortoise is under shelter (that is, in a tortoise house or otherwise protected from dew, rain, or sprinklers). A doghouse with an incandescent red bulb provides heat, shelter, and a hiding place. Give your star tortoise hiding places and basking areas.

  Keep hatchlings and juveniles inside. Supply a long, low terrarium (see Chapter 3), using alfalfa pellets as substrate. Maintain a basking spot at 85 to 90 degrees, with the rest of the terrarium cooler. A fluorescent reptile light can supply needed UVB rays. As soon as the tortoise is large enough or you have a protected area, move the tortoise outside: These tortoises don't thrive indoors for long periods.

Star tortoises do better in a group, perhaps two males and several females. Don't mix them with other species of tortoises, however; they don't have resistance to diseases that are common in other species.

✔ **Diet:** This herbivorous species eats vegetables, fruits, commercial tortoise food, commercial iguana food, and flowers. Roses are a special treat.

✔ **Breeding:** Breeding usually occurs during or slightly after the rainy season in India and Sri Lanka. You may have to induce breeding with artificial "rain showers." Males aren't aggressive toward one another, although sparring sometimes occurs. Three to six eggs are laid per clutch and should be incubated at 86 degrees with 50 to 70 percent humidity.

The incubation period for just one nest varies from 47 to 147 days. Never throw out an egg unless it has obviously gone bad.

Burmese Star Tortoise (Geochelone platynota)

This rare tortoise is related to the star tortoise but is seldom seen. Its carapace is dark brown to black, with radiating yellow stripes on each scute. The plastron is yellow with dark brown or black blotches, while the skin is yellowish tan. Males have longer, thicker tails than females. The average length of this tortoise is about 10 inches.

✔ **Geographical origin:** Burma. (Unfortunately, this tortoise is used as a food source in its native land.)

✔ **Native habitat:** Woodlands and forests.

✔ **Captive environment:** In captivity, this tortoise can be kept in an outdoor enclosure that's heavily planted but retains a few basking spots in the sun. Supply water in a shallow plant saucer.

Keep hatchlings and juveniles indoors in a long, low terrarium (see Chapter 3). Use alfalfa as bedding in the cage, provide a basking spot that's at least 85 to 90 degrees, and create some hiding places.

Like their cousins, Burmese star tortoises do better in small groups. Don't mix them with other chelonian species, however; they have poor immunity to diseases and parasites that other species may carry.

✔ **Diet:** Burmese star tortoises are herbivores and eat a variety of plant matter, including grasses, leaves, shrubs within reach, fallen fruits, and berries.

✔ **Breeding:** Very little is known of this species' breeding behaviors, although the process is assumed to be very similar to that of the star tortoise. More research needs to be conducted.

Radiated Tortoise (Geochelone asterochelys radiata)

This attractive tortoise (see Figure 12-1) has an elongated carapace with a dark brown background. Each scute has radiating yellow or orange stripes, while the plastron is yellow with black blotches and black stripes. The skin is light tan to yellow with darker shadings. The maximum length of this tortoise is 16 inches. Males have longer tails and more protruding *gular scutes* (the plastral projections under the chin) than females.

Figure 12-1:
The radiated tortoise
(Geochelone asterochelys radiata).

✔ **Geographical origin:** Madagascar, mostly south coastal.

This attractive tortoise is exploited for its shell, for the pet trade, and as a food source. A CITES Appendix I listing has protected it somewhat, although those people native to Madagascar are still eating it, and recent illegal exports to China for the food market have cause a population collapse.

✔ **Native habitat:** Dry woodlands, grasslands, scrublands, and thorn brush.

✔ **Captive environment:** This tortoise can live well in a standard terrestrial enclosure that's kept somewhat dry. A doghouse with an incandescent red bulb can serve as shelter, providing heat and a hiding place. Low-growing plants can also provide spots for hiding.

✔ **Diet:** This herbivorous species eats just about anything in an herbivore diet, including fruits, vegetables, alfalfa hay, and flowers. Dethorned cactus is a special treat. Red foods, such as tomatoes, strawberries, and red flowers, are more attractive to these tortoises than foods of other colors are.

✔ **Breeding:** This species breeds well in captivity. Courtship begins with the male following the female around, smelling her *cloaca* (intestinal, urinary, and reproductive opening). The male then rams the female. When he mounts her, he places his front feet securely on her carapace, lifting his rear feet from the ground while swinging the rear half of his body toward the female, smacking the rear of her shell with his plastron. He then copulates with her.

Six to twelve eggs are laid per clutch and should be incubated at 86 degrees with 70 to 80 percent humidity. The eggs should hatch between three and fifteen months later.

Geometric Tortoise (Psammobates geometricus)

The carapace of the geometric tortoise is domed and elliptical, with the widest point in the rear. The carapace is dark brown, and the center of each scute is slightly elevated, giving a tented or pyramid effect. Each scute also has a yellow center with radiating stripes. The plastron is yellow with brown or black pigment along the seams. Geometric tortoises average between 6 and 10 inches in length. Males have longer, thicker tails and concave plastrons.

✔ **Geographical origin:** Cape Province, South Africa.

✔ **Native habitat:** Dry grasslands with short shrubs.

Long ago, this tortoise was widespread, found all over South Africa and neighboring countries. Unfortunately, because of habitat loss due to farming, this beautiful tortoise is now one of the most endangered in the world.

Don't buy a geometric tortoise unless you know that doing so is legal in your area and that the tortoise was either legally imported or captive-bred.

✔ **Captive environment:** These tortoises do well outside in a large terrestrial tortoise enclosure. A dry substrate with rocks, plants, and hiding places is best. Provide a basking area in the sun, as well as water in a shallow plant saucer. These small tortoises don't like extreme heat.

✔ **Diet:** The geometric tortoise is herbivorous. Feed a varied herbivore diet consisting of vegetables, some fruits, commercial tortoise food, and commercial iguana food.

✔ **Breeding:** Captive breeding of this species has been extremely successful. Two to four eggs are laid per clutch and should be incubated at 88 degrees and 70 to 80 percent humidity. The eggs should hatch between 150 to 210 days later.

Leopard Tortoise (Geochelone pardalis)

This is the fourth largest tortoise species in the world (following the Galapagos, Aldabra, and sulcata tortoises). Some adults of this species, especially captive-bred adults, have reached 100 pounds in weight. Females are often much larger than males; for a period of time, the largest known male was 26 inches long, with the largest female over 28 inches long. Well-fed captive-bred tortoises may exceed these lengths.

The leopard tortoise is brightly marked, attractive, and personable. You can find two subspecies: *Geochelone pardalis pardalis* and *Geochelone pardalis babcocki.* In both subspecies, the carapace is highly domed, often with the centers of the scutes somewhat elevated, creating a pyramid effect. *Geochelone pardalis pardalis* has a slightly less domed carapace that's slightly flattened along the top. *Geochelone pardalis babcocki* has a higher-domed carapace. Females are more oval in shape, and males are more elongated.

The carapace is white to yellow or bone-colored with dark markings along the growth seams (see Figure 12-2). *Geochelone pardalis pardalis* has brighter, more distinct markings. The markings vary among individuals: Some have quite a few blotches, spots, or other markings, while others have few. The skin is yellow, tan, or bone-colored.

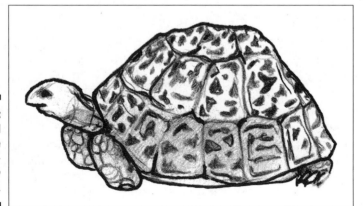

Figure 12-2: The leopard tortoise (Geochelone pardalis).

Leopard tortoises very rarely hibernate, so they need indoor housing for the winter. The minimum size is 10 feet x 10 feet for a 12-inch adult, and proportionally bigger for larger adults. Anything smaller is cruel. The cage also needs light and heat. Larger adults do poorly when kept inside, so keep this in mind when deciding whether to add a leopard tortoise to your family.

- **Geographical origin:** Africa, from Ethiopia south through eastern Africa to South Africa.

  The leopard tortoise is threatened in many parts of its range. Warfare, hunting, and overcollection have depleted its numbers. If you buy a leopard tortoise, make sure that it's captive-bred or that it hasn't been illegally imported.

- **Native habitat:** Leopard tortoises inhabit grasslands, savannas, and low thorn scrublands.

- **Captive habitat:** This large tortoise needs a lot of room to forage, graze, and roam. A large outdoor enclosure (a minimum of 10 yards x 10 yards) is necessary. Hiding spots are needed, as is a shallow water pan. Provide a doghouse with an incandescent red bulb for heat, shelter, and a hiding place.

  This powerful tortoise is capable of pushing through fences, destroying landscaping, and crushing flowerbeds. Make sure that the enclosure is solid and escape-proof!

- **Diet:** This herbivorous species is not at all picky about what it eats. A varied herbivore diet is fine. Dethorned cactus is a treat, as are roses. Watermelon, cantaloupe, bananas, strawberries, tomatoes, and commercial tortoise food all are eaten eagerly, but make grass the animal's primary food. These tortoises like to graze, and a good-quality grass such as Bermuda can and should supply the foundation of this tortoise's diet. A vitamin/mineral supplement is a necessity, because these rapidly growing tortoises need calcium.

- **Breeding:** This species (like most other tortoises) needs male competition prior to breeding. However, be careful, because the males can flip each other over.

  The males are very vocal when breeding. Eight to twelve eggs are laid per clutch and should be incubated at 82 to 86 degrees and 80 percent humidity. The eggs won't hatch for a long time; between 120 and 150 days is normal, but even longer isn't unheard of. All the eggs in one clutch won't necessarily hatch at the same time. Often, one egg will hatch, and then another a day or two later. An entire clutch of 12 eggs may take a couple of weeks to hatch! A female can lay several clutches throughout the summer, with most females spacing clutches four to six weeks apart.

Part III
Welcome Home! Creating a Safe and Healthy Environment

The 5th Wave By Rich Tennant

@RICHTENNANT

"Okay Margaret, Billy's coming back in. Move away from the basking light, put down the heating pad and step out of the soaking tub so I can change the water."

In this part . . .

After you decide on a turtle or tortoise and bring it home, how can you keep it safe and secure? Turtles and tortoises, unfortunately, make poor bedfellows, so your pet needs its own home. The chapters in this part walk you through the process of setting up a cage or enclosure for your turtle or tortoise. You can also find out what environmental conditions, such as light, heat, humidity, and water, are important to your pet. So read on and get up to snuff on turtle homebuilding!

Chapter 13

Making a Home for an Aquatic or Semi-Aquatic Turtle

. . . .

In This Chapter
▶ Finding a container to hold water
▶ Discovering what your turtle's home needs to have in it
▶ Making your turtle's home easy to clean

. . . .

*P*rofessionally, you may be a computer programmer, an exotic dancer, or a writer, but after you decide to get an aquatic or semi-aquatic turtle or two (see Chapters 5 and 6), you become a turtle homemaker. After all, your turtle needs a home!

This chapter gives you tips to consider when choosing a container, information to keep in mind when buying fancy extras for your turtle's home, and methods for keeping the home clean.

Keeping Your Turtle's Head Above (Or Under) Water

An all-glass or Plexiglas aquarium is the most attractive way to keep aquatic turtles and enables you to see your turtles swimming, eating, and basking — see Figure 13-1. In fact, an aquarium with aquatic turtles can be just as attractive and relaxing as an aquarium full of tropical fish.

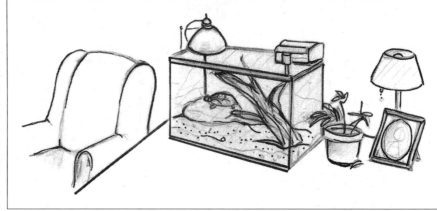

Figure 13-1:
An all-glass aquarium allows your turtle to be an integral part of your life.

However, a large all-glass aquarium can be expensive, and if you have a few turtles, you may want to use something that costs less. Plastic tubs, plastic cement mixing containers, and children's wading pools (see Figure 13-2) can make suitable aquatic turtle homes. Just make sure that the container is new, clean, and waterproof.

Figure 13-2:
A children's wading pool makes a great home for aquatic turtles.

© Bill Love

Purchase an aquarium or container that's large enough for your turtle (as an adult) to have plenty of room to swim, eat, explore, and bask. The minimum-sized aquarium is a 20-gallon tank with long, low sides (as compared to high sides), which gives the turtle more usable floor space. Add an additional 10 gallons of capacity per additional turtle. Extra-large turtles, of course, need more room.

An aquarium of this size is heavy after being filled with water — water weighs almost 8½ pounds per gallon — so make sure that the aquarium is where you want it to be after you finish setting it up. Don't try to move it after it's full of water! Make sure that the stand, table, or counter on which you set the tank is strong enough to hold the tank, too. A 30-gallon aquarium with water, land mass (see the "Making the House a Home" section, later in this chapter), and a turtle may weigh upwards of 300 pounds. If you're using a plastic tub instead of an aquarium, the same rule applies: Make sure that it's where you want it to stay before you fill it.

No matter what kind of container you use, the water should be deep enough for swimming. For most species, it must be at least as deep as the turtle's shell is long. For a good swimmer, such as a red-eared slider *(Trachemys scripta elegans),* the water can be as deep as you can make it, as long as the turtle can easily climb out of the water onto his basking area. Some aquatic turtles, like the matamata *(Chelus finbriatus),* are poor swimmers, though, and these turtles need shallow water.

Making the House a Home

Many elements come together to create a turtle's home. Because water quality is important, choose a filter to keep the water clean, and add some aquatic plants. For many species, you also need to heat the water with an aquarium heater. Your turtle will also need some land area for basking, and because so many turtles are escape artists, you need a cover for the tank. In addition to the information in this chapter, be sure to meet your turtle's needs for sunlight (Chapter 16), heat (Chapter 17), and water (Chapter 18).

A *vivarium* is exactly what you're creating here — a tank with both land area and water. A *terrarium* (a more familiar term) is all land without water.

When constructing basking areas and land masses, think simple. Although plants, tri-level basking areas, and assorted stones are attractive, they can be difficult to keep clean. As you put this turtle home together, keep in mind that you're going to have to clean it regularly.

Choosing a filter

Many turtles defecate in their water. This behavior may seem gross to you, but the turtle isn't thinking about where its next drink is coming from. In the wild, if a turtle defecates in water, the movement of the water flushes it away. No problem! In captivity, you need to pay attention to housekeeping. If your turtle is aquatic or semi-aquatic, a water filtration system, which filters and treats the water, should keep up with the housekeeping chores. If you're supplying water in a shallow bowl or saucer, you must change that water daily or after the turtle defecates.

Several different kinds of filtration systems are on the market. Some work better than others, and some are more expensive than others. Some filters use charcoal to condition the water; others use an ammonia-removing mineral called zeolite; still others use a combination of both. Others, such as Bio-Wheel filters, are biological and count on naturally occurring flora to help with debris decomposition. Beneficial bacteria cultures, which eliminate toxic ammonia from the water, flourish in the filter itself.

- ✔ **Canister filters:** Canister filters sit outside the tank with both inflow and outflow tubes carrying water to and from the filter. These filters are more expensive than other filters but are very effective at keeping turtle tanks clean. In my experience, a canister filter is far and away the best filter for aquatic and semi-aquatic turtle tanks.

- ✔ **Sponge filters:** Sponge filters normally sit in the tank itself (in the water), and the air flow from the pump forces water through the sponge. This filter works well if the air flow is strong enough. If you're going to use a sponge filtration system, buy a medium- or higher-priced air pump that has a good strong flow of air through the filter. A small, inexpensive pump will not be able to do the job. Sponge filters also need to be cleaned frequently.

- ✔ **Power filters:** Power filters sit outside the tank and draw water up and out of the tank, through the filtration system, and then back into the tank. They are very effective but have certain limitations in turtle tanks. You must maintain the water at a certain level so that the filter continues to operate. In turtle tanks, the water level is usually lower than in fish tanks (so that the turtle can climb out of the water to get to basking areas — see the following section), so power filters often don't work.

- ✔ **Undergravel filters:** Undergravel filters are situated under aquarium gravel and filter wastes through the gravel. These biological filters work with a microbial action. They're relatively inexpensive, but I don't find them particularly effective: It's much too easy for a turtle to pick up a piece of gravel and swallow it, with potentially dangerous results. I also like to keep the bottom of the water portion of the tank bare, free of any *substrate* (such as aquarium gravel or sand), so that I can see when it needs cleaning. If you have a large tank and only one or two small turtles, however, an undergravel filter may work.

As with so many things, you get what you pay for when buying a filtration system. Go to your local pet store or tropical fish store and ask the salesperson about filters. Look at some of the available filters and check out the prices. Don't skimp here; buy the very best filter you can afford.

Creating a basking area

If your turtle is aquatic, like a red-eared slider *(Trachemys scripta elegans),* it will need something to bask on but will not necessarily need a land mass. The basking area, site, or platform should be low enough in the water that the turtle can easily climb out, yet elevated enough that it will remain dry. The turtle needs to be able to bask in the heat and dry out completely.

You can make a basking platform in several different ways:

- ✔ Use a large, smooth rock that's big enough so that the top of it remains out of the water. A rock that big is heavy, though; make sure that it won't break the glass or plastic bottom of your aquarium.
- ✔ Place a small piece of a log (or half a log split lengthwise) above the water to make a good platform.
- ✔ Use a brick, a piece of wood, or a portion of cork bark as a platform.

Ideally, the basking platform is at one end of the tank so you can heat that end (and the platform) to a slightly warmer temperature than the rest of the tank. Use a heat lamp made specifically for reptiles (see Chapter 17). Install the lamp over the basking area or land mass, making sure that the lamp is situated so that it can't fall into the water. Using a thermometer, check the temperature in the basking area. For most aquatic species, a basking area temperature of 85 to 88 degrees is fine. (See Chapters 5 and 6 for detailed information about your type of turtle and the basking temperatures it prefers.)

Don't forget to decorate!

You can decorate a vivarium to be as simple or as complicated as you can care for and keep clean. For example, you can use flat stones (such as slate) and silicone aquarium adhesive to stack the stones. Simply glue them together to keep them in one position so that they don't tumble on top of your turtle. You can also build caves, steps, and two- and three-level basking areas. Just make sure that your turtle can walk through all the areas safely and can easily reach both the water and the basking area.

Making a land mass

If you're making a home for a semi-aquatic turtle, such as the common map turtle *(Graptemys geographica)* or the more rare bog turtle *(Clemmys muhlenbergii)*, you need to divide the aquarium so that there's sufficient swimming room and some land mass. This land mass is also used for basking, so you want to situate it at one end of the tank.

How much land mass do you need? Unless you have lots of turtles in the tank, a division of three-quarters water and one-quarter land mass is usually sufficient. For several turtles, create enough land mass that each turtle in the tank has room to bask if all of them get out of the water at the same time.

Build the land mass in one of the two following ways:

✔ Measure the width of your tank, and then have your local hardware store cut a piece of Plexiglas to fit so that you can divide the tank with it. Make sure to measure accurately; the Plexiglas must fit tightly because it will hold back water. Secure this piece of Plexiglas in place with aquarium silicone adhesive and let it set for 24 hours. Then fill behind the Plexiglas with clean potting soil. After the soil is in place, all you need is a small piece of log or cork bark for the turtle to use as a bridge (or ladder) from the water to the land mass, as shown in Figure 13-3.

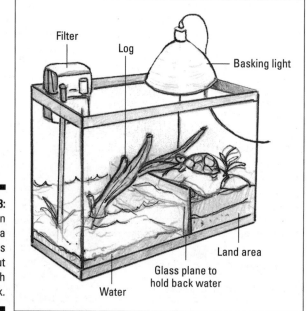

Figure 13-3:
You can create a land mass without doing much work.

Filter

Log

Basking light

Land area

Glass plane to hold back water

Water

✔ Buy a commercial kit specifically designed to divide your tank into swimming area and land mass. These kits are much prettier than homemade dividers and usually include a small waterfall and a stream. Viquarium produces one such kit, called Water's Edge Viquarium. Look for these kits at your local pet store.

Heating a turtle home

Your aquatic turtle tank needs a heat source for the water, which for most species needs to be in the mid to high 70s, or even into the low 80s. An aquarium underwater heater (also called a *submersible heater*) works very well. These heaters have built-in thermostats. Be sure to limit the power of the heater to 15 to 25 watts.

When you fill the tank with water, install the heater according to the directions and then turn it on. Let the heater warm the water for 48 hours before putting your turtles into the tank. Heaters need time to work, and you need to watch the heater and adjust it, warmer or cooler, as it heats the water. Tropical fish keepers have learned that you can't rush a water heater; if you do, it may just overheat and boil your pets! Even if you have a built-in thermostat, keep a water thermometer in the water so that you can double-check the temperature. See Chapter 17 for details on heating units.

While your heater warms up, you can treat the water to remove chlorine and any other additives that your local water company adds. Water also ages after coming out of the tap; some chemicals evaporate. Call your local water company to find out what you need to do to make your water safe for your pet. Chapter 18 covers the subject of water in great detail.

Finding hiding places

Your turtle needs places to hide. Many tropical fish stores sell aquatic plants that you may want to add to your turtle's new home. Some safe aquatic plants are listed here:

✔ **Arrowhead:** This aquatic plant is easy to grow and tolerates different water conditions.

✔ **Crystalwort:** This plant spreads quickly.

✔ **Eel grass:** This plant requires a lot of light, does well in shallow water, and spreads quickly.

✔ **Hair grass:** This hardy plant does well in cooler water.

✓ **Java fern:** This hardy, vigorous plant withstands turtle nibbling well.

✓ **Water hyacinth:** This plant is considered a weed and a pest by many people (and is illegal to grow in some states — be sure to check your local laws), but it has large, floating leaves that turtles enjoy. Many herbivorous turtles like to munch on water hyacinths.

✓ **Water lettuce:** This attractive, vigorous tropical plant does well in warmer tanks.

Unfortunately, turtles can be quite destructive and may look upon aquatic plants as combination playground and snack bar. For this reason, you may want to invest in some plastic home furnishings for your turtle as well. Plastic plants, a ceramic skin diver with a water stone that releases bubbles, and even a backdrop for the tank makes the tank look more like a home.

Covering your bases

The tank or tub needs a cover of some kind. If you're using an aquarium, a cover probably came with it. If you're using a plastic tub, a square of hardware cloth with ½-inch squares will work fine. *Hardware cloth* is wire woven into squares, much like a screen with wider openings. It's made of metal — not aluminum like most screens — and therefore will not melt if you place a hot basking light above it.

A cover isn't just to keep turtles in, but also to keep other creatures out. Don't let your dog drink out of the turtle's tank or the cat play pat-pat with the turtles. Keep the kids' fingers out, too, or they may get nibbled!

The cover also works as a platform for the heat lamp and for the fluorescent reptile light that supplies the necessary ultraviolet rays. See Chapters 16 and 17 for more information.

Making Sure You Don't Muddy the Waters

An aquatic or semi-aquatic turtle setup requires maintenance. There's no way around it. But you can make the process a little easier by using the tips in this section.

✔ **Supplies:** Keep supplies in a central location so that you don't have to go searching for stuff. Have extra supplies, cleaning products, water treatment, and everything else in one place.

✔ **Water quality:** You're going to have to change the water in the turtle tank every once in a while — how often depends on the size of your tank, the strength of your filtration system, and the number of turtles you have. Clean it as often as is necessary to keep the water in the tank clear and clean. If you see a lot of debris in the water and/or the water smells, the tank is overdue for a cleaning.

Because water quality and temperature are so important, you may want to fill a new, clean plastic trashcan with clean water before cleaning your tank. If you set up this trashcan two days before tank cleaning, you can treat the water as needed, and if you get a second water heater, you can even heat it so that it's ready for your turtles.

Making complete water changes isn't always necessary. If the water level is down a little or the water is a little dirty but not too bad, clean the filter in your filtration system, drain out part of the water, and then add some clean, pretreated water.

✔ **Tank cleaning:** To clean the tank, catch your turtles and set them aside in a dry container. Siphon, scoop, or dump out the old water. With a scraper, clean the sides of the tank, scraping off any debris. Do not use kitchen, bathroom, or other household cleaners! However, if the tank was really dirty or if sick turtles were in the tank, you can scrub it with a mild 3 percent bleach solution (20 parts water to 1 part bleach). Rinse out the debris, and then rinse again. Add clean, treated, preheated water. Double-check the water temperature, and if the temperature is okay, you're ready to add your turtles.

Think good hygiene as you clean the tank. Wash your hands before touching your face. Don't clean any turtle stuff in the kitchen sink, and disinfect everything afterward with a mild bleach solution.

If you set up a regular routine, maintaining the tank won't get out of hand. If you set aside one hour every Saturday morning for cleaning the turtle tank, for example, you (and other family members) will expect it and maintain the tank the way you complete any household chore. In that hour, you can replace the water, make partial water changes, clean the filter, replace some of the potting soil in the land mass area, or scrub down the basking area log.

Chapter 14

Making an Indoor Home for a Terrestrial Turtle or Small Tortoise

. . . .

In This Chapter

▶ Building an enclosure for your turtle or tortoise

▶ Furnishing your turtle or tortoise's home

▶ Maintaining the cage with minimal effort

. . . .

Making an indoor home for a terrestrial turtle or small tortoise can be a challenge, because these active chelonians need more room than you may think. In this chapter, I take a look at different types of cages or enclosures, cage furnishings, and cage covers so that you can make and keep your turtle's or tortoise's cage safe and healthy for it.

Home Sweet Home: The Cage or Enclosure

There are a number of different ways to house your terrestrial turtle or tortoise. Glass aquariums, commercially designed reptile cages, home-built wooden enclosures, and plastic swimming pools are options. However, before you decide which type of cage to use, you need to figure out how big the cage should be. In addition, you need to make the cage escape-proof. The following sections show you how.

Making it large enough

Terrestrial turtles and small tortoises are active. In the wild, they forage for food and like to explore, climb, burrow, and dig in leaf litter. In captivity, their cages (often called *terrariums*) must allow them some of these same activities or they'll be scrunched (see Figure 14-1).

Figure 14-1:
Don't try to
squeeze a
turtle or
tortoise into
a small
terrarium.

Guidelines are as follows:

- ✔ **For terrestrial turtles:** Allow each turtle 3 square feet of floor space for each 8 inches of turtle length. For example, if you have an adult box turtle that's 12 inches long, it should have a minimum of 4½ square feet of space to roam.

  If your turtle is captive-bred, this much space will probably work just fine. However, if your turtle is wild-caught, you may need to supply even more room before your turtle adapts to captivity.

- ✔ **For small tortoises:** Tortoises need even more room. Small tortoises need a minimum of 3 square yards of floor space for each 12 inches of length. For example, if you have a leopard tortoise that's 12 inches long from nose to tail, you need to supply an enclosure that's 9 feet long x 9 feet wide — in other words, a small bedroom! A 6-inch pancake tortoise, however, can do quite well in an enclosure that's about 4½ feet square or in one that's 2 feet wide x 9 feet long.

Choosing the proper materials

Most adult tortoises and terrestrial turtles, when housed inside, are kept in either a plastic swimming pool or a homemade enclosure.

- ✔ **A plastic children's wading pool** works well for many turtles and small tortoises. It's cheap to purchase, easy to replace, and easy to clean. Unfortunately, it does take up floor space — you can't just set it up on the counter!

- ✔ **A homemade cage** is as good (or bad!) as you are a carpenter. A simple wooden box with four sides and a floor can be a great cage. Be sure to paint or seal a wooden cage with a nontoxic paint or water sealant; otherwise, it will absorb wastes and become dangerous to you and your pet.

I'm not a fan of housing terrestrial turtles or tortoises in all-glass aquariums. Because the tanks are see-through all the way around, the turtles are constantly visible and suffer from the stress of being so visible. They often beat themselves against the glass, hurting themselves in an attempt to escape. If you do decide to use an all-glass aquarium, cover three sides with paper or cardboard and provide plenty of hiding places.

Many commercial reptile cages aren't made specifically for turtles or tortoises. Wire cages aren't suitable because tortoises and terrestrial turtles will either hurt themselves on the wire or tear up the cage. In addition, wire doesn't hold in the heat needed for many tortoise species. Plastic reptile cages, on the other hand, can work for smaller species or hatchlings. These cages are solid; have a molded plastic top, bottom, and three sides (with no seams); and usually include Plexiglas or glass sliding front doors. Plastic reptile cages are easy to heat, easy to clean, and easy on the wallet. However, they're not at all suitable for adult animals of larger species.

Preventing a great escape

No matter what kind of cage or enclosure you use, it must be escape-proof. Box turtles are wonderfully inventive escape artists! The males, especially, are quite tenacious. Don't assume that your adorable little pet won't climb; given the opportunity, it might!

Make sure that the sides of the cage are high enough to prevent escape and are as vertical as possible, with no slanting sides. Don't pile cage furnishings (covered in the following section) along the sides or in the corners. And every cage — even a swimming pool — should have a cover of some kind. Hardware cloth (mesh screening) of ½-inch squares works very well.

If you're building a wooden enclosure, make the height of the sides twice the length of the turtle. (If your turtle is 6 inches long, for example, the sides should be at least 12 inches high.) Plus, cut a triangular piece of wood for each corner and fasten it at the top of the corner, making a small triangular roof. If the turtle tries to escape by using the corners as a brace, it will be unable to do so.

Home Furnishings

Furnishing your turtle's or tortoise's cage or enclosure is just as important as selecting the cage itself. A perfect cage won't work if it isn't furnished correctly. In the following sections, I look at the furnishings that turn your turtle's or tortoise's cage into its home.

Feeling the heat

After you decide which type of cage or enclosure you're going to use, you need to decide how you will supply heat. Consider providing more than one source of heat, such as an incandescent light (which provides warmth and a place to bask in the artificial "sunshine") and belly heat — heat underneath your turtle or tortoise.

✔ An incandescent light is a good source of heat, and you can position it anywhere you want over the cage to make a hot spot — see Figure 14-2. Test the temperature of this spot by putting a thermometer in the light at a position where your turtle may rest: The temperature should be at least 85 degrees for most terrestrial turtles and even 90 degrees for many tortoises. (See Chapters 7 and 9 for information about the heating needs of specific terrestrial turtles and small tortoises.)

✔ If you have a glass aquarium, you can use an undercage heater for belly heat. These heaters attach to the bottom of a glass cage, sticking to the glass, and can be positioned at one end of the tank, providing a heat gradient. However, never use one of these heaters on a plastic cage (it will melt or crack the plastic) or a wooden cage (it could start a fire).

If you have a plastic or wooden cage, you may want to use a heat rock for belly heat. Bury the heat rock in the *substrate* (the stuff on the floor — see the next section) so that it doesn't overheat and burn the turtle's or tortoise's *plastron* (the lower shell covering the belly).

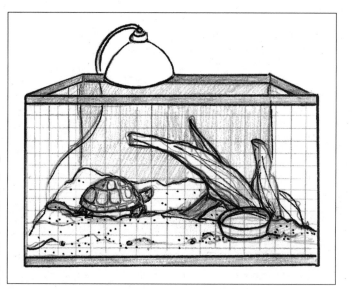

Figure 14-2:
Provide a heat source for your tortoise or terrestrial turtle.

Chapter 17 gives you gobs more information on keeping your turtle or tortoise toasty warm.

Getting in on the ground floor

What *substrate* (a fancy term for the stuff on the floor of the cage) should you use? The following list can help:

- ✔ **Bark:** For terrestrial turtles and tortoises that need slightly higher humidity, I like to use bark. Shredded bark can be moistened to retain water for a while, looks natural, smells good, is easy to replace, and is inexpensive. On the downside, bark doesn't hold heat well, so you have to compensate for that with your heat source(s). If you do use bark, avoid those with strong odors, such as cedar.

- ✔ **Alfalfa pellets:** For tortoises that need lower humidity, I use alfalfa pellets — rabbit food. Alfalfa pellets are inexpensive and smell good, and scooping feces out of them is almost as easy as scooping them out of cat litter. Besides, if a tortoise drops food in the pellets and eats some pellets by mistake, it's also good nutrition!

  Never use sand or cat litter in your cages. Although sand holds heat very well, it can cause an intestinal impaction if your tortoise ingests it. Cat litter is very abrasive and will harm your tortoise's plastron, skin, feet, and intestinal tract if it eats some.

- ✔ **Newspaper:** Many commercial breeders and keepers like to use newspaper. It's cheap and makes cleaning the cage easy. I don't like newspaper because it's ugly. I'm also not sure about the inks: Turtles and tortoises are long-lived pets, and researchers haven't yet studied the risks of long-term exposure to newspaper inks.

- ✔ **Commercial bedding:** Commercial bedding products (shredded bark, peat mixtures, and recycled paper products) are also available. Feel free to try the ones that are marketed for turtles and/or tortoises. Compare prices, though, because both bark and alfalfa pellets are relatively inexpensive.

Taking care of odds and ends

What else does your turtle or tortoise home need? A variety of odds and ends, as follows:

✔ **Water:** Provide water in a shallow bowl or a plastic plant saucer. Make sure that the bowl is shallow enough that your turtle or tortoise can climb out without flipping over. You can leave water in the cage of humidity-loving chelonians all day, but offer it just once a day to desert species and then remove it from the cage.

✔ **Cover:** The cage or enclosure needs a cover. If you're using an aquarium, a cover may have come with it. However, a swimming pool or homemade cage needs a cover, too, to keep kids, dogs, and cats out and turtles in. Hardware cloth with ½-inch squares works well. It's stiff enough to hold its shape, and you can bend it to form corners.

The cover also supplies a place to hold and position a heat lamp and a fluorescent light needed to supply those essential ultraviolet rays. (See Chapter 17 for more about ultraviolet rays.)

✔ **Hiding places:** Supply hiding places for your turtle or tortoise. In the wild, a turtle or tortoise out in the open is vulnerable. Hiding places give the animal a feeling of security. Hatchlings and young turtles, especially, need hiding places.

When laid on their sides, plant pots — either clay or plastic — make great, inexpensive hiding places, as shown in Figure 14-3. If the pots have been used for plants, make sure that they're well washed and that no fertilizer or pesticide residues remain.

Low-growing potted plants also make good hiding places and make the cage or enclosure look more natural. Keep in mind, though, that your pet doesn't really care about looks. A turtle or tortoise, even a small one, goes through or over anything in its path, and that may include your potted plant. Because tortoises seem to enjoy destroying plants, I use potted plants in the cages of hatchlings and very small turtles only. The bigger, stronger, and more tanklike turtles and tortoises can go without.

If you use plants in your turtle or tortoise cage, make sure that the plants are safe, clean, and nontoxic. See Chapter 19 for a list of poisonous plants.

✔ **Cage decoration:** A few rocks make for good cage decorations, and your turtle or tortoise will appreciate a flat rock positioned under the heat lamp. You may also want to add a small log or a pile of twigs or leaves. Turtles and tortoises do like to explore, and a naked cage is boring.

Tortoises in space

Did you know that the Soviets used tortoises in their space program? The Soviet interplanetary probe number 5, which traveled in October 1968, carried insects, some microorganisms, and several Russian tortoises (*Testudo* or *Geochelone horsfieldi*). These tortoises were the first vertebrates to circle the moon.

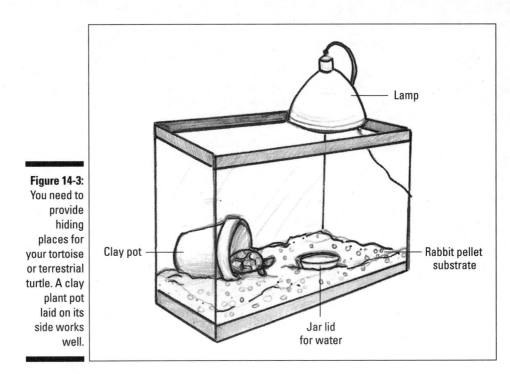

Figure 14-3: You need to provide hiding places for your tortoise or terrestrial turtle. A clay plant pot laid on its side works well.

Lamp

Clay pot

Rabbit pellet substrate

Jar lid for water

Making the Cage Easy to Clean

Cage furnishings are visually appealing, but be sure to balance the needs of an attractive environment with those of your tortoise, and then consider the ease of cleaning the cage with all this stuff in it. Make it look nice, but keep it easy to clean, too.

Your daily cleaning should take just a few minutes. Scoop feces daily or as soon as they appear. Pick up leftover food daily. Add more substrate when it's needed (you lose some when you remove feces). Keep it simple.

Every once in a while, clean the entire cage and replace the substrate. How often depends on the type of cage or enclosure, how many turtles or tortoises are in the cage, and how big they are. If the cage smells dirty, clean it. A good-sized cage with two or three box turtles kept on bark may need to be thoroughly cleaned once a month. A cage housing three small to medium-sized tortoises on alfalfa pellets may need to be thoroughly cleaned weekly.

When you clean the cage, take the turtles and tortoises out and put them in a safe spot (a plastic, escape-proof tub or cardboard box) while you work. Empty all the substrate and either throw it away or add it to your compost heap. Wipe out the last traces of the substrate and then scrub the cage with a mild solution of 20 parts water to 1 part bleach. Rinse the cage a couple of times, dry it, and then add clean substrate.

Chapter 15

Keeping a Turtle or Tortoise Outdoors

In This Chapter

▶ Securing a perfectly sized enclosure

▶ Building an outdoor house

▶ Keeping the area clean

If you have turtles and tortoises and a secure backyard, your chelonian friends will welcome some time outside. For just a few hours a week or all summer long, your pets will enjoy spending time in more natural surroundings — see Figure 15-1. And in some parts of the United States, especially Hawaii, Florida, and southern California, turtles and tortoises can stay outside year-round. Regardless of how much time they spend — 1 month per year or 12 — you must build a safe enclosure. This chapter shows you how.

Figure 15-1:
Most chelonians love spending time outdoors.

© Bill Love

Setting Up an Enclosure

Almost all turtles and tortoises enjoy spending time outside when the weather is good. Terrestrial turtles and tortoises prefer living outdoors in more natural circumstances, and even aquatic turtles like to bask in the heat of the sun (rather than that of a heat lamp) once in a while.

Evaluating the space you need

All turtles and tortoises require a secure enclosure, but the size may differ, depending on the residents:

- **Aquatic and semi-aquatic turtles:** If an aquatic or semi-aquatic turtle spends a few hours a day or a summer outside, its enclosure needs a turtle swimming pool and less land area. A child's wading pool set into the ground makes a great swimming pool for a 4- to 8-inch turtle; a larger turtle needs slightly more room. An enclosure just slightly larger (maybe a foot or two) than the pool is all these turtles need.

  Your aquatic or semi-aquatic turtle needs a ramp so that it can get into and out of the water. Make sure that the ramp and pool are far enough away from the outside walls of the enclosure that escape attempts don't occur.

- **Terrestrial turtles:** If the enclosure is for a terrestrial turtle, allow at least 3 square feet of ground per 8 inches of turtle length. Although 3 square feet is a minimum and is adequate, more room is always better.

- **Tortoises:** If the enclosure is for a small tortoise, you need to provide more space. If the enclosure is for a medium to large tortoise, 3 square yards per 12 inches of tortoise length is the absolute minimum, and 5 square yards per 12 inches of tortoise length is better.

Constructing the enclosure

You can construct an outdoor turtle enclosure in several different ways. To build a wooden enclosure, follow these steps:

1. **Dig a ditch at leash 6 inches deep and 6 inches wide, outlining the walls (perimeter) of the tortoise enclosure.**

   Before you dig, make sure that the enclosure is located exactly where you want it and is the proper size.

2. **Measure wooden planks for the walls of the enclosure and cut them to size.**

   The height of the walls should be at least twice the length of the largest turtle or tortoise in the enclosure. (If the largest turtle is 8 inches long, the walls should be at least 16 inches high.) When figuring the height, don't forget to add 6 inches for the depth of your ditch. The planks lie on their edges, lengthwise.

3. **Cut a 4-inch x 4-inch post for each corner.**

4. **Fasten the planks to each 4 x 4.**

   You now have a wooden box (with no top and no bottom) lying in an open ditch.

5. **Take a 6-inch-wide strip of chicken wire or hardware cloth and staple or nail it to the bottom of the planks (in the ditch).**

6. **Spread out the rest of the 6 inches perpendicular to the planks in the ditch, pointing inward into the enclosure.**

   The planks should form the back of an L, with the chicken wire as the base of the L. If a turtle decides to dig under the boards, the chicken wire will stop it.

7. **Fill the ditch with dirt and pack it down.**

8. **Cut four triangular pieces of wood to fit as small ceiling pieces for the top of each corner of the enclosure.**

   With a ceiling, the turtles are less apt to try to climb out.

Wood, unfortunately, does rot eventually, and a wooden enclosure needs to be replaced regularly. Other turtle and tortoise keepers have built concrete block walls for their enclosures, which can be more permanent and look like part of the landscaping (see Figure 15-2), especially if you also have concrete block raised garden beds.

Turtle trivia

The Arizona-Sonora Desert Museum has one of the most extensive living collections of native reptiles in the United States. Some of these reptiles are threatened, some are endangered, and some need special management. The zoo is consistently listed as one of the ten best in the country. The museum also manages a Tortoise Adoption Program to serve the needs of desert tortoises in captivity.

Figure 15-2:
A concrete block enclosure can fit right into your landscape.

If you decide to build a concrete block enclosure, make sure to dig down at least 6 inches for the first layer of blocks and lay at least a 6-inch-wide strip of hardware cloth or chicken wire at the base of the first layer of blocks. Doing so helps prevent escapes.

Don't build an enclosure out of see-through material, such as chicken wire. The residents will constantly try to escape, fit through, or climb the fence. Turtles and tortoises believe the adage, "The grass is always greener on the other side." A solid fence that they can't see through or over will reduce escape attempts.

If you have small turtles and tortoises — box turtles or Russian tortoises, for example — provide some sort of cover for the enclosure. You want to protect your pets against predators: raccoons, coyotes, hawks, and owls, as well as dogs and cats. Depending on the size of the enclosure, a 4-x-8-foot piece of framed wooden lattice can be a sturdy, lift-off cover. Hardware cloth (¼-inch to ½-inch mesh screening) or chicken wire can also make a satisfactory cover.

A ranger who has worked at the Guajome Park in northern San Diego County notes that Western pond turtles *(Clemmys marmorata)* are food for several different predators. All the larger predatory birds, including the hawks, owls, herons, egrets, ravens, and crows, catch and eat hatchlings and small turtles. Coyotes eat larger turtles when they can catch them on land. Many animals, including raccoons, opossums, skunks, coyotes, and large birds, consider the eggs a delicacy.

Going Househunting

If your turtle or tortoise is going to spend more than a few hours at a time outside, it needs a dry, warm house. A wooden box elevated slightly from the ground works well, but I've found that the commercially produced plastic doghouses work even better. Plastic doghouses don't leak in bad weather, don't deteriorate as they age the way wood does, and hold in heat quite well.

If you have one or two small turtles or tortoises, the smallest size of dog-house will do. If you have bigger tortoises, choose from a variety of larger sizes. When choosing a doghouse, make sure that your turtle or tortoise can climb in easily. Some plastic doghouses have a lip at the doorway that could hamper entry. Make sure, too, that the doorway is wide enough for your turtle or tortoise; measure your tortoise's width before you go shopping!

Your turtle or tortoise won't know that this big plastic thing is its house; you need to teach it. Find your turtle or tortoise in the enclosure and place it in the house. At first, it may just turn around and run back out. That's okay during the day, but at night, put it in the house and then block the entrance so it can't go back out into the nighttime weather, at a time when predators are more active, too. Unblock the doorway in the morning — if you don't, your chelonian will overheat during the day. The turtle or tortoise will learn very quickly that the turtle house is warm and cozy.

I like to use bark as a *substrate* (the stuff on the floor of the cage) for outdoor turtle and tortoise homes. It's inexpensive and easy to replace, and when it's soiled, I use it as mulch around my roses. Spread a couple of inches of shred-ded bark on the floor of the turtle house.

I also like to have supplemental heat available in the turtle house. I hang an incandescent reptile light with a red bulb (for heat and not light) from the inside top of the plastic doghouse/turtle house. By running the cord through the vent at the top of the house, I can turn the light on and off depending on the weather. Or, if I want, I can put the light on a timer, turning the light on at dusk and off in the morning.

If you have a turtle or tortoise species that originates from a climate much like your own, you don't need to provide supplemental heat. However, if you have a desert or tropical species and your climate is not similarly desert or tropical, supplemental heat is a necessity.

Knowing What Else the Enclosure Needs

Your terrestrial turtle or tortoise needs water, of course. You can supply that in a low, shallow plant saucer. Make sure that it's shallow enough for your pet to climb into and out of without flipping itself over, as shown in Figure 15-3.

Provide hiding places, too. If your turtle or tortoise is small, is young, or has been inside for a period of time, it will hide more often than not. You may have to search the enclosure for it. However, as it gets older, gets bigger, and feels more secure, it will spend more time out in the open. Hiding places can be anything that won't trap your turtle. Plant pots on their sides, half-buried in the dirt, work well. Have two or three in different parts of the enclosure. Safe, nontoxic, low-growing shrubs also provide hiding places, as shown in Figure 15-4. Your turtle or tortoise will quickly learn to use its house as a hiding place, too.

Figure 15-3:
Provide a
small
container
of water
(relative
to your
chelonian's
size).

© Liz Palika

An aquatic or semi-aquatic turtle also needs a hiding place in the water. Some big-leafed water plants works, as does a narrow board over one portion of the pool. The turtle can either bask on the board or hide under it.

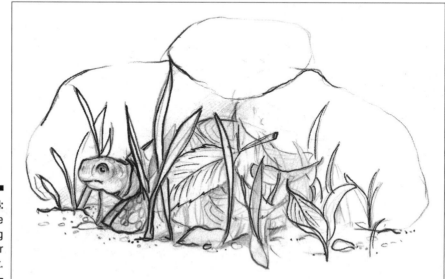

Figure 15-4:
Provide
hiding
places for
your pet.

You may also want to add a few things to the enclosure for your turtle or tortoise to climb on, such as small sticks, small logs, or a few rocks. Chelonians like to explore and investigate things, so make sure that whatever you leave in the enclosure is safe. Turtles and tortoises also like to see whether things are edible, and they do so by biting. Don't leave plastic kids' toys or gardening equipment in the enclosure!

All the varieties of box turtles, sulcatas *(Geochelone sulcata),* Russian tortoises *(Testudo* or *Geochelone horsfieldi),* and gopher tortoises *(Gopherus polyphemus)* like to dig. Providing something for them to dig in may prevent them from trying to dig out of their enclosure. For my Russians and box turtles (in their own separate enclosures), I dug up a small area (about 3 feet x 3 feet, deep enough for each tortoise to cover itself). When the soil was turned over and soft, I dumped a big bag of large chunk bark. I mixed the bark with the soil and left it heaped up. The box turtles and the Russians quickly learned that digging and burying themselves in this soil was much easier than it was in the grass.

Many tortoises aren't as prone to digging if they have enough hiding places. Sulcatas usually dig in the heat of the summer when there isn't enough shade. If you provide a shady hiding place, you eliminate the need to dig. If you need motivation to provide a variety of hiding places, just think about how much soil a 200-pound male sulcata can move!

In addition, if you decide to breed your turtles or tortoises — or, more likely, if your turtles and tortoises decide that it's time to breed — the females will need soft, sandy soil in which to lay their eggs.

Keeping It Clean

Keeping an outdoor terrestrial turtle or tortoise enclosure clean isn't difficult at all. A dog pooper-scooper (the kind with a rake and a shovel) works well for picking up turtle or tortoise feces. In addition, complete the following tasks:

- ✔ Rake bark from the turtle house that has been tracked outside back into the house or add it to a compost heap.

- ✔ Rake up leftover food and throw it away or add it to a compost heap.

- ✔ Dump out dirty drinking water, rinse the water saucer, and refill the saucer.

- ✔ Clean the pool for aquatic turtles by removing the water, rinsing the plastic basin, and refilling the pool.

- ✔ Once a week, rake the enclosure, water the grass, and trim the shrubs.

Chapter 16

Lighting Up Your Chelonian's World

*R*esearchers who specialize in human medicine have discovered that many people suffer from a seasonal disorder (Seasonal Affective Disorder, or SAD) that causes them to become depressed, moody, and lethargic in winter. These people are affected by the shorter daylight hours, less sun, and increased cloud cover. When the sufferers are exposed to lights of a specific type, the effects of this disorder are greatly reduced.

Light is even more important to reptiles. Light, heat from light, and natural *photoperiods* (cycles of light and dark, such as daylight and nighttime) affect every part of a reptile's life, including its appetite, eating, sleeping, and reproduction. This chapter sheds the light on your turtle's or tortoise's needs.

Providing Natural Sunlight

When you stay out in the sun too long without sunscreen, you get sunburned, a malady that's caused by the sun's ultraviolet rays. These particular rays are also being blamed for many skin cancers caused by overexposure to the sun. Ultraviolet rays come in two varieties:

✔ **UVA:** Plants need UVA rays. The florescent lights sold as grow lights for greenhouses (or for houseplants) are UVA lights.

Reptiles deprived of UVA rays often show signs of mental illness, including aggression. Even experts don't know why this happens. UVA rays also stimulate appetite, and an ill or injured turtle or tortoise that is not eating often begins to eat when given fluids and exposed to UVA light.

✔ **UVB:** Some turtles and other reptiles require UVB rays to synthesize vitamin D3. Some turtles and tortoises, like most reptiles, can't synthesize vitamin D3 in their bodies. The ultraviolet wavelengths found in natural sunlight enable them to manufacture vitamin D3, which is necessary for them to utilize the calcium in their food. Without D3, calcium would simply pass through the body unused, causing innumerable health problems, including soft-shell syndrome.

If you're going to house your turtle or tortoise outside where it can soak up the sun's rays, you don't need to provide additional light. However, if you're going to keep your turtle or tortoise indoors at all, additional lighting is necessary.

If you house your turtle or tortoise inside and you have a temporary outdoor enclosure, a few hours of sunlight per week will satisfy your pet's needs. When you put your turtle or tortoise outside, don't leave it sitting out in the sun without shade or protection. Ideally, you want to give it access to both sun and shade and let it go back and forth between the two so that it doesn't get overheated.

Make sure that the sunlight is unfiltered. *Unfiltered* means that the sun can reach your turtle or tortoise without passing through glass, Plexiglas, plastic, or any other covering. Sunlight passing through most glass loses up to 98 percent of its UV light due to refraction.

Using Commercial Reptile Lights

A variety of lights are available commercially to meet your turtle or tortoise's UV needs. Several companies produce fluorescent tubes that supply UVB rays. Keep in mind, though, that not all fluorescent tubes produce UVB, nor do all "full-spectrum" lights supply both UVA and UVB. Look for fluorescent lights specifically labeled as "UVA and UVB for reptiles."

✔ The Reptile Daylight, distributed by Energy Savers Unlimited, is a full-spectrum fluorescent tube designed specifically for reptiles. It produces UVA in the 315 to 400 nanometer range and UVB at 310 nanometers. It is available in 18-, 24-, 36-, and 48-inch sizes. Energy Savers Unlimited also carries a number of different fixtures to mount the fluorescent tubes. Energy Savers Unlimited lights are available through pet stores.

✔ Zoo Med sells several fluorescent tubes for reptiles. The Reptisun tube produces UVB at 310 nanometers, as does the Repti Iguana Light. Zoo Med encourages potential buyers to write for a copy of their independent lighting research. Write to Lighting, c/o Zoo Med Laboratories, Inc., 3100 McMillan Road, San Luis Obispo, CA 93401.

Zoo Med also has a number of hoods and fixtures for fluorescent tubes to fit a variety of cage sizes, from 24 to 72 inches long. Zoo Med products are available from pet stores.

✔ Ultraviolet Resources International offers two fluorescent tubes for reptiles. One produces a 3 percent UVB output; the other an 8 percent output. If you can't find these lights at your local pet store, call Ultraviolet Resources International at 800-247-3251.

✔ National Biological Corporation also produces a fluorescent light (Reptile D-Light) that produces an 8 percent UVB concentration. You can reach National Biological Corporation at 800-891-5218.

Mount the lights over your turtle's or tortoise's cage or enclosure, no lower than 12 inches and no higher than 18 inches from the top of your pet's shell, unless the manufacturer's directions specify otherwise. Make sure that no glass or plastic (which could block UV light) is between the fluorescent tube and your turtle.

These fluorescent tubes lose effectiveness with age, so mark your calendar and replace the tubes every six months, even if the tube hasn't burned out.

When shopping for a fluorescent fixture or hood, look for a multipurpose hood, too. Some manufacturers make hoods with three fixtures in them. One is for the fluorescent tube, one is for a white daylight incandescent light bulb, and one is for a red or black nighttime bulb. A fixture like this can lessen some of the mess that several fixtures would make on top of your pet's cage or enclosure.

Photo What? Understanding Photoperiods

All the Earth's creatures (including humans) have what are called _circadian rhythms_. These physiological and behavioral actions are associated with the Earth's 24-hour rotation. Eating, sleeping, basking, and even reproduction are all governed by (or affected by) the hours of daylight. One cycle of daylight and nighttime is one _photoperiod_.

If an artificial light is on constantly over a captive turtle or tortoise, within a short time the animal's natural rhythms will be disturbed. The turtle or tortoise may stop eating, may not reproduce, may try to sleep constantly, or may not sleep at all. Eventually, the stress might even cause death.

The intervals of light and darkness that you can create by turning lights on and off over the turtle's cage are also called _photoperiods_. You can use these photoperiods to mimic natural conditions (as much as possible). If you aren't breeding your turtles or tortoises, or if you're raising young chelonians that are not yet old enough to breed, a 14-hours-on, 10-hours-off schedule works well.

If your turtles and tortoises are in the house and you enjoy watching them in the evening when you come home from work, make sure that their schedule of light is such that you can enjoy them with the lights on. Set up a timer so that the lights over the cage come on at 8:00 a.m. and go off at 10:00 p.m. when you're ready to go to bed. That way, your turtles or tortoises have a good photoperiod schedule, and you can still enjoy them.

You can find timers at your local hardware store for about $10. You plug the power cord to the light into the timer. You can then set the timer so that the light turns on and off at specific times. You can then have lights on for 14 hours and off for 10 hours, or lengthen or shorten the photoperiods during other seasons.

If your turtle normally hibernates or becomes somewhat dormant in the winter, you can prepare it for hibernation by making the artificial daylight hours shorter. When spring comes, you can lengthen the hours of light, mimicking spring's increasing daylight. (See Chapter 22 for the lowdown on hibernation.)

Natural photoperiods are especially important if you're planning to breed your turtles or tortoises (see Chapter 21), because much of breeding behavior is keyed to specific times of the year. In the wild, if eggs are laid at the wrong time of year and the young hatch when inadequate supplies of water or food are available, the species doesn't survive — and turtles and tortoises instinctively know this. Naturally, in captivity, you're there to care for the eggs and the young, so the time of year may not seem important to you. However, if the photoperiods aren't correct, many species simply won't breed.

How do you know how to set the photoperiod schedule? Try the following:

✔ If you live in North America and your turtle or tortoise is a species native to North America (such as an eastern box turtle or a California desert tortoise), follow the guidelines of the sun. Keep the lights on as long as the sun is up, and turn them off when the sun goes down.

✔ If you have a European or Asian species from approximately the same latitude as North America, follow the same sunup, sundown schedule.

✔ If the species is from south of the equator, such as South America or southern Africa, the seasons are reversed. Because it would be difficult (if not impossible) to fool your turtle into thinking that winter is summer and summer is winter, simply let your pet adapt to the northern hemisphere's schedule by turning the lights on and off with the local daylight and nighttime hours (sunrise and sunset).

✔ Species native to areas close to the equator require less-extreme photoperiods. A 12-hours-on, 12-hours-off schedule works well for most tropical species.

Chapter 17

Keeping Your Turtle or Tortoise Warm and Toasty

. . . .

In This Chapter
▶ Recognizing the importance of heat
▶ Using optimum temperature ranges
▶ Considering commercial heat sources

. . . .

*L*ike other reptiles, turtles and tortoises are *ectothermic* — often called "cold-blooded." This means that these animals can't produce their own body heat as mammals do and instead rely on heat sources in the environment.

In all animals, reptiles included, some body processes work better at certain temperatures. Enzymes, for example, require heat to perform their critical chemical conversions, which include breaking down carbohydrates and fats and working with proteins and vitamins to make sure that the body is well fed. Without body heat, these reactions slow down — and even stop! While mammals produce their own body heat and can maintain enough heat for all necessary functions regardless of the external temperature, reptiles can't produce enough body heat for those processes and must find outside sources of heat.

Turning Up the Heat

The need to maintain body heat is one of the most important factors in any turtle's or tortoise's life. In hot climates, such as North American, African, or South American deserts, maintaining a higher body temperature is relatively easy for a turtle or tortoise. That could be why so many turtles and tortoises are found in these environments.

Turtles and tortoises found in cooler climates are experts at finding warm places. A rock in the sunshine heats the body quickly; a dark-colored log in the sun is warmer than a light-colored log. For this reason, turtles are often found out of the water basking in the sun: the ultimate sun worshippers!

If the temperature is too cool, your chelonian may stop eating. With very few exceptions, turtles and tortoises don't eat if the temperature is less than 65 degrees. The food in the digestive tract rots (instead of being digested), which slowly poisons the chelonian. In addition, low temperatures slow the activity level, breeding behaviors cease, and, when cool enough, the chelonian becomes motionless.

If the temperature is too cool, the turtle or tortoise may hibernate (depending on the species). Box turtles, for example, hibernate when the temperature cools down in the fall. Leopard tortoises, however, come from a climate that's warmer year-round and don't hibernate. If a leopard tortoise gets too cool for too long a period, it will die.

Optimum Temperatures

Temperature needs vary among species. The optimum temperature — the best temperature for eating, digestion, and good health — for many turtles and tortoises is about 88 degrees Fahrenheit. However, I don't think there's an environment on the face of this Earth where the temperature is always 88 degrees. Temperatures vary from day to night, from season to season, and because of the weather. In addition, in their native habitats, turtles and tortoises live in a variety of climates and temperatures.

When establishing an environment for a turtle or tortoise, your goal should be to set up a cage or enclosure in which your pet can live comfortably and thrive in your care. Many times, you need to supply supplemental heat. See Figure 17-1.

Figure 17-1:
Your aquatic turtle needs a heated home.

✔ The African mud turtle *(Pelusios subniger)* thrives in temperatures between the mid-70s and the mid-80s. The striped mud turtle *(Kinosternon baurii)* does well when temperatures are in the low 80s, as does the yellow mud turtle *(Kinosternon flavescens)* and the eastern mud turtle *(Kinosternon subrubrum)*.

✔ Most freshwater aquatic and semi-aquatic turtles need their aquarium water heated to between 70 and 75 degrees. A protected submersible aquarium heater works well at maintaining this temperature. The ambient temperature of the cage should be between the mid-70s and high 80s.

✔ The Chaco side-neck turtle *(Acanthochelys* or *Platemys pallidipectoris)* thrives in water conditions in the high 70s and air temperatures slightly higher, as does the matamata *(Chelus fimbriatus)*.

✔ The angulated tortoise *(Chersina angulata)* does well in temperatures in the low to mid-70s. This species doesn't care for high temperatures. The leopard tortoise *(Geochelone pardalis)* is active and eating when temperatures reach the high 60s but prefers temperatures in the 70s to 80s.

✔ Many tortoises need slightly higher temperatures, thriving in the mid to high 80s. Species from desert areas obviously need higher temperatures. The Aldabran tortoise *(Geochelone* or *Aldabrachelys gigantea)* eats when temperatures are as low as the low 60s, but optimum temperatures are in the mid 80s. The radiated tortoise *(Geochelone asterochelys radiata)* shares these temperature requirements. See Figure 17-2.

✔ The red-footed tortoise *(Geochelone* or *Chelonoidis carbonaria)* likes higher temperatures and thrives in daytime temperatures in the mid-80s. The sulcata *(Geochelone sulcata)* also does well in higher temperatures.

Figure 17-2:
A small tortoise requires a carefully monitored climate.

Too much heat can be as dangerous as too little. An environment kept too warm with no escape can rapidly dehydrate or overheat a turtle, with tragic and fatal results.

Evaluating Heating Sources

Turtles and tortoises regulate their body heat by moving back and forth between the sun and the shade, warming up in the sun and cooling off in the shade. In this way, they can prevent themselves from cooling down too much or from overheating.

I watch this temperature regulation each day with my outdoor turtles and tortoises. In the morning, all my turtles and tortoises find a nice sunny spot in their enclosure and bask. Even though each turtle and tortoise house has a nighttime heat lamp, they really do prefer the sun. Because the sunshine is good for them (providing vitamin D3), that's fine! As they warm up, the tortoises begin to graze on the grass in their enclosures, and the box turtles drink or search for worms in the compost heap. Their daily activities begin as their body temperature rises.

(Note that I maintain a compost heap in one of my outdoor turtle enclosures. I recycle yard wastes and at the same time raise earthworms for feeding the turtles. The turtles quickly learned that the compost heap produces heat, and on many cool mornings I find several turtles soaking up the heat on top of the decaying vegetation.)

Later, toward noon, all the chelonians have found some shade. At this time of day, they would overheat if they continued to bask in the sun. Later in the afternoon, they're active again, getting a last bite to eat before night. When the sun goes down, there isn't a turtle or tortoise to be seen; all have put themselves away for the night under the nighttime heat lamps in the turtle and tortoise houses.

Temperatures vary between night and day as well. Many species are keyed to cooler nighttime temperatures, slowing down their activity and sleeping. Other species are very active in the morning and later in the evening, foraging for food at those times and resting or basking in the sun during the heat of the day.

In a captive environment, you need to provide similar situations. If the entire cage or enclosure is heated to 88 degrees, a turtle or tortoise can't cool itself off if it becomes too hot. By supplying areas in the enclosure that are warmer than others, you give the turtle or tortoise a choice.

You can find a variety of different heating supplies:

✔ **Undercage heaters** attach to the bottom of a glass aquarium and heat to specific temperatures. When you place an undercage heater under one end of the tank, that end becomes warmer, with the unheated end of the tank becoming cooler, creating a heat gradient. Undercage heaters are to be used only with glass-bottomed aquariums, not with wooden or plastic cages.

✔ **Heat rocks** are manufactured stones or bricks with heating elements inside. They heat to specific temperatures and can be used alone as a heat source buried in the cage bedding to warm a specific area (not the entire cage). Some heat rocks have thermostats so that you can set specific temperatures.

✔ **Incandescent light bulbs** produce heat, and several bulbs on the market are specifically for reptiles. By placing one above one end of a turtle or tortoise enclosure, you can create a warm area for basking. During the day, you can use a clear or white incandescent bulb that produces light and heat. At night, when the reptile needs darkness, use a red bulb that produces red light (which reptiles have difficulty seeing) and heat.

The wattage of the incandescent bulb you should use varies, depending on how much heat you need to provide and how far from the light fixture the basking area sits. When setting up the cage or enclosure, place a thermometer in the spot you're trying to heat and turn on the light. In five minutes, check the temperature. If it's too cool, you need a higher-wattage bulb. If it's too hot, you need a lower-wattage bulb.

The bulb you use at night should be of a lower wattage than the bulb you use during the day. Most reptiles, including most chelonians, need a slightly cooler nighttime cycle — maybe 10 degrees.

Because incandescent lights get very hot, always set up the bulb *outside* or *above* the enclosure. Don't put it where the turtle or tortoise can touch it or knock it down. And make sure that nothing else can touch the bulb.

✔ **Ceramic heat emitters** screw into light bulb sockets (like incandescent bulbs). Because they don't produce light, just heat, you can use them 24 hours a day. Heat emitters are more expensive than incandescent light bulbs, but they usually last much longer. Just as incandescent bulbs come in different wattages, so do heat emitters. Use a thermometer to test the temperature in the hot spot.

A heat emitter, like an incandescent light, can burn your turtle or tortoise if touched, so take care to set up the heat emitter above your chelonian's reach.

When incandescent bulbs burn out, it's obvious because they produce no light. However, because heat emitters don't produce light, it's not quite as obvious when they burn out. It's important that you check the emitters on a regular basis.

Use ceramic (instead of plastic) light bulb sockets with either light bulbs or heat emitters. Ceramic light sockets are slightly more expensive but are much safer. Also, don't use an inexpensive plastic lamp (plastic socket and plastic shade) for your heat source; these lamps aren't made to be on for hours at a time and may overheat, melt, and possibly even start a fire. Finally, don't use standard heat lamps (such as you may use to warm up under after a shower) on your turtles and tortoises. These lamps are too hot and will burn your pets.

If your house is normally at 72 to 74 degrees or cooler, you may need to supply an underwater heater and a basking light for aquatic turtles. For tortoises, an undercage heater and a basking light may be sufficient. If you house your tortoises outside, you can't control the weather. However, you can supply your tortoises with a tortoise house (perhaps a plastic doghouse) with an incandescent reptile lamp inside.

Regardless of what you use to heat your turtle or tortoise cage, invest in a few thermometers. Place one regular thermometer at the cool end of the cage or enclosure and one at the hot end. These will tell you what the actual temperature is at any given time. The thermometers that register a 24-hour low temperature and a 24-hour high temperature are invaluable. You can see exactly how cool it gets during the night and how hot it gets by mid-afternoon. Knowing this, you can make adjustments to your pet's habitat.

As you choose heating devices for your turtle or tortoise, keep in mind that all of them require electricity. Your monthly utility bill can, quite literally, shoot sky high! From personal experience, I found that ceramic heat emitters use quite a lot of electricity. Depending on the species, I use an undercage heater or a heat rock (not both) and an incandescent basking lamp. You may want to watch your electric bill closely as you start to use some of these different devices. If your bill goes up too much, try something else.

Heating supply sources

Because heat is such an important aspect of keeping reptiles, a variety of heating supplies are available from a number of different companies. Manufacturers have said the following about their products:

- **Zoo Med** sells several different kinds of heating devices. Several different kinds of heat rocks are offered in different sizes and temperature ranges. Zoo Med Reptitherm under-tank heaters come in different sizes, from small (about 4 inches x 6 inches) to very large heaters that can heat 20- and 30-gallon aquariums. Zoo Med has a variety of incandescent heat/light bulbs as well. The basking spot bulbs produce a lot of heat and bright light. The Repti Infrared Spot bulb produces heat but no light for use at night. Zoo Med offers ceramic heat emitters, too. These light bulb–shaped heating devices screw into light bulb sockets and produce heat. They can get quite hot and produce a lot of heat without producing light.

  Zoo Med also offers a variety of thermometers, including high/low thermometers and thermostats. Zoo Med products are available in pet stores.

- **DuroLite** offers basking lights for reptiles in four sizes: 30 watt, 50 watt, 75 watt, and 100 watt. Ask for DuroLite bulbs at your pet store.

- **Hagen** makes an undercage heater called Heat-Wave for mounting at one end of an aquarium, like the Zoo Med undercage heater. The Heat-Wave comes in several different sizes to fit different-sized tanks. Look for this heater in your local pet store.

- **Helix Controls** sells several different products for heating a reptile cage. One is the Space Heater, a small warm-air circulator. The Basic System provides day and night temperature settings, maintains temperature, and synchronizes lights with the temperature cycle. For more information, call 619-566-8335.

- **Bush Herpetological Supply** makes the Biostat DP, a heating system with a proportional thermostat that monitors the temperature in a cage or enclosure. The temperature remains at preset settings. For information, call Bush Herpetological Supply 316-325-2250.

- **MTS Electronics** offers a variety of supplies to help you heat your turtle or tortoise enclosure, including thermostats, thermometers, FlexWatt Heat tape for under the aquarium, and light bulbs. Call 610-588-6011 for details.

Many Internet pet stores carry reptile supplies, including fluorescent tubes, hoods and light fixtures, incandescent bulbs, heat emitters, and undercage heaters. You may find that the online pet stores have a wider selection of equipment than your local pet store carries. When you compare prices with your local pet store, remember to take into account the cost of shipping.

Chapter 18

Water: The Magic Liquid

*T*he bodies of most reptiles are more than two-thirds water. Blood is more than 80 percent water, muscles are over 70 percent water, and the brain is 75 percent water. Even bones are 20 percent water. Water is required for the normal functioning of every cell in a turtle's or tortoise's body. Respiration, digestion, metabolism, and elimination all require water. Water is needed to dissolve and transport nutrients.

A certain amount of water is lost each day through respiration and elimination and must be replaced. Some desert tortoises have tough, armored skin that aids in retaining water. The amount of water that each species needs can vary depending on the chelonian's size, its activity level, and the climate, especially the temperature and humidity.

The type of chelonian also determines its method of elimination and how much water it loses during elimination. For example, most tortoises excrete a fairly bulky, somewhat drier stool and chalky urine. In comparison, aquatic turtles pass more fluid urine and softer, less bulky stools.

Water needs also vary depending on the chelonian's natural climate. Many desert species have been genetically programmed to conserve water and may go months without drinking. Instead, they may obtain water from the food they consume, or the animal may *estivate* — that is, become dormant during the summer, through a heat spell, or through a drought. Many desert species can also "recycle" water from urinary wastes.

This chapter distills these details about water into easy-to-manage sections.

Understanding Your Pet's Water Needs

Turtles are, by definition, chelonians that live in or near water. Not all turtles live in the water all the time. Some, like the red-eared slider *(Trachemys scripta elegans),* are very aquatic. Some, like the spotted turtle *(Clemmys guttata),* are semi-aquatic, living in and near the water but sometimes spending time on land, too. Other turtles, like the various box turtles, are terrestrial but usually live within walking distance of water. (See Part II for details on which turtles like which environments.)

These chelonians must have water in their cages or enclosures all the time. The aquatic species needs enough water for swimming and foraging and just enough land area for basking. The semi-aquatic species need both water and land areas, whereas the terrestrial species do well with simply a shallow bowl of water.

Tortoises, on the other hand, are terrestrial creatures that can't swim — they would sink like rocks if they tried! Many tortoises will freely drink from shallow saucers and water puddles but won't enter water, even to soak, while a few tortoises seem to enjoy soaking in water. The Galapagos tortoises are often seen soaking in water, sometimes with only their heads showing.

How do you know whether your tortoise should have just drinking water or needs soaking water? Look at the area where the species originated. As an example, my leopard tortoises *(Geochelone pardalis)* are from Kenya or Tanzania and live in dry, arid grasslands. These tortoises may drink from puddles during rainstorms but otherwise have little access to water, getting most of their moisture needs from their food. I have found that my leopard tortoises will drink from a shallow water bowl and from puddles on the ground but will never soak or bathe in water. My sulcata *(Geochelone sulcata),* another African desert species, rarely drinks water and never soaks in water. My Russian tortoises *(Testudo* or *Geochelone horsfieldi)* drink occasionally, never soak in the water, and, like the other desert species, get most of their moisture needs from their food. The box turtles, however, bathe and soak in the water daily, sometimes for hours at a time. My Gulf Coast box turtles *(Terrapene carolina major)* even like to eat in the water!

One of the easiest ways to determine what climate your turtle or tortoise came from is to get a tourist guide for that region or area. Tourist guides list temperatures and other weather particulars, as well as geographical information. This info will give you a good idea as to your turtle's or tortoise's needs.

Aquatic and semi-aquatic turtles must have an aquatic cage or enclosure, obviously, and terrestrial turtles may do well with a shallow bowl for water and bathing. Every tortoise should be offered water on a daily basis; however, don't leave water in the cages of species that originated in dry grasslands, arid terrain, and desert areas (see Part II for details).

Many turtles and tortoises have drowned because their bowls' sides were too steep or slick. If a turtle or tortoise is trying to climb out of the bowl and flips over, it will drown, so make sure that the bowl is shallow, with equally shallow sides. The shallow plastic plant saucers used under potted plants work very well as shallow water bowls. You can use small saucers for smaller turtles or tortoises and bigger ones for larger chelonians.

Monitoring Water Quality

Water, water, everywhere, but is it safe to drink? Water pollution is a problem that the United States has been dealing with for some time. Twenty years ago, most of the rivers and lakes in the continental United States were polluted to some extent. In fact, some were so badly polluted that they were considered dead; no life existed in those bodies of water.

Recent research has shown that water pollution affects people more than suspected. A report published in *New Scientist* by Roger Masters of Dartmouth College stated that toxic metals in drinking water were linked to crime rates. He found a link between pollution amounts and incidences of murder, assault, and robbery.

The effect on turtles

If pollution has this effect on people, what does it do to the native life in those bodies of water? Is there a turtle out there robbing its buddies? Probably not, but pollution does kill. The food chain suffers when pollution kills off the fish, amphibians, and insects inhabiting the body of water or when it reduces those species' reproductive rates. If by chance an adult turtle can survive the pollution and can find enough food to eat (see Figure 18-1), it still stands a greater risk of dying of cancer or illness. In addition, reproductive rates are greatly decreased.

Most drinking water comes from lakes, rivers, and reservoirs, some of which are exposed to pollution on a daily basis. Other drinking water comes from ground wells. Originally thought to be the best water available and safe from pollution, many wells across the United States have been shut down because they're polluted. Chemicals and pollutants dumped on the ground or into sewers have seeped into local water tables, polluting nearby wells.

Water also contains dissolved minerals, organic molecules, and a wide variety of living organisms, including larvae, protozoans, bacteria, and viruses. The majority of these organisms will never cause a problem, either to people or to pets. However, occasionally something does happen. Floods that overwhelm water treatment plants make headlines because the public's water supply becomes polluted.

Figure 18-1:
Polluted waters decrease the quality of life for turtles.

So how safe is your water? By the time the water in a reservoir reaches your home, it has gone through several filtration systems and has had a number of different chemicals added to it to purify it. Most water treatment plants add chlorine for purification and fluorine to prevent cavities in children's teeth. Does that make your water safe? Does that make it healthy for you and your turtles? It's hard to tell. Some experts feel that drinking water is dangerous — that it contains too many chemicals and pollutants. (Researchers in Finland found that rats exposed to high levels of MX, which develops from organic compounds in chlorinated water, get a number of different types of cancer.) Other experts argue just as strongly that the water supply is safe.

Assessing the chemicals in your water

It's important to know what has been added to your water so that you can protect your turtles. Some aquatic turtles are very sensitive to chlorine and other water additives. Call your local water supplier (either your city or the local water district) and ask these specific questions:

- ✔ What has been added to the water during and after processing?
- ✔ Are those additives safe for reptiles?
- ✔ How can I remove those chemicals from the water before I put my turtles in it?

Keepers of tropical fish learn quickly to treat their water while cleaning the aquarium. If they don't treat the water, the fish will die as soon as they're exposed to the chlorine. Commercial products are available from tropical fish and aquarium supply stores that remove chlorine from water. However, if other chemicals have been added, make sure that your turtles will be safe before putting that water in their enclosure.

Tetra, a company specializing in aquarium products, sells several different water test kits, including the TetraTest Kit, the Complete Hardness Kit, and the pH Kit. All of these kits enable you to test your water for chemicals, acidity, alkaline (both of which refer to the pH balance of the water), and hardness. After you've tested the water, additional supplies enable you to treat the water.

Some people assume that bottled water (often called spring water or purified water) is better or safer than water from the tap. Unfortunately, that's an unsafe assumption. Bottled water must meet certain standards; however, it is often the same water that comes out of your tap! In many areas, local companies filter and bottle the water, add a label, and sell it under a fancy name. If you're using bottled water because you think that it's safer or more pure, read the label first, and if you have any questions, call the company bottling the water and ask.

In some regions, turtle keepers set up water barrels to catch rainwater. These barrels can then be used as water supplies for turtles. But this water, too, is only as good as it is clean. Is acid rain a problem in your area? Does factory soot pollute your area? Air pollution affects the quality of the rainwater.

Ultimately, using the water out of your tap may be easiest. Just make some telephone calls first, asking about the quality of your water, what has been added to it, and how you can treat it so that it will be safe for your chelonians.

Humidity: Water in the Air

Humidity is water vapor in the air. How much water vapor is in the air depends on many different circumstances. If you live near the ocean, your relative humidity will probably be much higher than that of your relative who lives in an arid inland valley. However, it's not quite that simple. Phoenix, Arizona is located in the desert, and you may expect the humidity levels to be quite low, but that's not the case. There is so much agriculture and irrigation in and around Phoenix now that the humidity levels have risen drastically in the last few decades.

Many turtles and tortoises have specific humidity needs. Most desert tortoises can't tolerate high humidity levels; that's one reason you should offer water once a day but not leave it in these chelonians' enclosures. (A water bowl raises the humidity levels in the enclosure.)

Species that thrive in low humidity include the following:

- ✔ Desert tortoise *(Gopherus agassizii)*
- ✔ Pancake tortoise *(Malacophersus tornieri)*
- ✔ Russian tortoises *(Testudo* or *Geochelone horsfieldi)*
- ✔ Star tortoise *(Geochelone elegans)*
- ✔ Texas tortoise *(Gopherus berlandieri)*

Species that prefer higher humidity include the following:

- ✔ Most turtles
- ✔ Burmese brown and black tortoises *(Manouria emys)*
- ✔ Elongated tortoise *(Indotestudo* or *Geochelone elongata)*
- ✔ Red-footed tortoise *(Geochelone* or *Chelonoidis carbonaria)*
- ✔ Serrated hingeback tortoise *(Kinixys erosa)*

For species that do need higher humidity, you can raise the humidity level in a cage or enclosure by spraying or misting the cage as needed or by adding standing water (such as in a water bowl).

Part IV
Open Wide!
Turtle and Tortoise Health

The 5th Wave   By Rich Tennant

"I'm sorry, Mr. Mathews. Your turtle is gravely ill. I don't think he's got much more than 30 years left."

In this part . . .

So you've decided to own a turtle or tortoise, you've selected a pet, and you've built him a house. Now what?

The four chapters in this part explain how to keep your new pet happy and healthy and answer all your questions about turtle health. In this part, you can find out about nutrition, diseases, injuries, and hibernation. And if you'd like to hear the pitter-patter of tiny turtle or tortoise feet, you can find out about breeding, too.

Chapter 19

Making Sure Your Pet Eats the Right Things

In This Chapter

▶ Understanding basic nutrition

▶ Becoming acquainted with the terms *herbivore, carnivore,* and *omnivore*

▶ Deciding whether to use commercial reptile foods

▶ Feeding your turtle or tortoise

For as long as turtles and tortoises have existed, they have foraged for themselves. Some aquatic turtles catch and eat small fish; some turtles eat insects and plants. Most tortoises eat plants, although some also scavenge when they get the chance. Some chelonians live in rich, fertile areas where food is plentiful, while others survive in harsh, arid deserts where food is often hard to find.

Captivity has changed the way many turtles and tortoises eat. An aquatic turtle that in the wild would eat a variety of small fish and aquatic creatures may exist solely on a diet of goldfish. A tortoise used to eating cactus and wild grasses may graze on well-nourished fescue and Bermuda grasses in captivity.

Are these changes healthy? Will a problem develop later in that turtle's or tortoise's life or with that turtle's or tortoise's offspring? What about a tortoise being fed commercial pellet food? As turtle and tortoise ownership increases, many researchers are looking at the foods fed to pets, and more research is being done on reptile nutrition. The more you know, the better you can care for your pets. This chapter helps you make sense of a vast amount of information.

Understanding What Nutrition Is

Nutrition is the relationship between food and the health of the body consuming the food. Proper nutrition means that the food being eaten supplies all the body's essential nutrients — proteins, fats, carbohydrates, vitamins, minerals, and water — in a form that the body can use.

Good nutrition is needed for a strong immune system, reproduction, and normal growth. Food supplies the substances that act as regulators for the body's many processes, including organ development and functions and disease resistance. Food also provides energy so that the body can function from day to day.

However, a variety of factors affect a turtle's or tortoise's nutritional needs:

- **The type of turtle or tortoise:** Each species has its own nutritional needs: Some need fish, some need meat, and some need plants. The variety is considerable, and you must take it into account when formulating a diet for your turtle or tortoise.

- **The turtle's or tortoise's age:** Nutritional needs vary dramatically with a chelonian's age. Active, rapidly growing hatchlings often require more food or significantly higher protein levels than do older, more sedate adults. Sometimes even the foods they eat may change. Hatchling box turtles, for example, often refuse to eat anything except live foods, while adult box turtles relish fruits and vegetables.

- **The turtle's or tortoise's state of general health:** A chelonian stressed by injury, illness, or parasites needs more support from its food to provide for the increased needs of the immune system and for healing. Good nutrition can also prevent problems by keeping the immune system running properly.

- **Reproduction:** Good nutrition is necessary for both the male and the female prior to and during breeding. A male that's not well nourished may not produce viable sperm and may even have a reduced desire to breed. If a female isn't well nourished, she may not ovulate properly, may not release eggs, may not have the reserves to adequately nourish the eggs, or may not have the calcium to cover the eggs with a strong shell.

- **Activity levels:** Some turtles and tortoises are more active than others. Some herbivorous tortoises browse for hours two to three times a day looking for and eating the best foods. Some turtles are active long enough to eat and then bask in the sun for hours at a time. Reptiles that are more active need more nutritional support from their food to maintain their energy level.

- **Stress:** A wild-caught turtle or tortoise goes through a great deal of stress when adapting to captivity. Turtles and tortoises may be stressed in other ways, too. An inappropriate environment causes stress, as does overcrowding or too much activity near the animal's cage or enclosure. Although good nutrition can help a turtle or tortoise deal with some stress by keeping the body well nourished, stress affects some chelonians more than others.

✔ **Food:** The food that your turtle or tortoise eats can also cause stress, especially if it's the wrong food for that particular species or if it's of poor quality. Too little food can also cause stress.

No single thing can ensure good health through nutrition. For most turtles and tortoises, good health requires the proper food, correct lighting, adequate temperatures, proper humidity, and the right size and design of cage or enclosure.

The building blocks of good nutrition

The food that your turtle or tortoise eats contains eight basic building blocks of nutrition. Each of these nutrient building blocks has its own purposes and functions, which the following sections cover.

Water

Chapter 9 discusses water, and I must mention its importance here as well. Water is vital to the digestive process. Without water, food can't be digested, nor can nutrients be absorbed into the body. Even desert tortoises need water. If it isn't available to drink, it must be available from the foods they eat.

Provide water to all turtles and tortoises — even desert species — whenever you offer food.

Enzymes

Enzymes have numerous functions in a chelonian's body; so many, in fact, that your turtle or tortoise can't survive without them. Enzymes are made up of two parts: One is the protein molecule, and the other is called a coenzyme. The coenzyme may be a vitamin, a mineral, or the chemical derivative of a vitamin or mineral.

In the digestive process, each enzyme is capable of breaking down one specific substance. For example, an enzyme designed to break down fat doesn't work with carbohydrates. Enzymes (including their coenzymes) work by initiating a chemical reaction so that other substances can do their jobs. The digesting and metabolizing of food requires a complex system of thousands of enzymes, each performing its individual job so that thousands of chemical reactions happen as they should.

Because enzymes are made up of proteins and other substances, usually a vitamin or mineral, the number of enzymes available for use by the turtle or tortoise can vary depending on what the chelonian is eating.

Protein

Proteins are one of the most important elements of food for growth and development, repair of body tissues, sexual maturation, and metabolism. Proteins are vital parts of the blood, the immune system, the digestive system, hormone production, and other systems.

Carbohydrates

Carbohydrates make up almost three-quarters of the dry matter in most plants. Like proteins, when eaten, carbohydrates have more than one function in the body. The most important function is to provide energy to the body for both bodily functions and muscular energy. Carbohydrates also assist in the digestion of other foods.

Fats

Dietary fats, also called *lipids,* are a group of compounds that aren't soluble in water and have a number of different functions in the body. One of the most important is that of carrying the fat-soluble vitamins, including A, D, E, and K. Fats are also involved in a number of chemical processes in the body and are necessary for growth, healthy blood, and normal kidney function. Fats are also a good source of energy.

Fiber

Fiber, the cellulose in the plants that your chelonian eats, is necessary for intestinal health. Fiber absorbs water and aids in the formation and elimination of feces.

Vitamins

Vitamins are organic compounds found only in plants and animals. With very few exceptions, your chelonian's body can't synthesize vitamins; they are supplied in the food that it eats. Vitamins work together with other compounds (each other, minerals, or enzymes) to perform different functions. Vitamins are involved in digestion, metabolism of food, growth, reproduction, cellular reproduction and oxidation, and many other functions. They are responsible for thousands of different chemical reactions.

- **Vitamin A:** This fat-soluble vitamin has two forms: carotene and vitamin A. Carotene, which is found in plants, must be converted to vitamin A before the body can use it. *Preformed vitamin A* is the result of that chemical conversion and is found in animal tissues. Because A is fat soluble, the excess is not excreted through the urine and instead is stored in the liver, fat tissues, lungs, and kidneys. Vitamin A is an important antioxidant, helps in growth and body tissue repair, and keeps the immune system strong.

  A vitamin A deficiency causes slow or retarded growth, reproductive failure, and skin disorders. Secondary infections are common, as are eye disorders. Too much vitamin A has been associated with bone deformities, joint pain, and bleeding.

Vitamin A is found in green leafy vegetables, yellow and orange vegetables, fish oils, and animal liver. Most commercial reptile food manufacturers claim to add vitamin A to their foods.

✔ **B complex vitamins:** The B vitamins include B1 (thiamin), B2 (riboflavin), B3 (niacin), B5 (pantothenic acid), B6 (pyridoxine), B12 (cyanocobalamin), and B15 (pangamic acid). The B complex also includes biotin, choline, folic acid, and a few other important vitamins. The B vitamins are all water soluble; excess isn't stored in the body but, instead, is excreted through the urine.

The B vitamins have so many functions in the body that your chelonian literally can't live without them. Some of these functions include protein and fat metabolism, normal functioning of the immune and nervous systems, and the development of good muscle tone and healthy skin. Each of the individual B vitamins has its own functions, all of which are vital to good health. Because the B vitamins work together, a deficiency in one can have repercussions in the functions of others. The B complex vitamins are found in grains, including whole-grain bread, and brewer's yeast.

✔ **Vitamin C:** This is often called a "wonder vitamin" because it has such a beneficial effect on the body. Vitamin C helps form blood corpuscles, aids in a healthy immune system, fights bacterial infections, helps in healing, and does much, much more. Vitamin C is water soluble, and excess is excreted through the urine.

Chelonians are able to synthesize a certain amount of vitamin C internally; however, it is also available from dark green vegetables and fruits.

✔ **Vitamin D:** Often known as the "sunshine vitamin," D is absorbed from exposure to sunlight. Of the three forms of vitamin D (D1, D2, and D3), mammals use the first two forms of the vitamin, and some reptiles need D3. The D vitamins are necessary for normal growth and healthy bones. They work with vitamin A, and a deficiency in either one can lead to bone deformities, rickets, soft-shell syndrome or other bone diseases, and deformities. Vitamin D is fat soluble, and excess is stored in the liver, brain, and skin.

Chelonians can get adequate D3 if they're allowed to bask in the sun daily. Those kept inside should have a fluorescent reptile light that provides UVA and UVB rays. Supplements are also a source of vitamin D.

✔ **Vitamin E:** E, a fat-soluble vitamin, is vital to healthy blood. As an antioxidant, it is also thought to protect both the pituitary and adrenal hormones from oxidation. *Tocopherols* are a form of vitamin E and are often added to commercial reptile foods as preservatives. Natural sources include leafy green vegetables, soybeans, nuts, and seeds.

✔ **Vitamin K:** This fat-soluble vitamin is needed for proper blood clotting and calcium metabolism. You can find vitamin K in alfalfa, kelp, and supplements.

Feeding your turtle or tortoise foods that contain vitamins isn't always enough. Many vitamins that work closely together should be eaten together so that they can perform their functions.

Some of the vitamins that work best with a partner include the following:

- ✔ Vitamin A works best when eaten with vitamin B complex, vitamin D, and zinc.
- ✔ Vitamin B complex works best with vitamin A, vitamin C, vitamin E, calcium, and phosphorus.
- ✔ Vitamin C works best with a wide range of other vitamins and minerals.
- ✔ Vitamin D works best with vitamin A, vitamin C, calcium, and phosphorus.
- ✔ Vitamin E works best with vitamin A, vitamin B complex, and vitamin C.

As you can see, most vitamins work closely together, and no one vitamin should be emphasized over the others. Excess or toxicity of any one vitamin can affect the functioning of all the other vitamins and some of the minerals.

Minerals

Minerals originate in the earth but pass through plants and eventually are present to some extent in the tissues of all living things. Minerals make up part of the bones, muscles, blood, and nerves. They work with vitamins, enzymes, and each other to perform their functions.

Just as many vitamins are more effective when paired with certain other vitamins or minerals, many minerals work best with partners:

- ✔ Calcium is more effective with vitamin A, vitamin C, and vitamins D and D3.
- ✔ Copper is most effective with cobalt, iron, and zinc.
- ✔ Iron is most effective with vitamin B complex, vitamin C, calcium, copper, and phosphorus.
- ✔ Phosphorus is most effective with vitamin A, vitamin D and D3, calcium, and protein.

Galapagos tortoises and occasional Indian Ocean giant chelonians need iodine to prevent goiter.

Maintaining a balance

When looking at your chelonian's nutritional needs, remember that no one vitamin, mineral, or nutritional element (such as protein or fat) functions alone. Each has its own place in the system, and each is dependent on the others. A deficiency or excess of any one nutrient can threaten the others.

Should you use supplements?

Most nutritionists consider a supplement anything you add to a reptile's diet on a regular basis. That may include a vitamin, mineral, or vitamin/mineral combination. As with so many other aspects of reptile nutrition, experts don't agree as to whether supplements are necessary. Some experts feel that a varied natural diet is all chelonians need. The makers of commercial reptile foods say that their food is "complete and balanced" and that no other supplementation is required. Other experts say that those points of view don't take into consideration each reptile's unique needs.

A vitamin/mineral supplement with a calcium: phosphorus ratio of 2:1 is minimally beneficial for most turtles and tortoises.

If your turtle or tortoise is eating a varied diet appropriate to its species, adding a vitamin/mineral supplement that's also in balance won't disturb the biological value of the diet itself. Supplements alone won't cure nutritional problems; they are simply one piece of the nutritional puzzle.

Clarifying What Herbivore, Carnivore, and Omnivore Mean

Turtles and tortoises are often classified by what they normally eat. Some are called herbivores, while others are called carnivores or omnivores. By classifying them this way, pet owners can more easily understand the feeding needs of particular species. The following sections define these three classifications.

What's an herbivore?

Herbivores eat plants and plant products, such as grasses, leaves, vegetables, fruits, and grains. In their native habitat, herbivores eat the plants found in their particular geographical location. For example, desert tortoises *(Gopherus agassizii)* that live in the wild eat grasses, cactus pads and blossoms, shrubs, and other desert plants. (Most herbivores are tortoises.)

Herbivores are nothing if not adaptable. That same desert tortoise will readily eat and thrive on fescue, Bermuda grass, bluegrass, and rye grass found in the backyard, with supplemental feedings of common vegetables and commercial tortoise foods. The majority of chelonian herbivores can also thrive on a captive diet as long as it's balanced and varied and is supplemented with vitamins and minerals at least twice a week.

Safe, nutritious plants for herbivores (omnivores and carnivores, too — see the following section) include the following:

- **Alfalfa:** Fresh, dried hay, meal, pellets
- **Apple:** Fresh — no core or seeds
- **Banana:** Peeled fruit
- **Barley:** Leaves, hay, meal, flour, sprouted seeds
- **Beans:** Leaves, stems, sprouts
- **Beets:** Stems, flowers, grated roots
- **Blackberries:** Fruit
- **Blueberries:** Fruit
- **Broccoli:** Fresh, raw heads; grated stems
- **Brussels sprouts:** Fresh, raw heads
- **Cactus:** Dethorned pads (leaves) and blossoms
- **Carrots:** Root, chopped or grated
- **Clover:** Leaves, blossoms, hay
- **Corn:** Kernels off the cob
- **Dandelion:** Leaves, stem, flowers (flowers are especially good for tempting a tortoise that's ill or hasn't been eating well)
- **Grapes:** Fruit
- **Grass:** Fresh but without insecticides, herbicides, or fertilizers
- **Hibiscus:** Flowers, leaves
- **Kale:** Leaves
- **Millet:** Leaves, meal or flour, hay
- **Mustard:** Leaves, flowers
- **Nasturtium:** Leaves, stems, flowers
- **Okra:** Fresh or frozen/thawed
- **Parsley:** Fresh leaves
- **Pea:** Pods, fruit
- **Pumpkin:** Fruit, flowers
- **Soybean:** Leaves, hay, meal, flour
- **Spinach:** Fresh leaves
- **Squash:** Blossoms, fruit
- **Strawberries:** Fruit

✔ **Sunflower:** Seeds (unsalted), meal, flour

✔ **Timothy:** Fresh, hay

✔ **Tomato:** Fruit only (the leaves are poisonous)

✔ **Turnip:** Leaves, grated root

✔ **Wheat:** Sprouted seeds, fresh leaves, bran

✔ **Zucchini:** Fruit, blossoms

If you're lucky enough to live in a temperate region where your herbivore can spend some time outside, let it do so. Let your tortoise graze — the grass is more like a natural diet, and the sunshine will be good for your pet. As an added treat, offer some clean rose blossoms (see Figure 19-1), hibiscus flowers, nasturtiums, and dandelions.

Figure 19-1:
A tortoise munching on a rose bloom.

However, make sure that the plants in your outdoor landscaping are safe. Many commonly used landscaping plants are poisonous. Here's a list of some dangerous plants:

Amaryllis	Boxwood	Croton
Anemone	Buttercup	Cyclamen
Avocado (leaves, not fruit)	Calla lily	Daffodil
Azalea	Cherry (seeds)	Dieffenbachia
Belladonna	Christmas cactus	Dogwood
Bird of paradise	Common privet	Eggplant (foliage)
Bottlebrush	Crocus	English ivy

Foxglove	Milkweed	Potato (foliage)
Hemlock	Mistletoe	Privet
Holly	Morning glory	Rhododendron
Horse chestnut	Mushrooms (some wild ones, including toadstools)	Rhubarb
Hyacinth		Sage
Impatiens	Oleander	Snapdragon
Iris	Peach (seeds)	Sweet pea
Jasmine	Pennyroyal	Tomato (foliage)
Jimson weed	Poinsettia	Tulip
Larkspur	Poison ivy	Verbena
Lily of the valley	Poison oak	Wisteria
Locoweed	Poison sumac	Yew
Marijuana	Pokeweed	

You can also find food for your herbivore in your refrigerator. Fresh spinach, kale, romaine lettuce, grated carrots, chopped parsley, and grated summer squash are all good foods (see Figure 19-2). Tomatoes, sweet potatoes, and yams are also good, as are mustard greens, collard greens, and Swiss chard. Most herbivores, as well as many omnivores and carnivores, eagerly eat strawberries, raspberries, blueberries, and grapes. Other good fruits include papaya, bananas, melons, apples (cored with seeds removed), and kiwis.

Iceberg lettuce has little or no nutritional value, but herbivores love it. If you have an herbivore recovering from an illness or injury, use iceberg lettuce to make sure that your herbivore eats its vitamins or medication. Chop up the lettuce, mix in the medication or vitamin, and feed your tortoise. Feed this lettuce sparingly, though, because some herbivores like it so much that they refuse other foods.

Take care not to feed too many plants from the cabbage family, such as broccoli, cauliflower, Brussels sprouts, and cabbage. These foods are known to interfere with thyroid function and calcium absorption in turtles and tortoises. Because they provide good nutrition, don't eliminate them from your feeding program altogether — simply feed them in small amounts every other week or so.

Figure 19-2:
Your
chelonian
can munch
on food from
your fridge.

© Liz Palika

Many herbivores are also opportunists, eating what's available. Some normally herbivorous tortoises have been seen to eat scavenged meats; some eat insects; and some even eat the feces of both carnivorous mammals and herbivorous mammals. Some researchers believe that a tortoise eats what's available and what its body needs. Perhaps a tortoise that's eating meat needs more protein in its diet?

The majority of herbivores, however, prefer to eat what they would be eating if they lived in the wild. Recommended foods for herbivorous tortoise species include the following:

✔ **Chaco or Argentine tortoise** (*Geochelone* or *Chelondoidis chilensis*): Flowers, fruits, vegetation, some insects

✔ **California desert tortoise** (*Gopherus agassizii*): Grass for grazing, hay, cactus pads, flowers, fruit, some meat or canned dog food

✔ **Egyptian tortoise** (*Testudo kleinmanni*): Fruit, flowers, vegetation, some insects

✔ **Elongated tortoise** (*Indotestudo* or *Geochelone elongata*): Vegetation, flowers, some fruit, some insects

- ✔ **Galapagos tortoise** (*Geochelone* or *Chelonoidis elephantopus*): Vegetation, flowers, fruit, insects, some meat

- ✔ **Florida gopher tortoise** *(Gopherus polyphemus)*: Vegetation, flowers, fruit, insects, some meat or carrion

- ✔ **Greek tortoise** *(Testudo graeca ibera)*: Vegetation, flowers, some fruit, some insects (in particular, snails)

- ✔ **Hermann's tortoise** *(Testudo hermanni)*: Grass for grazing, weeds, some flowers, chopped or mixed dark green vegetables, grated squash, succulent plants

- ✔ **Hingeback tortoises** (*Kinixys* species): Vegetation, some flowers, fruits, snails, meat

- ✔ **Leopard tortoise** *(Geochelone pardalis)*: Grass for grazing, alfalfa, weeds, flowers, some fruit, mixed dark green vegetables, variety of common household vegetables

- ✔ **Marginated tortoise** *(Testudo marginata)*: Grass for grazing, weeds, flowers, dark green vegetables

- ✔ **Pancake tortoise** *(Malocochersus tornieri)*: Grass for grazing, weeds, seeds, succulents, alfalfa, dark green vegetables

- ✔ **Radiated tortoise** *(Geochelone asterochelys radiata)*: Grass for grazing, weeds, some flowers, fruits, dark green vegetables

- ✔ **Russian tortoise** *(Testudo* or *Geochelone horsfieldi)*: Fleshy vegetables (zucchini, squash, and so on), fruit, flowers, some meat or carrion, soaked dry dog food

- ✔ **Sulcata torotise** *(Geochelone sulcata)*: Grass for grazing, hay, weeds, cactus, succulents, some fruits, some grated vegetables

- ✔ **Star tortoise** *(Geochelone elegans)*: Grass for grazing, weeds, some flowers, some fruits, dark green vegetables

- ✔ **Yellow-footed tortoise** (*Geochelone* or *Chelonoidis denticulata*): Grass for grazing, weeds, clover, some fruits, some fleshy vegetables, some dark green vegetables

Some turtles are herbivores. The painted terrapin *(Callagur borneoensis)*, an aquatic turtle, is a vegetarian, as is the crowned river turtle *(Hardella thurjii)*. The yellow-headed temple turtle *(Hieremys annandalei)* is also an herbivore, eating fruits, green vegetables, and aquatic plants.

What's a carnivore?

Carnivores are, by definition, meat eaters. "Meat" includes mammals, fish, birds, and other reptiles. Many turtles, especially aquatic turtles, are carnivores. In this book, I also include *insectivores* (insect eaters) in the classification of carnivores, because many of the turtles that eat insects also eat meat.

Nutritional values of common foods

Knowing the nutritional values of various foods can help you decide what to feed your chelonian. Following are the nutritional values of some foods that are commonly fed to herbivores and omnivores:

- ✔ **Alfalfa sprouts (1 cup):** 10 calories, 1g protein, 1g carbohydrates, 0.5g fiber, 51 IU vitamin A, 13mg B complex, 10mg calcium, 23mg phosphorus.

- ✔ **Banana (one whole):** 105 calories, 2g protein, 27g carbohydrates, 1g fiber, 92 IU vitamin A, 2mg B complex, 7mg calcium, 22mg phosphorus.

- ✔ **Bread, mixed whole grain (one slice):** 257 calories, 10g protein, 47g carbohydrates, 1g fiber, trace of vitamin A, 5mg B complex, 104mg calcium, 212mg phosphorus.

- ✔ **Broccoli (1 cup):** 24 calories, 2.6g protein, 4.6g carbohydrates, 1g fiber, 1,356 IU vitamin A, 62mg B complex, 42mg calcium, 58mg phosphorus.

- ✔ **Carrots (1 cup):** 48 calories, 1g protein, 11g carbohydrates, 1g fiber, 30,942 IU vitamin A, 15mg B complex, 30mg calcium, 48mg phosphorus.

- ✔ **Collard greens (1 cup):** 35 calories, 3g protein, 7g carbohydrates, 1g fiber, 6,194 IU vitamin A, 2mg B complex, 218mg calcium, 29mg phosphorus.

- ✔ **Prickly pear cactus (one large pad about 130g in weight):** 42 calories, 1g protein, 10g carbohydrates, 2g fiber, 53 IU vitamin A, 1mg B complex, 58mg calcium, 25mg phosphorus.

- ✔ **Tofu (3.5 ounces):** 72 calories, 8g protein, 3g carbohydrates, less than 1g fiber, 0 IU vitamin A, 0mg B complex, 100mg calcium, 176mg phosphorus.

You can find a wide variance in the nutritional values of foods available to your chelonian. By feeding your turtle or tortoise a variety of foods, you are better able to feed a nutritionally complete diet.

In the wild, carnivores catch and eat their prey by using a variety of hunting techniques. Some hold still and wait for their prey to come to them, while others actively hunt for their prey.

In captivity, the foods that carnivorous turtles eat vary. You can use canned dog food as a treat or give it in addition to other foods, but you don't want to use it as a diet staple: It's too high in fat. Soaked dry dog food can be an added ingredient, and commercially available insects, such as crickets, mealworms and waxworms, are good foods to offer. Most carnivorous turtles accept goldfish, guppies, and other commercially available feeder fish.

In general, a good diet for most aquatic or semi-aquatic turtles, which are primarily carnivorous, may include the following:

- ✔ Live feeder fish
- ✔ Earthworms — see Figure 19-3
- ✔ Snails
- ✔ Commercial aquatic turtle food (as a part of, but not the entire, diet)

✓ Shredded lettuce, grated carrot, grated squash, strawberries, and diced apple (the added vegetables and fruits help contribute to a well-balanced, nutritionally complete diet)

Figure 19-3:
A turtle grabbing up a long, thick earthworm.

My husband loves to tell people that his wife is a bug hunter. He thinks I'm funny for going out in the yard at night with a flashlight, hunting for bugs for my turtles. I take my bug hunting very seriously, though, because the bugs I catch add a lot to my turtles' diet. In my backyard, I catch sowbugs and pill-bugs, earthworms and night crawlers, slugs and snails, beetle larvae and aphids. I don't feed my turtles spiders, bees, wasps, or caterpillars. And to guarantee that I catch only bugs that are poison-free, I don't use any insecticides, fungicides, or herbicides in my yard.

Specifically, carnivorous turtles in captivity, listed by species as follows, prefer certain foods:

✓ **Indochinese box turtle** *(Cuora galbinifrons)*: Earthworms, fish, meat, canned dog food.

✓ **Chinese three-striped box turtle** *(Cuora trifasciata)*: Earthworms, crabs, fish, canned dog food.

✓ **Spotted pond turtle** *(Geoclemys hamiltonii)*: Snails, insects, fish, amphibian larvae.

✓ **Malayan snail-eating turtle** *(Malayemys subtrijuga)*: Snails, worms, aquatic insects, small fish.

✓ **European pond terrapin** *(Emys orbicularis)*: Insects, crustaceans, mollusks, worms, amphibians, frogs, fish.

✓ **Barbour's map turtle** *(Graptemys barbouri)*: Mussels, snails, insects, crayfish, fish. Females are plant eaters.

✓ **Alabama map turtle** *(Graptemys pulchra)*: Clams, insects, snails. Females are plant eaters.

✔ **Diamondback terrapin** *(Malaclemys terrapin)*: Snails, crabs, clams, insects, fish, canned dog food.

Feeding a carnivore can be a challenge. If your turtle is genetically programmed to eat snails, clams, and crabs, how can you duplicate that diet in captivity? Many carnivorous turtles have done quite well on a diet consisting of feeder fish (guppies or goldfish), commercially purchased insects (earthworms, waxworms, mealworms, and crickets), insects from the backyard (sowbugs, pillbugs, earthworms, night crawlers, snails, slugs, beetle larvae, and aphids), and a commercial turtle food with vitamins and minerals added. Such a variety of foods can help prevent nutritional deficiencies that may arise from a more selective diet, such as an all-fish or all-insect diet.

Insects can provide your omnivore or carnivore with a number of valuable nutrients if — and only if — the insects themselves are well fed. Any insects you purchase commercially (mealworms or crickets, for example) should be fed for at least two days prior to feeding to your turtle. Think of it this way: During shipment, the insects will not have been fed, so if you feed these insects right away to your pet, you will be giving your turtle a hungry insect with little or no nutritional value. However, if you feed the insects first, the turtle will get the nutritional value of the food the insects have eaten. This process of feeding the insects first is called *gut loading.*

To gut load, buy commercially available insect-feeding foods or feed the insects yourself. Grated carrots, yams, squash, and dry oatmeal or cornmeal are all good foods.

✔ **Mealworms:** Mealworms, scientifically known as *Tenebrio molitor,* are the larvae of a beetle known to be a pest of stored grains. However, to your turtle, these hard-shelled worms (when gut loaded) are a valuable food source. You can buy them from your pet store, or if you're feeding several turtles, buy them in bulk. See Appendix B for resources.

Keep bulk mealworms in a 5-gallon aquarium. Put about 3 inches of wheat or oat bran in the bottom of the tank, and then drop in the mealworms. Supply moisture by slicing a potato or yam and laying the slices on top of the bran. The worms will eat the vegetable, leaving the skin. Replace the slices when needed so that you always have a few in the tank.

Mealworms have four life stages: egg, larva (when they look like worms), pupa, and beetle. The mealworm you buy is at the larva stage and, if kept warm, will quickly change into a pupa. The pupa will shortly turn into a beetle. Leave the beetles in the tank; they will lay eggs and replenish your mealworm population.

✔ **Crickets:** Crickets have been domesticated for the pet trade for many years. You can buy small quantities at your local pet store, and again, as with mealworms, you can buy larger amounts in bulk.

Use a 10- to 20-gallon tank to keep crickets. The tank should have a secure lid, because crickets are escape artists. Put an inch or two of sand in the bottom of the tank and add some sticks, bark, or an egg crate or two to provide hiding places. A jar lid with a wet sponge can provide water. (Don't give crickets open water; they drown easily.) Feed the crickets anything except meat or fat. Apple peels and cores, dry oatmeal, grated carrots, grated yams, bread crusts, and cereal are all good foods. Just keep in mind that what the crickets eat, your turtle will eat, too!

Female crickets lay their eggs in the sand. The babies are tiny little bugs smaller than the head of a pin. You may see them crawling around on the floor of the tank, maturing in five to six weeks.

You can enhance the nutritional value of mealworms or crickets by dusting them with a vitamin/mineral supplement prior to giving them to your turtle. Open a plastic bag and drop in a handful of insects. Shake some vitamin/mineral supplement over them and then shake them up — like Shake 'n' Bake! Promptly feed the dusted insects to your turtles.

What's an omnivore?

Omnivores are opportunists, eating whatever is available. Bears, pigs, and, yes, people are omnivores. Reptilian omnivores include a number of turtles. Depending on the species, these turtles eat fruits, vegetables, insects, and meat. Nutritional problems are rare in omnivores when they have an adequate selection of foods of different types.

The suggested diet for semi-aquatic or terrestrial omnivorous turtles (aquatic turtles are almost always carnivorous) includes the following:

✔ Crickets

✔ Snails

✔ Slugs

✔ Sowbugs (small bugs that run away when startled)

✔ Pillbugs (small bugs that roll into a tight ball when startled)

✔ Earthworms

✔ Canned dog food

✔ Commercial turtle food

✔ A variety of berries, grated carrot, diced fruit, and tomatoes

Most omnivorous species have particular eating preferences, as follows:

- **Asian leaf turtle** *(Cyclemys dentata)*: This species eats both plant matter and meat when small and is mostly vegetarian after it reaches 6 inches in length.

- **Black-breasted leaf turtle** *(Geoemyda spengleri)*: Little is known of these turtles in the wild; however, captives eat both plant and animal matter and tend toward being carnivorous.

- **Spotted turtle** *(Clemmys guttata)*: Feed worms, snails, slugs and other insects, frogs, earthworms, grubs, fruit, and aquatic greens. This turtle tends to be carnivorous.

- **Wood turtle** *(Clemmys inscupta)*: Algae, moss, *lichens* (small plants that grow on rocks and trees), and grass are accepted. A wood turtle will eat leaves, soft fruits, and vegetables. Insects (including earthworms), canned dog food, and hard-boiled eggs are also good foods to offer. This species tends to be carnivorous.

- **Bog turtle** *(Clemmys muhlenbergii)*: Feed insects, earthworms, snails, slugs, seeds, aquatic greens, fruits, and berries. This species tends toward being carnivorous.

- **Western pond turtle** *(Clemmys marmorata)*: Feed water lily pods and other aquatic greens, insects, worms, and crustaceans (such as lobster, shrimp, and crab). I have seen these guys eat greens when I've kept them.

- **Coahuilan aquatic box turtle** *(Terrapene coahuila)*: Feed fish, worms, insects, fruits, and canned dog food.

- **Eastern box turtle** *(Terrapene carolina carolina)*: Offer snails, slugs, insects, crayfish, frogs, lizards, small snakes, carrion, fruits and berries, and tomatoes.

- **Ornate box turtle** *(Terrapene ornate ornata)*: Insects, including snails and slugs, dung beetles, grasshoppers, carrion, fruits, and berries are all accepted.

- **Painted turtle** *(Chrysemys picta)*: Feed insects, fish, animals, carrion, fruits, berries, aquatic greens and other vegetation, and canned dog food.

Offer a variety of foods to keep your omnivore healthy. Also, remember to feed a good balance of foods — insects, meat, vegetables, and fruit — that are appropriate to the species. This variety, plus a good vitamin and mineral supplement, helps keep an omnivore healthy.

Using Commercial Reptile Foods

Researchers haven't yet studied the long-term effects of feeding a turtle or tortoise a commercially prepared diet. Most commercial reptile foods have been on the market for only ten years, and many more are much newer. With many turtles and tortoises living for 30, 40, 50, or more years, scientists simply don't know what these foods do to chelonian pets in the long run. That doesn't mean that you shouldn't use these foods — they can provide good nutrition — but use them as only *part* of a varied, balanced diet.

Until more is known about them, don't use commercial reptile foods as a sole food or complete diet for your turtle or tortoise. Commercial foods can also be quite expensive, especially when compared to more natural food sources. Using them as a part of the diet shouldn't affect your budget too badly, though.

Commercial reptile food comes in the following four varieties:

- ✔ **Dry:** One of the most common forms of commercial reptile food is *dry extruded* (or pelleted) food. Dry food usually has a moisture content of 10 to 12 percent and contains grains and grain products, vegetables, and other ingredients, often including meat. Dry foods usually have a good shelf life (three to six months) and are reasonable in price. When this food is soaked in water, turtles and tortoises usually accept it readily.

- ✔ **Canned:** You can find several commercially available canned reptile foods. Canned foods have a much higher moisture content than dry foods do and usually contain meat, vegetables, and sometimes even fruit. Most turtles and tortoises readily accept them. Be forewarned, though: Canned foods can be quite expensive.

- ✔ **Frozen:** Frozen foods come in many different forms, from frozen worm cubes to frozen vegetable burgers (for herbivores) to frozen fish, whole mice, and mice substitutes. Frozen foods, when thawed, are sometimes accepted by turtles and tortoises.

- ✔ **Live:** Carnivores more readily notice and eat live foods, including crickets, mealworms, waxworms, fish, and mice. Quite a few companies are now in the business of raising insects and rodents for the reptile trade. Most large pet stores and reptile specialty stores carry these live foods. You can buy other live foods, such as night crawlers and earthworms, at a local fishing supply store or bait shop.

Feeding Your Turtle

Getting your turtle or tortoise to eat is usually not a problem as long as the environment — especially the heat — is correct and your chelonian is healthy. Indoors, you just put the food in front of your turtle and watch it disappear. Outside, you can feed your turtle or tortoise on the ground if you have a grassy spot. If the turtle or tortoise picks up some grass with its food, fine! If you have sand, dirt, or bark on the ground, however, feed your pet on a paper plate so it doesn't pick up anything that could cause problems with its digestive system.

If you're feeding a turtle live foods, such as mealworms, earthworms, or waxworms, offer them in a plastic lid (like those on peanut butter jars). These lids hold the worms in place for a few minutes, until your turtle gets a chance to eat.

Most aquatic turtles eat only in the water. You can hand-feed your turtle by dropping the worm, feeder fish, or other food directly into its mouth, or you can simply drop it into the water in front of your turtle. If you can teach your turtle to eat on land, do so; the water in your aquarium will stay cleaner longer.

Most tortoises like to eat during the heat of the day in spring and fall. During summer's heat, however, they normally sleep during the day and eat in the morning and late afternoon. Box turtles and others are ready to eat after a rainfall. If you don't have enough natural rain, sprinkle their enclosure with water from the hose — they won't know the difference! Beware, though: Rainfall also stimulates breeding behavior in the spring and summer.

Recognizing and Treating a Malnourished Turtle or Tortoise

Sometimes a turtle or tortoise won't eat. The stress of capture, shipment, and captivity causes many chelonians to reject food. A simple lack of familiar food is sometimes the problem. Disease, parasites, illness, or injury could cause anorexia.

A malnourished turtle or tortoise appears dehydrated; its skin is wrinkled and dry on the neck and inside the shell at each leg. Its eyes are sunken. If the causes of malnutrition aren't clear, see a veterinarian to check for underlying causes of the condition. However, if the turtle or tortoise has simply been neglected and not fed, you need to make it eat.

Some turtles show more interest in food after being misted with warm water. This approach is especially effective with box turtles. Others show more interest after being soaked in lukewarm water or after basking in the sun.

To treat a malnourished turtle or tortoise, you first need to get some liquid nourishment into it. Doing so can be difficult because a starving chelonian may no longer have a desire to eat. Here's your best way to approach getting nourishment into a malnourished turtle or tortoise:

1. **Buy Nutrical from your local pet store or veterinarian.**

2. **Dissolve about an inch of Nutrical in a small bowl with about ¼ cup of warm water.**

3. **After the Nutrical dissolves, pull some of the liquid up into a needle-less syringe or an eyedropper.**

4. **Get as much of the Nutrical solution as you can into the chelonian's mouth.**

   You may need to get its head out first. Sometimes a turtle or tortoise will put its head out if allowed to soak in a warm bath, so fix a lukewarm bath that's no deeper than the chelonian's nose when resting. When the chelonian pokes its head out, grab it firmly but gently behind the jaw-bones and hold on!

   With the head out of the shell, you should be able to get some of the mixture into the turtle's or tortoise's mouth. If you can't, use the edge of a spoon to pry the mouth open.

5. **After you've put several syringes full into the turtle or tortoise, let it relax and bask in a warm spot.**

6. **In a couple of hours, repeat the procedure.**

By the second day of treatment, you're going to want to get a little more nutrition into the chelonian so that it will begin eating.

✔ **For an herbivorous tortoise** (see the following section), take a few alfalfa pellets (rabbit food) and mix them in with the Nutrical formula. Let them dissolve and add some more water until you have a green, liquid mush. You need a wide-mouth syringe or dropper or even a poultry baster for this. Get as much as you can into the tortoise (a teaspoon into a hatchling or several tablespoons into a large adult tortoise) without drowning the tortoise. Repeat this process every two or three hours for a day or two, or until the tortoise begins eating on its own.

✔ **For an omnivorous or carnivorous turtle** (review the following section for definitions), mix half a jar of chicken or turkey baby food with the Nutrical solution and feed the turtle this mixture. As with an herbivorous tortoise, repeat the process every two or three hours until the turtle is willing to eat.

Usually, after a chelonian has some food in its system and the digestive process begins again, the turtle or tortoise begins to eat on its own. This can take a few days, however.

Chapter 20

Monitoring Your Turtle's or Tortoise's Health

In This Chapter
▶ Tracking down a veterinarian
▶ Preventing illness before it happens
▶ Understanding where in the body illness occurs

A s your turtle's or tortoise's caretaker, you are ultimately responsible for its good health. You aren't able to hear directly from your turtle or tortoise when it is unwell or has been hurt. In fact, your turtle or tortoise is genetically programmed to hide illnesses and injury, because in the wild, predators prey upon the weak.

However, if you set up a regular routine of examining your pet, you can spot problems before they get too serious. And if you select a veterinarian who's knowledgeable about the care and treatment that chelonians require, you'll have someone to turn to if a problem occurs.

Finding a Veterinarian

Not all veterinarians are skilled in treating reptiles. Finding a veterinarian who likes turtles and tortoises and is knowledgeable about their care is vital — it's something you need to do *before* an emergency happens.

Some veterinarians who like working with exotics (including reptiles) advertise that fact in their ads in the Yellow Pages. In addition, if you have friends with turtles or tortoises, they may be able to recommend a vet to you. Local turtle and tortoise clubs also maintain listings of reputable veterinarians.

The Association of Reptilian and Amphibian Veterinarians (ARAV) is for veterinarians who have an interest or specialize in working with reptiles. This association may be able to help you find a qualified veterinarian in your area. Write to ARAV; care of Wilber Amand, DVM, Executive Director; P.O. Box 605; Chester Heights, PA 19017; or visit the ARAV Web site at www.arav.org.

You can also call the American Veterinary Medical Association at 800-248-2862 and ask for assistance in finding a qualified reptile vet in your area.

There's a difference between a veterinarian who's knowledgeable about reptiles, one who likes working with reptiles, and one who's actually a specialist. For a veterinarian to be called a specialist, he or she must pass a specialty board in that particular specialty.

After you find a vet who is experienced, is knowledgeable, and/or specializes in reptiles (or turtles and tortoises), make an appointment to talk to him or her before you have an emergency. Introduce yourself and tell the vet about your pets and your plans for them. (Are they pets only, or do you plan to breed them?) Ask the vet about his or her policies regarding appointments, emergencies, billing, and so on.

A veterinarian is your partner in pet ownership. Having a veterinarian you can call not just in emergencies, but whenever you have concerns, will help you take care of your pets in the best way possible.

Ask to see the vet's facilities as well. Do you see cages for reptiles with supplemental light and heat, or are reptiles kept in dog and cat cages? Is the hospital equipped to use Isoflourane gas (currently the best anesthesia for reptiles)?

Talk to the vet, too, about his or her charges. What do a normal office call and an exam cost, and how much are the most common tests, including fecal tests for internal parasites? In some areas, veterinary charges are as expensive as physicians' charges! Make sure that you can afford this vet's services.

Preventing Illness

Keeping your pet healthy is the best way to prevent illness. Correct caging, heating, lighting, humidity, and nutrition are vital to your pet's overall good health — if you don't deliver even one of these needs, your pet's health can suffer. But preventing illness involves more than that. Keeping your pet's environment clean is also important, and by keeping the environment clean, you can prevent the spread of salmonella — a potential threat to you as well as your pet.

Vaccinations aren't yet available for turtles or tortoises, but your pets can live a long life without them. It's up to you to make sure that happens!

Maintaining a clean environment

In the wild, turtles and tortoises have a home range or territory, but they move around. They don't stay in the same spot day after day after day, and they certainly don't eat anywhere near their feces. In a cage or enclosure, a turtle or tortoise defecates and eats in close proximity, which can cause significant health problems.

Keep the cage or enclosure clean. Scoop feces daily (if not more often) and replace cage *substrate* (the stuff you put on the floor of the cage) often. Replace water and throw out food that has been soiled with feces, is old, or contains meat. See Chapters 13, 14, and 15, respectively, for tips on keeping aquariums, terrariums, and outdoor enclosures clean.

Preventing the spread of salmonella

About 20 years ago, selling turtles less than 4 inches long was made illegal. This was the result of many cases of salmonella that were associated with tiny red-eared slider turtles *(Trachemys scripta elegans),* which were sold everywhere, even at five-and-dime stores. Some of the cases of salmonella (but certainly not all) were probably directly related to the turtles, because turtles can carry salmonella.

Of course, salmonella can be carried in other ways, too, including through other animals and feces. People have been infected from improperly refrigerated foods and foods contaminated during processing. Even contaminated water can carry salmonella. However, salmonella can be carried by reptiles and is found in aquatic turtles, box turtles, and iguanas.

Don't take salmonella lightly. Although healthy adults can fight off a mild case without showing any significant symptoms, young children, elderly people, and those with suppressed immune systems are at grave risk. The symptoms include cramps, diarrhea, vomiting, bloody stools, and fever. Severe cases may turn into meningitis and encephalitis. If you or someone in your home becomes unexpectedly ill and you have a new turtle, make sure to tell your physician about your turtle!

Although many turtles show no signs of illness when carrying salmonella, some turtles with weakened immune systems may become ill from it. Veterinarians can test to see whether a turtle has salmonella, but unfortunately, treatments are rarely effective. Most animals carrying the disease are euthanized, although salmonella is sometimes treatable with antibiotics.

You can prevent salmonella infections by keeping cages and enclosures very clean and by picking up leftover food and feces right away. Always dispose of feces in a sealed plastic bag; don't add feces to your backyard compost heap. Wash cage furnishings and dishes someplace other than the kitchen sink. Use bleach when cleaning the cage furnishings and dishes and rinse them well. Always wash your hands thoroughly after handling your pet or touching anything in the cage. And teach other family members, especially kids, to do the same.

Investigating Your Pet's Anatomy

Pay attention to your turtle or tortoise. Look at it thoroughly, all over, at least once a week. Look for anything out of the ordinary or anything different. Make note of those things; write them on your calendar even. If problems do develop, the more you can tell your vet, the better: "Three days ago, Sherman tortoise had a small cut behind his left front leg. I washed it and put some ointment on it, but now there's a bump there." Your vet can use those clues to try to solve the problem.

I make it a point to look at my turtles and tortoises as I feed them. Once a week, I hand-feed a strawberry or something else that the animal considers special, and when it stretches out to grab the strawberry, I look carefully at its eyes, nose, and head. As the chelonian opens its mouth to grab the berry, I peek inside. I look for anything out of the ordinary and anything signaling trouble. This quick and easy exam causes no stress and, in fact, is a special time for my pet.

If your pet is vomiting, it may have intestinal blockage, kidney failure, a throat obstruction, or a breathing problem — in all cases, see your vet immediately. Vomiting may also be a sign of poisoning. Search the cage or enclosure for clues and see your vet.

Your pet should have an attitude

A healthy turtle or tortoise should have an attitude. Not a bad attitude — a certain joy in life. When you pick up your pet turtle or tortoise, unless it was asleep and basking in the sun or under a heat lamp, it should be bright and alert. When you feed it, it should be hungry and eager to eat. Lethargy in a turtle or tortoise may be a sign that something is wrong.

The first thing to look at is the temperature in the chelonian's environment. Cold turtles and tortoises are lethargic, move slowly, and may refuse to eat. Most aquatic and semi-aquatic turtles prefer a water temperature of at least the mid to high 70s, with the low 80s even better. A basking area should be in the high 80s. Terrestrial turtles and tortoises need a basking area in the high 80s to low 90s.

The eyes

A turtle's or tortoise's eyes should be clear and bright — see Figure 20-1. Desert species sometimes have a clear, tearlike drainage from the eyes; this is a normal flushing mechanism. However, the eyes shouldn't be crusty.

Figure 20-1:
A strong, vigorous tortoise has clear and bright eyes.

© Liz Palika

If the eyes are red, are slightly swollen, and have matter in them, the turtle or tortoise probably has some form of conjunctivitis. Apply a small amount of a triple antibiotic ophthalmic ointment to the eyes three times a day for ten days. If this doesn't clear up the problem, see your veterinarian.

Turtles are sometimes prone to eye problems when suffering from a vitamin A deficiency (see Chapter 19). The eyes will be closed, swollen, and full of matter. You approach this problem both nutritionally and medically. Increase foods that contain vitamin A, including canned fish cat food, grated carrots, and fish oil supplements. Wash the eyes daily and apply ophthalmic antibiotic ointment three times a day for ten days. If you see no significant improvement, consult your veterinarian.

If opaque white caps are covering your turtle's or tortoise's eyes so that you can't see them, take your pet to the vet right away. That cap is caseated pus and must be removed. The eyes then need to be treated with an antibiotic ointment.

The nose

A turtle's or tortoise's nose should be clean and dry. You should see little or no crusty material at the nose and no discharge.

If your turtle or tortoise has bubbles at its nostrils, pay attention! Tortoises are prone to upper respiratory infections, especially when kept at cooler temperatures; too often, these infections lead to pneumonia. Severe infections or pneumonia cause the animal to breathe through its mouth, have bubbles at the mouth, or breathe heavily. If you see bubbles at the nose or any of these other symptoms, immediately separate this tortoise from others and increase the temperature at your tortoise's basking site to the low to mid-90s. Call your veterinarian and get your tortoise on an antibiotic program. You need to medicate this tortoise and any others it has been exposed to.

Mouth breathing, sneezing, and a runny nose may also signal an allergic reaction. See your vet to determine the cause.

If your turtle has a clear, bubbly discharge from the nose (with no discoloration of the mucus) and swollen eyes, it may have a vitamin A deficiency. Treat the eyes as I explain in "The eyes" section and increase its intake of foods high in vitamin A.

The ears

A turtle's or tortoise's ears aren't very visible, but your pet may have problems with these little-seen sensory organs. Your turtle — especially if it's a box turtle — may swell around the areas of the cheek behind the jaw (it can be quite pronounced) and also be reluctant to eat. This problem is caused by a bacterial infection of the middle ear. Your veterinarian must treat it, because the area needs to be lanced, cleaned, and packed with antibiotic ointment.

The mouth

Your turtle's or tortoise's mouth also can be a source of problems. An overgrown *beak* (the upper part of the mouth) on some turtles and tortoises can cause eating problems. If the turtle is eating many soft foods and too few hard foods, the beak may not be wearing down. Sometimes a malformed skull causes the beak to grow irregularly. In any case, the beak can be trimmed much like the beak on a large bird. Ask your veterinarian to show you how so that you can do it in the future.

Many reptiles can get a mouth infection called *infectious stomatitis* or *mouth rot*. It shows up as discoloration in the mouth, loss of tissue, excess salivation, and secretions. Antibiotic treatment is always needed for this potentially fatal problem.

If you see drooling or a deformed jaw, your pet may be eating too many soft foods or fruits or could have had trauma to the mouth or jaw. See your vet as soon as possible.

The skin

The skin of a turtle, and especially a tortoise, may look tough and impervious to harm, but it's really not as tough as it looks. The skin can be damaged, torn, or injured and must be treated as you would treat your own wounds.

Check the skin at the base of the neck and each leg for *ticks,* blood-sucking parasites that often carry disease. They dig into soft skin — which is why they're found on the neck or the upper part of the legs. After they've dug in, they suck the chelonian's blood. Ticks that are full of blood look swollen and may be larger than a pencil eraser. Ticks are the most common external parasites seen on chelonians, and if your turtle or tortoise spends time outside, it can easily pick them up.

If you can reach the tick with a pair of tweezers or forceps, remove it by grasping it and slowly pulling it out. Do so gently. If you yank it out, you may leave the head in the skin, which can cause an abscess. After removing the tick, clean the wound with hydrogen peroxide and apply antibiotic ointment. Watch to make sure that the wound heals without becoming infected.

Mites are tiny relatives of spiders that bite a turtle or tortoise, getting blood with each bite. Smaller than a pinhead, mites can reproduce rapidly, causing stress and discomfort. Other reptiles, especially snakes, can transmit their mite population to chelonians. If you suspect a mite infestation, remove the turtle or tortoise from its cage or enclosure and bathe your pet in a lukewarm bath with a mild antiseptic (povidone-iodine, for example). Thoroughly clean the cage and enclosure, throw away all substrate and bedding, and scrub the cage or enclosure with a bleach solution.

You can also treat an outdoor enclosure with a mild insecticide if you're able to keep the turtles or tortoises out of the enclosure for at least 24 hours after you treat it. I don't recommend doing so unless it's absolutely necessary, though. Repeat the process again in a week.

Aquatic and semi-aquatic turtles sometimes have peeling skin, which can be a sign of poor water quality, too cool a basking spot, or even too small a basking spot. Improve your pet's environmental conditions and see if the problem clears up. Some turtles also have peeling skin if they have been supplemented with too much vitamin A. Cut back slightly on the fish oil and spread an antibiotic ointment on the peeling skin.

Swollen spots on your turtle's or tortoise's legs could be signs of an injury or abscess that may require treatment. Because of their slow metabolism, reptiles heal slowly, and what may appear to be a minor wound can easily become a major problem. Pay attention to even minor wounds; medicate them and watch for abscesses.

Open wounds must be examined carefully, washed out with peroxide or Betadine, and then smeared with an antibiotic ointment. Watch open wounds carefully to make sure that flies don't lay eggs in them. If you see maggots in a wound, remove the maggots with tweezers and then wash, flush, and medicate the wound.

The shell

Unless it's a soft-shelled aquatic turtle (see Chapter 5) or a pancake tortoise (see Chapter 9), your turtle's or tortoise's shell should be hard and firm to the touch — see Figures 20-2 and 20-3.

A soft shell or a feeling of give when you press gently on the shell is a symptom of *metabolic bone disease,* or what used to be called *soft-shell disease.* Metabolic bone disease (MBD) is caused by an inadequate diet, a lack of vitamin D3, inadequate heat, or a combination of these risk factors. The initial symptoms of MBD may include a loss of appetite, swelling in the jaws or legs, a soft shell, and sometimes a swollen tail. The *carapace* (the top shell covering the back) may even lose major scutes, and if scutes are lost, death from a blood infection often follows within days. See your vet immediately if you notice your pet losing scutes.

To treat MBD, flip to Chapter 19 and feed the turtle or tortoise a complete and varied diet appropriate to its species. Supplement the diet with calcium. Make sure that your pet is exposed to unfiltered direct sunlight a couple times a week or has a fluorescent light over its cage (no higher than 12 inches away).

If your turtle's or tortoise's shell has some eroded, rough areas that may be soft or discolored, it may have *shell rot.* Shell rot, or *ulcerative shell disease* in terrestrial turtles or tortoises, can take two forms, caused by either a bacteria or a fungus. Increase the heat in your pet's enclosure and wash the affected area thoroughly with Betadine daily for three weeks. If you don't see any change, consult your veterinarian.

Figure 20-2:
This ornate box turtle (*Terrapene ornata ornata* — see Chapter 8) has a firm shell.

© Liz Palika

Figure 20-3:
This Galapagos tortoise (*Geochelone* or *Chelonoidis elephantopus* — see Chapter 11), though rare, displays a healthy shell.

© Liz Palika

Rescue 911

Early one morning, a telephone caller asked if I was the turtle rescue lady. After I answered yes, the caller said that he had picked up a turtle that had been hit by a car. He said it needed care, but he couldn't afford the vet bills for an animal that wasn't his. Sighing, I said that I would take it. This poor box turtle had been hit by a car so hard that its carapace had a tennis ball–sized indentation in it, but amazingly, the animal was still alert and active. So I took her to my vet, who repaired the shell with fiberglass patches. The vet didn't give the turtle much hope for recovery, saying that the injuries were quite severe.

The rescued turtle did heal over time, though, although her shell will always be somewhat deformed. The next summer, the turtle laid three batches of eggs, all of which hatched into adorable, active little baby turtles.

Don't let this condition go untreated; it may progress to or be caused by a *generalized septicemia*, or a blood infection. If you see signs of blood under the keratin layer of the shell, especially on the *plastron* (the lower shell covering the belly), your turtle or tortoise may have septicemia. If these signs appear along with listlessness, closed eyes, and lack of vigor, see your veterinarian right away; antibiotic treatment is needed immediately.

Aquatic turtles can have ulcerative shell disease, too. This condition is usually caused by injuries to the shell, either from abrasions or aggression from tank mates. Treatment is much like that for terrestrial turtles: Wash with Betadine daily. If you don't see any improvement, veterinary care is needed.

A cracked or broken shell can spell death for your turtle if a veterinarian doesn't treat it right away. Your vet can stabilize the broken shell with fiberglass patches or bone cement. Healing takes a long time, but even severely damaged shells can heal if the internal tissues are protected.

Appetite

Your turtle's or tortoise's appetite is a good reflection of its overall health. A healthy turtle or tortoise maintained in the proper conditions at the right temperature will always be ready to eat. Sometimes I'm amazed at how much these pets of mine can eat! A turtle or tortoise that has been eating well for a period and stops eating for no apparent reason should be examined carefully for problems. If you don't see anything wrong and you know that your pet's environmental conditions are right, consult your veterinarian.

Female turtles and tortoises may stop or slow their eating just before laying eggs. Failure to eat can be a sign that egg laying is near.

If, in the fall, your turtle or tortoise seems to slow down, doesn't eat well, or appears listless, it is probably getting ready to hibernate. See Chapter 22 for more information on hibernation.

The following guidelines may help you improve a temporary loss of appetite:

- **Gravid (pregnant) female:** Provide an egg-laying box or place.
- **Breeding-season male:** Symptoms will go away on their own, and appetite for food will return.
- **Environmental stress:** Maintain a stable, quiet environment.
- **Environment too crowded:** Decrease the number of chelonians in the cage or enclosure.
- **Infection:** See your vet, clean the cage, and improve your pet's care.
- **MBD:** See your vet, improve your pet's diet, and add UVB light.
- **Parasites:** See your vet and improve your pet's care.
- **Intestinal blockage:** See your vet.

Weight

Weigh your turtle or tortoise regularly. Doing so is an even better way to keep track of health than monitoring appetite. If a young turtle or tortoise has been steadily gaining weight and stops, or if an adult suddenly loses weight, something is wrong. When you pick up your turtle or tortoise, it should feel heavy for its size — like it has a shell full of water.

Feces

Because your turtle or tortoise can't tell you when it doesn't feel good or has a bellyache, you need to pay attention to things you would rather ignore, like your pet's stools (feces). Know what's normal and what isn't. If you see worms, mucus, or blood in the stools, take a sample to your vet.

Ask your vet how often he or she wants you to check your pet's feces for pests. In some areas, once a year may be adequate; in more tropical regions, quarterly checks may be better. Pay attention to anything out of the ordinary, and call your vet if you do see something unusual.

Parasites

Even if you don't see anything unusual in your chelonian's feces, have your veterinarian examine feces samples regularly for internal parasites. Parasitic infestations are the third leading cause of death of captive reptiles, after nutritional problems and bacterial infections. The most common parasites include roundworms, hookworms, tapeworms, and pinworms. Whipworms can also be a problem, especially in the Sunbelt states. Other internal parasites include protozoans and flagellates. All these pests can cause significant health problems.

General signs of a parasite infestation include loss of appetite, weight loss, listlessness, failure to thrive, and failure to reproduce. Specific symptoms include vomiting, mucus and blood in the stools, dehydration, and depression.

Parasites are, as their name suggests, organisms that live and feed on other creatures. Internal parasites live either in the digestive tract (the most common spot) or in other organs. Most parasites don't kill their host; after all, if their host dies, so will they! They do, however, often harm their hosts by doing the following:

✔ Sucking blood and causing blood loss (hookworms)

✔ Causing nutritional deficiency (roundworms and others)

✔ Absorbing intestinal contents directly (tapeworms)

✔ Destroying the host's cells (coccidia)

✔ Obstructing the intestinal tract (roundworms)

✔ Obstructing the liver bile ducts (roundworms)

✔ Producing toxic substances (several parasites)

✔ Triggering allergic reactions (several parasites)

✔ Causing intestinal tract inflammation and infection (several parasites)

✔ Suppressing the immune system (all parasites)

All parasites require a host; that's what parasites are. They don't and can't live alone. In addition, many parasites require more than one host during their life cycle; they are called *intermediary hosts.* For example, hookworms — a common parasite in the Sunbelt states — can infect people as well as dogs, cats, reptiles, and wildlife. Adult hookworms produce eggs in a host. These eggs are passed out of the host via the feces. In the soil where the feces are deposited, the eggs hatch and release larvae. The larvae attach themselves to new hosts (or the old one again) by invading a cut on the skin or by being ingested along with grass or water.

In captivity, you can interrupt this life cycle by keeping cages, terrariums, or outside enclosures very clean. However, if you allow feces to remain on the ground for any length of time, the cycle remains.

Check wild-caught chelonians for overall good health and parasitic infestations before introducing them to turtles or tortoises at home. In fact, I suggest that you quarantine new arrivals. Check captive-bred new turtles and tortoises as well, and also check long-term pets.

An excellent reference for turtle owners who want to know more about parasites is *Understanding Reptile Parasites* by Roger Klingenberg, DVM (published by Advanced Vivarium Systems, 1993).

Constipation and diarrhea

If you notice that your pet is constipated, try the following tips:

- ✓ **Diet:**
  - *Not enough fiber:* Change your pet's diet; add roughage.
  - *Overfeeding:* Reduce the amount you feed.
  - *Obesity:* Reduce the amount you feed.
  - *Anorexia:* See a vet.
- ✓ **Kidney disease:** See a vet.
- ✓ **Imminent egg laying:** Provide an egg-laying box or place.
- ✓ **Internal parasites:** See a vet.
- ✓ **MBD:** See a vet.

For diarrhea, try the following:

- ✓ **Internal parasites:** See a vet.
- ✓ **Diet:**
  - *Too many fruits:* Change your pet's diet.
  - *Not enough roughage:* Change your pet's diet.
- ✓ **Bacterial infection:** See a vet.
- ✓ **Salmonella infection:** See a vet.

Toenails

Overgrown toenails can be trimmed, much like a dog's toenails can. Make sure not to cut into the *quick* (where the nail attaches to the toe). If you do cause the nail to bleed, put pressure on it for a couple of minutes or use a commercial product to stop the bleeding. If you're worried about cutting your pet's nails, ask your vet to show you how.

Sexual organs

When sexually excited, male turtles and tortoises sometimes extend the penis. The penis is a large tube extending from the *cloaca* (the internal chamber where the urinary, digestive, and genital canals empty their contents). In most cases, the male retracts it on his own with no problem; however, if it dries while extended, he may suffer. In that case, lubricate the penis with Vaseline, Neosporin, or another lubricant and gently push it back into the cloaca. Don't force it, though. If a problem persists, call your veterinarian for help.

Female turtles or tortoises sometimes have problems laying their eggs. If your pet doesn't have an appropriate place to lay her eggs (see Chapter 16), she may not feel comfortable enough to lay them. Sometimes soaking the female in warm water for an hour or so and slightly increasing the heat in the enclosure helps. If she still doesn't lay her eggs in a day or two, call your veterinarian.

If your turtle or tortoise is *egg bound* (failing to lay eggs) and you're not sure of the cause, try the following:

✔ Provide a large box filled with potting soil.

✔ Make sure that your pet is gravid — you can feel eggs by gently pressing on her abdomen through the skin above the back legs (between the back legs and the shell surrounding it).

✔ Make sure that the eggs weren't reabsorbed. If this happens, see your vet, improve your pet's diet, and check her for parasites.

Planning First Aid for Your Turtle or Tortoise

No matter how careful you are, accidents are likely to happen. Perhaps your chelonian will catch a nail on something and break the nail. Perhaps a turtle will chip its shell or have a small wound on its skin. Accidents happen, but you can be prepared — or as prepared as humanly possible!

When something does happen, or if you suspect that something is wrong, call your veterinarian. Provide as much detail as you can. If the vet wants to see your pet, take it in. Granted, the office call and treatment may cost more than you paid to purchase your turtle or tortoise, but that doesn't matter. When you took in that turtle or tortoise and made it a home, you assumed the responsibility for its care, and that includes medical care. Veterinary care can help your pet live a long, full life.

Putting together a first-aid kit

Keep the following items in your first-aid kit in an easy-to-reach place at home:

✔ Gauze pads (in a variety of sizes) for cleaning, wiping, or putting pressure on a wound

✔ Gauze or elastic wrap to hold a gauze pad or splint in place

✔ Butterfly tape to hold a wound closed

✔ Bandage tape to hold a gauze pad, splint, or butterfly

✔ Cotton swabs to clean wounds or apply medications

✔ Nutrical (a nutritional supplement)

✔ Betadine to wash wounds

✔ Hydrogen peroxide to clean wounds

✔ Scissors

✔ Nail trimmers (dog or cat sizes)

✔ Tweezers (large and small)

✔ Saline eye wash

✔ Styptic powder to stop bleeding

✔ Gloves to protect your hands

✔ Towels to wrap the turtle or tortoise

Check your first-aid kit often, replacing used materials and throwing away expired items. In addition, keep a box or plastic carrier on hand to carry an ill or injured turtle or tortoise to the veterinarian's office.

Knowing what to do in an emergency

An injured turtle or tortoise isn't going to want to cooperate with you and may close itself totally within its shell. Sometimes, if you turn the turtle or tortoise over (on its back or side), it will move its legs and head out of its shell to try to right itself. If it does, you may be able to take advantage of this and see where it's hurt and what needs to be done. However, a severely traumatized chelonian may keep itself closed in its shell even when turned over. If it doesn't try to right itself in a few minutes, turn it right side up again; don't leave it turned over.

Don't hesitate to call your vet in an emergency; especially if your turtle or tortoise is closed up in its shell. Your vet can anesthetize the turtle, relax it, and then examine the turtle without stressing it.

Nursing Your Chelonian Back to Health

Although many reptiles can be quite delicate, a sick turtle or tortoise isn't necessarily a dead one. Your pet can potentially live a long life after an illness or injury — it just needs your help.

- ✔ Make sure to follow your veterinarian's advice regarding your pet's care. If you're supposed to give a medication for ten days, give it for the full ten days! Don't stop just because your pet looks better. The full course of medication is prescribed for a reason.

- ✔ Keep your vet posted regarding any changes in your pet. The changes may or may not be important, but tell the vet anyway. Let him or her sift through the information to decide what's pertinent to your pet's care.

- ✔ Keep your turtle or tortoise warm. Warmth is needed for a strong immune system. In addition, reptiles can't run a fever naturally. In the wild, a sick reptile searches out the warmest environmental conditions around to increase its body temperature, so offer your pet a warm cage and a hot basking light.

- ✔ Don't let your pet dehydrate. Keep some Gatorade or Pedialyte on hand. You can put it in the drinking bowl or saucer or offer it with an eyedropper.

- ✔ Offer a varied, nutritious diet and keep some food in front of your pet.

- ✔ Keep stress to a minimum. Don't fuss with your turtle or tortoise every five minutes. Do everything you need to do all at once, and then give your pet peace and quiet for a few hours until the next round of medication is due.

Chapter 21

Breeding Your Chelonians

. . . .

In This Chapter

▶ Deciding whether to breed your pet

▶ Finding a suitable mate for your chelonian

▶ Taking care of eggs and hatchlings

. . . .

*T*he wild populations of many turtles and tortoises are declining rapidly. Pollution, warfare, human hunger, human recreation, overpopulation, and habitat destruction are taking their toll. For many turtle and tortoise species, captive breeding may be the only way to survive.

North America box turtles (Terrapene carolina), discussed in detail in Chapter 8, have recently been placed on the CITES list as a threatened and potentially endangered species. (CITES stands for Convention on International Trade in Endangered Species — see Chapter 4.) Habitat destruction is part of the problem, but overcollection for the European pet trade is another. However, box turtles breed readily in captivity. Within a few years, I would love to see all the box turtles offered for sale being bred in captivity.

The U.S. Fish and Wildlife Service estimates that 25,000 to 30,000 box turtles are exported every year. Because, on average, only two offspring of any given turtle survive to adulthood in the wild, this rate of export is unsustainable and may endanger the survival of the species.

Breeding Your Turtle or Tortoise

If you decide to breed your turtles and tortoises, your pets will be happy. Reproduction is the natural way of life, after all. But why do you want to breed them? To make them happy? Your male turtle or tortoise will be happier if a female is in his enclosure with him, and he'll be much less likely to try to escape from his enclosure; however, that's not enough of a reason to breed. Breeding involves too much work and money.

Breeding your turtle or tortoise to help save turtles and tortoises from extinction is a worthwhile goal and a goal that many people strive toward. However, the reality isn't so simple.

Breeding turtles and tortoises isn't easy. It may require a financial investment in adult breeding stock. With many species, one adult of each sex is not adequate; groups of animals have a better breeding success rate. In some species, the males must battle with other males prior to breeding. This battling may cause injuries to one or both males, sometimes requiring veterinary care. Females sometimes get *egg-bound* (retaining their eggs), which may require treatment and sometimes requires surgery.

Don't count on a financial windfall after breeding your turtles or tortoises. Many people have tried to build a retirement fund by breeding chelonians only to find that it requires an investment of time, money, and effort with nothing guaranteed in return. For example, the eggs must be incubated, requiring either a homemade or a commercial incubator. Hatchlings require special care to survive, and United States law dictates that you keep hatchlings until they're at least 4 inches in length (see Figure 21-1). For many species, that's one, two, or even three years.

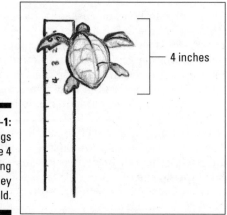

4 inches

Figure 21-1:
Hatchlings must be 4 inches long before they can be sold.

What will you do with all the babies once they reach a sellable size? Although some turtles and tortoises, such as the pancake tortoise *(Malacochersus tornieri)*, discussed in Chapter 9, lay only a few eggs, others lay lots of eggs! The sulcata tortoise *(Geochelone sulcata* — see Chapter 11) may lay 20 eggs five to six times per year.

If all those eggs hatch, what on Earth are you going to do with them? Do you have the room to care for them until they reach a sellable size? Do you have enough people who want to own and care for those little turtles or tortoises?

Before breeding your turtles or tortoises, think about the end result: all those adorable babies.

Same-species breeding

When planning to breed your turtles and tortoises, make sure that you have chelonians from the same species and, where appropriate, the same subspecies. Although dogs from different breeds reproduce and produce viable offspring, turtles and tortoises may not. Plus, if you're breeding in the hopes of selling the offspring as well as continuing a threatened species, a mixed breed (or hybrid) chelonian is worthless.

It's very important that you do the following:

- ✔ Keep different species (or subspecies) in different cages and/or enclosures.
- ✔ Don't breed individuals that you can't identify without a doubt as belonging to a specific species or subspecies.
- ✔ Keep good records as to all attempted breedings, actual breedings, and any resulting eggs and offspring.

When Mr. Right meets Ms. Right

Long before breeding season, you need to make sure that your breeding group is adequate. Do you have one or more males and one or more females? Does the species you have require multiple animals of each sex, or is the species more solitary, with only one male and one female needed?

North American box turtles *(Terrapene carolina),* covered in Chapter 8, have a much higher breeding success rate when at least two males are in the group. The males often battle, sometimes quite vigorously, and on occasion you may need to save the smaller or less dominant male from harm. However, the males do seem to need the stimulus of this competition.

Leopard tortoises *(Geochelone pardalis),* discussed in Chapter 12, also need more than one male in the breeding group. Male gopher tortoises, although loners for much of the year, battle as well. The larger (or more aggressive) male will flip his opponent over onto his back, sometimes stranding him fatally.

Some tortoises do not need a group for successful breeding. Sulcatas *(Geochelone sulcata),* explored in Chapter 11, breed very well with just one male and one female. In fact, many male sulcatas won't tolerate another male and will fight, sometimes to the death of the less-aggressive male. Most aquatic and semi-aquatic turtles (see Chapters 5 and 6) breed well with simply one male and one female.

Which is male and which is female? Can you tell them apart? Several clues tell you who's who. In most species (but not all), the adult male has a slightly concave *plastron* (the lower shell covering the belly). This dip in his shell allows him to mount the female's shell. The male of most species also has a longer, thicker tail than the female. His penis comes out of the *cloaca* (the internal chamber where the urinary, digestive, and genital canals empty their contents) and must be able to reach the female for penetration, which explains the longer tail. In many species, the male is also smaller than the female. In aquatic species, the male may have longer front claws so that he can wave them at the female as they court underwater.

Another point to consider when organizing your breeding stock is that not every animal may be ready to breed at a given time. If you have only one male and one female, what if she isn't ovulating? What if he isn't mature enough? Perhaps she's too stressed by a change in location, or he's inexperienced. At least 1,000 reasons explain why breeding may not be successful, so if you're adamant about breeding, your chances of success greatly increase if you have several adult females and at least two adult males.

When you acquire your breeding stock, make sure that all the chelonians are from the same species, subspecies, or geographical location. For example, many different types of box turtles exist (see Chapters 7 and 8). Don't breed a Gulf Coast box turtle *(Terrapene carolina major)* to an Eastern box turtle *(Terrapene carolina carolina).* They may be able to breed, but the offspring won't be true to either subspecies.

An excellent resource for people planning to breeding turtles and tortoises is *Keeping and Breeding Tortoises and Freshwater Turtles* by A. C. Highfield (published by Carapace Press, Krieger Publishing Co.).

Assessing breeding stock

One thing that rarely needs to be considered in the wild but must be taken into account with captive breeding is the suitability of the prospective parents. In the wild, the strong survive to live to adulthood and reproduce. In captivity, animals that are weaker than their siblings are often coddled and nurtured, and therefore they also survive. Granted, pet owners want them to survive, and that's fine. But should those animals be allowed to breed? Only you can answer this question.

Another issue that needs some thought is the relationship between the two prospective parents. Are they related? At some point in a captive breeding colony, a male and a female who are related may breed. Should you allow that? Should you bring in an outside male or female? Breeding related animals is called either *inbreeding* or *line breeding*, depending on the closeness of the relationship. When two animals from the same lines are bred, and those animals share close genetic material, their offspring will be very much like the parents. This serves a good purpose when the characteristics are good, but it can also lead to problems. The popularity of purebred dogs today is facing severe problems as a result of these breeding practices; many purebred dogs have severe, often life-threatening genetic problems.

Prebreeding

Long before breeding season begins — in fact, the summer prior to breeding — start conditioning both the males and females. Check (and, if necessary, treat) both the males and females in your breeding group for internal parasites. Pay particular attention to diet, making sure that each animal is eating enough of a well-balanced, varied diet that's appropriate to its species. Also provide a vitamin/mineral supplement with calcium. I let my females have access to a bird's *cuttlebone* — almost pure calcium.

Some species need to hibernate prior to breeding. Most North American box turtles (*Terrapene carolina* — see Chapter 8) should hibernate, as should Russian tortoises (*Testudo* or *Geochelone horsfieldi*), covered in Chapter 9. Most of the North American gopher tortoises (reviewed in Chapter 10) need to hibernate. As a general rule, turtles and tortoises that originate in temperate climates need to hibernate, but turtles and tortoises from tropical climates don't hibernate.

If your turtles or tortoises don't hibernate, you still want to keep the males away from the females. House them separately for the winter. Keep in mind the adage, "Absence makes the heart grow fonder." See Chapter 22 for more information about hibernation.

Introduce the males to the females in the spring as weather starts to warm up. Immediate breeding attempts may or may not occur. At this point, let nature take its course!

The ultimate goal of every species is to survive and pass on the strongest individual's genetic code. With turtles and tortoises, this instinct often leads to battles prior to courtship. As breeding season approaches, usually after hibernation or in the spring as the days grow longer, males begin searching for females of their own kind. When they encounter a male of their own kind, sparring often occurs, as shown in Figure 21-2. Depending on the species and the ritual behaviors of the species, the males may bob heads at each other, circle each other while bobbing heads, and even bite at each other.

Many male tortoises have an extended forward portion of the plastron called the *gular.* In California desert tortoises *(Gopherus agassizii* — see Chapter 10) and a few other species, the gular is quite pronounced, and the males use it as a battering ram. If one male can get his gular under the plastron of the other male, he can flip the other male. Being flipped over takes all the fight out of a male because this position is potentially life-threatening. The male who did the flipping then leaves — with a heightened ego! — and continues his search for a female.

Wood turtles *(Clemmys insculpta),* which are normally passive, become quite aggressive during breeding season. Males fight quite vigorously, to the point of biting each other seriously. See Chapter 6 for more on wood turtles.

When the male finds a female, he courts her. Courtship behaviors are ritual-ized within each species: The male performs a particular behavior, and the female responds in a particular way, to which the male responds again in a certain way. These rituals vary from species to species and help ensure that males and females from only their own species breed. If the courtship rituals aren't answered correctly, the courtship actions cease.

Some males have quite elaborate or energetic courtship rituals. Male sulcata tortoises *(Geochelone sulcata* — see Chapter 11) circle the female, nudging her, bobbing their heads, and trying to stop her forward movement. Leopard tortoise males *(Geochelone pardalis* — discussed in Chapter 12) also circle the female but are quite a bit more energetic about getting her to stop walk-ing forward. The smaller male may plant himself in her path — hoping to stop her — because he can't mount her while she's walking!

Male map turtles *(Graptemys* subspecies, covered in Chapter 5) are the Romeos of the chelonian world. The male, while courting his chosen female, swims with her and, while swimming above her, gently strokes her face and head with his long front claws. Apparently, the females think this gesture is quite romantic!

When courtship is successful and the male is able to mount the female (see Figure 21-3), rituals continue to vary from species to species. Male sulcatas are loud, grunting and groaning while copulating. Leopard tortoise males breathe very heavily while the female continues to graze — ignoring her hard-working suitor! The male North American box turtle of all species (*Terrapene carolina* — see Chapters 7 and 8) places his long back claws into the back hinge opening of the female on each side so that he can anchor his position, and then leans backward, sometimes to the point that he is actually lying on his back while copulating! Red-eared sliders (*Trachemys scripta elegans*) and other aquatic turtles (see Chapter 5) copulate in the water, coming up once in a while for a breath of air.

Figure 21-3:
Breeding
chelonians.

© Liz Palika

If your turtles or tortoises decide to breed, don't interfere; let nature take its course. If you interrupt those ritual responses, breeding may not occur.

Turtle breeding trivia

The good news: The Baltimore Zoo is the first zoo in North America to hatch the endangered Egyptian tortoise (*Testudo kleinmanni* — see Chapter 9). The Herpetology Department has other breeding programs for endangered species and has set many longevity records for captives. The extensive collection of reptiles represents many parts of the world.

More good news: The New England Aquarium has been working with the Massachusetts Department of Fisheries and Wildlife to preserve the Plymouth red-bellied turtle (*Chrysemys rubiventris*). Biologists are hatching the turtles, raising them at the aquarium and then releasing them into the wild. With this head start, the experts are hoping that the turtles will have a higher survival rate than babies hatched in the wild.

The bad news: Dade County, Florida has been losing beach sand. Sand imported from the Bahamas has a problem, though. The Bahamas' light sand is cooler, and because the incubation temperature determines the gender of turtles, eggs incubated in the cooler sand could potentially all be males. That would make environmentalists cranky and the turtles extinct.

Caring for a Gravid (Pregnant) Chelonian

After breeding, continue to feed the female a varied diet with a calcium supplement (see Chapter 19). I also allow my females free access to cuttlebones so that they can have as much calcium as their bodies need. Keep disruptions in the turtle's habitat to a minimum. If she's in an inside terrarium or vivarium, make sure that the UV fluorescent light is new and is producing the needed UVB rays, as per the manufacturer.

Helping with Eggs

When the female is ready to lay her eggs, she starts exploring her cage or enclosure, maybe even pacing. She may appear more active than normal and may even stop eating. She sniffs the ground, searching for just the right spot, as shown in Figure 21-4.

You can help her by having a spot already prepared. If your turtle or tortoise is an indoor pet, make a small box and fill it with clean sand or potting soil so that the soil is deeper than the female's back leg stretched out. Mount an incandescent reptile light over this box so that the temperature there is between the high 80s and the low 90s. Make sure that she can get into this box safely.

If your turtle or tortoise is outside, dig up a spot in the sun that's somewhat protected (maybe by a plant or a wall). Chop up the grass roots, break up clumps of dirt, and generally predig this spot for her. She may or may not use your spot, but at least you will have given her the option.

The female digs the hole for her eggs with her back feet — see Figure 21-5. Alternating feet, she scoops the dirt out and deposits it to one side. If the dirt is hard, she may urinate in the dirt to soften it. This effort may take her a while, sometimes hours. When the hole is deep enough and is to her satisfaction, she begins laying her eggs. After each egg has been laid, she carefully arranges it with her back foot until it is positioned as she wants it.

When she's through laying, she fills in the hole and covers it up. Some females are quite thorough, scraping grass back over the hole. Burmese black and brown tortoises *(Manouria emys)* collect leaf litter, pile it into a mound, and lay their eggs inside the mound, guarding the nest for about two days afterward.

After the eggs have been laid and the hole filled in, most female turtles and tortoises leave the eggs. A few species, such as the desert tortoise *(Gopherus agassizii* — discussed in Chapter 10), guard the nest for a short period. Eventually, though, the eggs are left to develop on their own.

If your turtle or tortoise has gone through the motions of looking for a place to lay her eggs and hasn't done laid them, she may be *egg bound*. This term refers to the condition in which a female has eggs and for some reason can't lay them. Perhaps an egg is too large and she can't pass it. Maybe she can't find the right spot to dig her hole, or maybe environmental conditions aren't right. In any case, consult a veterinarian right away, because those retained eggs can kill your pet.

Figure 21-5:
A female
digs a hole
for her eggs
before
laying them.

© Liz Palika

If you want to dig up the eggs and artificially incubate them, do so immediately. Leaving them in the ground is the natural way, but death is natural, too, and many eggs won't survive. Dogs, neighborhood raccoons, opossums, and other predators can dig up eggs. Also, when eggs are in your yard, you may discover their hatching by accident, perhaps when mowing your yard!

How many eggs?

The number of eggs laid in each clutch varies from species to species and sometimes even within subspecies. In addition, a young female may lay fewer eggs in her first reproductive season than she will later as a full-grown adult. Older females usually begin laying fewer eggs as they age.

However, each species lays an average number of eggs. Although your female may lay more or fewer, here's what you can expect in the number of eggs per single clutch:

- **African forest turtle** (*Pelusios gabonensis*): 20 to 25
- **Bell's hingeback tortoise** (*Kinixys belliana*): 4 to 8
- **Big-headed turtle** (*Platysternon megacephalum*): 1 to 2

- Blanding's turtle *(Emydoidea blandingii)*: 10 to 14
- Bog turtle *(Clemmys muhlenbergi)*: 2 to 6
- Eastern box turtle *(Terrapene carolina carolina)*: 4 to 6
- Florida cooter *(Pseudemys floridana)*: 10 to 20
- Leopard tortoise *(Geochelone pardalis)*: 8 to 12
- Painted turtle *(Chrysemys picta)*:: 10 to 15
- Red-eared slider *(Trachemys scripta elegans)*: 10 to 20
- Red-footed tortoise *(Geochelone or Chelonoidis carbonaria)*: 4 to 5
- Reeve's turtle *(Chrysemys reevesii)*: 4 to 7
- Russian tortoise *(Testudo or Geochelone horsfieldi)*: 3 to 5
- Spotted turtle *(Clemmys guttata)*: 4 to 6
- Sulcata tortoise *(Geochelone sulcata)*: 15 to 20
- Texas tortoise *(Gopherus berlandieri)*: 2 to 4
- Western pond turtle *(Clemmys marmorata)*: 3 to 10

Turtle and tortoise eggs can't be rotated the way bird eggs are. When you dig up the eggs, mark the tops carefully and don't allow them to roll. If development has already started, rolling will tear delicate capillary blood vessels, damaging or even killing the embryos.

What temperature?

Incubating turtle or tortoise eggs isn't difficult. Commercial incubators are available from several different companies. Lyon Electric Company (619-585-9900) has an incubator called the Reptile Incubation System: I've been using this particular incubator for several years with good success. If you have more than one adult female or are planning to breed regularly, I suggest that you get a commercial incubator; it will be much easier in the long run.

You can also build your own incubator. A large Styrofoam cooler works well. You need an aquarium heater with a thermostat and two thermometers, one specifically for water and the other for air. After collecting these products, do the following:

1. **Pour water into the cooler to the one-third mark.**

2. **Use the aquarium heater to heat the water to about 86 degrees.**

   Put the water thermometer in the water to give you a second temperature reading.

3. **Set a wire rack in the cooler at the halfway mark; it should be a few inches above the water.**

   With the lid on the cooler, this is your incubator.

4. **Use a plastic flat container for your eggs — a plastic shoe box with several holes drilled in it will work.**

5. **Put a layer of damp vermiculite in the container or shoe box and set the eggs (right side up) in the vermiculite, buried about halfway.**

6. **Put the other thermometer on the vermiculite next to the eggs.**

Humidity is vital to successful egg incubation. You need to add water to the cooler once in a while and maybe even to the vermiculite. Don't let either the cooler or the vermiculite dry out. Soft-shelled turtle eggs, such as box turtle eggs, need very high humidity; 100 percent is ideal.

Most pet stores have humidity gauges (they look like thermometers) that tell you what the humidity is. Look for these gauges in the reptile section of the store near the thermometers and thermostats.

Eggs need to be incubated between certain temperature ranges. Eggs incubated below 70 degrees normally will not hatch. Eggs incubated between 70 and 85 degrees will hatch all-male offspring. Eggs incubated at about 86 degrees will bear mixed sexes, and eggs incubated between 86 and 90 degrees will bring all females. Eggs incubated over 90 degrees may result in deformed or dead hatchlings.

Ideal temperatures and humidity for some species may vary. Examples are

- ✔ **Desert tortoise** *(Gopherus agassizii)*: 50 to 70 percent humidity at 85 to 88 degrees
- ✔ **Leopard tortoise** *(Geochelone pardalis)*: 80 percent humidity at 84 to 86 degrees
- ✔ **Malayan box turtle** *(Cuora amboinensis)*: 100 percent humidity at 83 to 87 degrees
- ✔ **Painted turtle** *(Chrysemys picta)*: 90 percent humidity at 80 to 84 degrees
- ✔ **Red-footed tortoise** *(Geochelone* or *Chelonoidis carbonaria)*: 75 to 80 percent humidity at 84 degrees
- ✔ **Reeve's turtle** *(Chinemys reevesii)*: 90 percent humidity at 82 to 86 degrees
- ✔ **Spotted turtle** *(Clemmys guttata)*: 100 percent humidity at 82 to 86 degrees

✔ **Star tortoise** *(Geochelone elegans)*: 50 to 70 percent humidity at 86 degrees

✔ **Sulcata** *(Geochelone sulcata)*: 80 percent humidity at 84 to 86 degrees

✔ **Wood turtle** *(Clemmys insculpta)*: 80 percent humidity at 82 to 86 degrees

I don't recommend handling the eggs during incubation. There's still too much we don't know. Will the oil on your hands affect the developing baby? How about the soap you used to wash your hands before touching the eggs? We do know that too much movement can cause the tiny capillary vessels to tear and bleed, causing harm and potentially death. It's much better just to look at the eggs without touching.

When you check the water levels in the incubator and in the vermiculite, remove any eggs that have gone bad. If an egg has collapsed, is broken, or smells bad, take it out and throw it away.

Incubation times vary among species. Some hatch fairly soon, and others seem to take forever. See the entries on individual turtles and tortoises in Part II for complete details. Here, however, are the incubation times for the most popular species:

✔ **Desert tortoise** *(Gopherus agassizii)*: 80 to 130 days

✔ **Leopard tortoise** *(Geochelone pardalis)*: 140 days or more

✔ **Malayan box turtle** *(Cuora amboinensis)*: 70 to 85 days

✔ **North American box turtles** *(Terrapene carolina)*: 60 to 90 days

✔ **Painted turtle** *(Chrysemys picta)*: 55 to 80 days

✔ **Red-footed tortoise** *(Geochelone* or *Chelonoidis carbonaria)*: 150 to 175 days

✔ **Reeve's turtle** *(Chinemys reevesii)*: 65 to 90 days

✔ **Spotted turtle** *(Clemmys guttata)*: 55 to 75 days

✔ **Star tortoise** *(Geochelone elegans)*: 75 days

✔ **Sulcata tortoise** *(Geochelone sulcata)*: 85 to 100 days

✔ **Wood turtle** *(Clemmys insculpta)*: 45 to 50 days

Watching incubating eggs is like watching grass grow; it happens and you want it to happen, but it's incredibly boring. You must be patient. Don't try to hurry the process and open an egg — you will kill the embryo. Just check on the eggs regularly, keep the vermiculite damp, and wait.

Caring for Hatchlings

When an egg starts to hatch, the baby turtle or tortoise will use its *egg tooth* (a tiny protrusion on its beak) to open a small hole in the shell. After the baby has taken a few breaths, it will probably remain in the shell for a little while (even a day or two) to gain strength and finish absorbing the yolk. Don't try to rush the baby and tear open the rest of the shell. Just leave it in the incubator, keep it damp, and continue checking on it. See Figures 21-6 through 21-9 for a step-by-step look at how hatchlings break free of their eggs.

However, if the baby seems to be sticking to its egg, mist it lightly with water. If, after a day or two, the baby has stopped trying to free itself from its egg and seems to be tired, mist it again and see if you can gently free it from its eggshell.

If several eggs hatch, but others in the same clutch don't, do not open the other eggs! All eggs don't necessarily mature at the same rate. If you open an egg prematurely, you will kill the embryo. Instead, be patient. As long as the egg hasn't obviously gone bad, continue incubating it.

When the baby comes out of the shell, remove it from the incubator. If some *yolk sac* (the soft, delicate, round structure that in premature hatchlings is under the plastron) is left, gently smear some KY jelly on the yolk so that it doesn't dry out, stick to the cage floor, or tear. If it does, the hatchling will die.

Place the hatchling in a previously prepared nursery cage for a few days. The cage should be heated to the same temperature as the incubator. The humidity should also be high, although not as high as in the incubator. Damp paper towels can serve as *substrate* (floor covering). You can also use a clean plastic shoe box with holes in it for air circulation and put it back into the incubator.

If a hatchling rips the yolk sac on edges of the shell as it climbs out, don't panic. You can still save the baby. Gently run warm water over the yolk sac and wash off any vermiculite, dirt, or debris. Then carefully smear a thick coat of antibiotic first-aid ointment over the entire yolk sac, making sure that all of the rip is covered. Keep this hatchling away from its clutch mates in a covered plastic container in the incubator. Use damp paper towels as substrate (see Figure 21-10). Replace the paper towels a couple of times a day to keep them clean, and replace the antibiotic ointment daily. The yolk sac should gradually be absorbed and dry off; when it does, the hatchling can join its clutch mates.

Figure 21-6:
A hatchling begins to break free of its shell.

© Liz Palika

Figure 21-7:
The hatchling's body starts to emerge.

© Liz Palika

Figure 21-8: The hatchling's feet finally work free of the egg.

© Liz Palika

Figure 21-9: The hatchling leaves the egg behind.

© Liz Palika

Figure 21-10:
Place the hatchling on damp paper towels under an incubator.

Eggs may not hatch for several reasons. Some have to do with the health of the parents, some with your care of the eggs. Sometimes, there is no visible reason; the eggs simply don't survive. Here are a few of the most obvious reasons:

- The male is infertile because he is too young, unhealthy, stressed, not adapted to the environment, or took a medication that made him temporarily infertile.
- The female was unable to produce viable eggs because of poor health, stress, or inadequate nutrition.
- The incubating temperature was incorrect.
- The incubating medium was too dry or too wet.
- The eggs were disturbed and/or turned during incubation.
- The male and female were genetically incompatible, or a developmental defect was present.

Experts seem to agree that in the wild, egg fertility can be expected to be anywhere between 60 and 80 percent of each clutch. Eight of ten eggs hatching is a perfectly normal and acceptable percentage.

When the yolk has finally been absorbed, the hatchlings can be moved to a cage with conditions like their parents. Heat, humidity, UVB light, and other conditions should be just as required for the adults of the appropriate species (see Part III for details). Substrate materials put on the floor can be shredded bark for terrestrial turtles or alfalfa pellets for tortoises. You can introduce baby aquatic turtles to a small aquarium with both swimming water and a basking area with easy access.

Offer the babies lots of little hiding places. A small plant pot lying on its side, half buried in the substrate, works well. A small pile of leaves or shredded bark works, too. Remember that in the wild, the baby turtle that can hide the best from predators is the one that will survive. As the baby grows, it will start to recognize you as the source of its food and will stop hiding as soon as it sees you.

Baby turtles and tortoises are especially sensitive to the cold. However, just because they need heat, don't turn the entire cage into a sauna. Too much heat will dehydrate the babies. Instead, create a basking area that's easily accessible.

Provide water to terrestrial turtles and tortoises in a shallow saucer that won't cause the babies to flip over and potentially drown. A jar lid works well. I save all plastic screw-on jar lids (like those off of peanut butter jars); they make great little water and food saucers. Replace the water daily and change or scrub out the water saucer.

When environmental conditions are right, most baby turtles and tortoises begin eating within 48 hours of hatching. If a baby is still absorbing some yolk, it may not eat until the yolk is totally absorbed. If a baby isn't eating, soak it in some shallow, warm water with liquid vitamins added, and then offer food.

In most instances, babies eat the same food as their parents (see Chapter 19):

- Herbivorous turtles and tortoises can be fed grasses, vegetables, and fruits. Simply chop most of the food into bite-sized pieces. Every once in a while, offer a piece of food that isn't chopped finely so that the baby can have something to chew on, wrestle with, and gain strength from.

- Omnivorous turtles can eat small insects, tiny bits of chopped meat, and diced or chopped vegetables.

- Carnivorous turtles can eat tiny insects, small feeder fish (baby guppies), or canned dog food.

Offer baby turtles and tortoises a variety of foods. If the baby imprints on a certain food, it may refuse other foods, and, in most cases, a variety of foods is best. Variety assures good overall nutrition better than a single-ingredient diet does.

All turtles and tortoises can be introduced to commercial turtle or tortoise foods. Canned food can be served as is; dry food should be soaked in water first.

North American box turtles (*Terrapene carolina* — discussed in Chapter 8) offer a different nutritional approach than many other species. Adult box turtles are omnivorous, eating insects, meats, fruits, and plants. Baby box turtles, however, are carnivores, eating only live foods. Although most baby box turtles are attracted to the movement of live foods, introducing them to other foods at a young age is good for them nutritionally.

If your babies are a species that normally hibernates, don't let them do so the first winter. Although hibernation is normal for many species, some chelonians do die during hibernation. Let your hatchlings get a head start on life by eating and growing throughout their first winter.

Baby turtles and tortoises are a lot of fun to watch. A tiny box turtle can be an amazingly fierce little creature when attacking a wiggling worm! Baby aquatic turtles swim naturally and show their joy of swimming from the beginning. I find baby turtles and tortoises better than tropical fish; fish may relax me, but baby turtles make me laugh!

Just as their momma will, you can keep track of your baby turtles' growth (see Figure 21-11). Draw a circle around the shell of the turtle or tortoise on a piece of paper. Identify each baby by markings, colorings, or the shape of certain spots. Once a month, check on growth by drawing another circle. How much have the babies grown? Also weigh the babies regularly and keep track of their individual weights.

Figure 21-11: Mom and several years' worth of babies.

© Liz Palika

Finding Homes for Your Babies

Federal law decrees that baby turtles and tortoises can't be sold until they're 4 inches long as measured from front to back along the plastron. You may, however, give turtles and tortoises away to new, caring owners who will give your babies a good home.

Finding new homes for the babies can be tough. I want to make sure that the people who take my baby turtles and tortoises are going to care for them as I care for mine. I would feel awful if I found out that some of my babies had died from neglect, were shunted from home to home, or had been turned loose in the wild somewhere. After all, I put the mom and dad together, and I helped bring these babies into the world, so I feel that it's my responsibility to make sure they get good homes.

Because of this, I screen people carefully and ask a lot of questions:

- Have you had reptiles as pets before?
- How long to you plan on keeping these chelonians?
- Do you know how long they live?
- What kind of environment do you have for this baby?

In addition, I ask them questions about books read and research reviewed. The more the prospective owner knows, the better care those babies will get.

Chapter 22

Sleeping the Winter Away

. . . .

. . . .

*A*t one time or another, you've probably seen an educational television segment showing hibernating bears. Researchers like to study bears while they hibernate, perhaps because they can safely get close to the bears at that time. But researchers study hibernation because it fascinates people. How can an animal do that? How can a bear sleep for two, three, or four months without dying?

Many turtles and some tortoises hibernate. Some hibernate for short periods; others for much longer. Some even hibernate underwater. And some species must hibernate so that breeding can be successful.

As researchers try to find out more about this mysterious process, this chapter shares specific ways in which you can help your pet through it.

Why Do Some Turtles and Tortoises Hibernate?

Hibernation enables turtles and tortoises to live in areas where the temperatures during winter would otherwise kill them. As *ectotherms* (cold-blooded creatures), turtles and tortoises rely on external heat sources for body functions. When the weather cools and sufficient heat is unavailable, body functions would slow or stop, and death would follow if the animal didn't or couldn't hibernate.

Hibernation — sometimes called *brumation* for reptiles — is a complex process. What's known about reptile hibernation is overshadowed by the vast amount that's unknown: How did they adapt to this process? What does the process entail? How does the turtle or tortoise stop eating, lower its temperature, and slow its body's processes? Why do many species need to hibernate to reproduce successfully?

One detail that *is* known is that when a species of turtle or tortoise has evolved to hibernate in its natural geographical area and is prevented from hibernating for several years, its health suffers. The results are a decline in reproductive success and an increased incidence of liver and kidney disease.

Which Species Hibernate?

The turtle and tortoise species found in most of North America and Europe, as well as some Asian species, hibernate. Most of the species found in subtropical and tropical areas don't hibernate. If that division seems overly simple, don't be fooled; it isn't. There are exceptions.

Some species hibernate in some parts of their range but not in others. The North African or Moorish tortoise *(Testudo graeca),* discussed in Chapter 9, is one example. The subspecies *Testudo graeca graeca,* found in Morocco, hibernates in colder, higher elevations and doesn't hibernate in warmer, lower elevations. North American box turtles *(Terrapene carolina)* are very similar; in most parts of their range, box turtles hibernate every year. However, many Florida box turtles *(Terrapene carolina bauri)* and many Gulf Coast box turtles *(Terrapene carolina major)* — both covered in Chapter 8 — don't hibernate.

So how do you know whether your turtle or tortoise will hibernate? First, check Part II for details on the species. Then watch your turtle or tortoise as the weather in your area cools and daylight hours shorten. If your pet shows signs of wanting to hibernate (slowing down, a decrease in appetite, and a desire to hide), you know to prepare it for the process. If your turtle or tortoise continues to be active, prepare a place for your pet to spend the winter awake.

Living in southern California, I can keep my adult box turtles outside (although the eggs are incubated inside, and I keep the hatchlings inside). When fall approaches, I bring in a big bale of hay and mound it in one area of the box turtles' enclosure. As daylight hours shorten, the turtles slow down and start to burrow under the hay. That is, all except my Gulf Coast box turtles *(Terrapene carolina major).* The Gulf Coast box turtles regularly bask under the heat lamp in the turtle house and are awake, active, and eating all winter long.

Species known to hibernate include the following:

- ✔ Blanding's turtle *(Emydoidea blandingii)*
- ✔ Bog turtle *(Clemmys muhlenbergii)*

✔ Bolson tortoise *(Gopherus flavomarginatus)*

✔ Desert tortoise *(Gopherus agassizii)*

✔ Eastern box turtle *(Terrapene carolina carolina)*

✔ European pond terrapin *(Emys orbicularis)*

✔ Florida gopher tortoise *(Gopherus polyphemus)*

✔ Marginated tortoise *(Testudo marginata)*

✔ Painted turtle *(Chrysemys picta)*

✔ Russian tortoise *(Testudo* or *Geochelone horsfieldi)*

✔ Texas tortoise *(Gopherus berlandieri)*

✔ Wood turtle *(Clemmys insculpta)*

Species that may or may not hibernate, depending on their range, include the following. (As with anything to do with reptiles — especially turtles and tortoises — you may find exceptions.)

✔ Chaco tortoise *(Geochelone* or *Chelondoidis chilensis)*

✔ Florida box turtle *(Terrapene carolina bauri)*

✔ Hermann's tortoise *(Testudo hermanni)*

✔ North African or Moorish tortoise *(Testudo graeca)*

✔ Ornate box turtle *(Terrapene ornata ornata)*

✔ Red-eared slider *(Trachemys scripta elegans)*

✔ Spotted turtle *(Clemmys guttata)*

Species that normally do not hibernate include the following:

✔ Aldabran tortoise *(Geochelone* or *Aldabrachelys gigantea)*

✔ Chinese box turtle *(Cuora flavomarginata)*

✔ Egyptian tortoise *(Testudo kleinmanni)*

✔ Gulf Coast box turtle *(Terrapene carolina major)*

✔ Leopard tortoise *(Geochelone pardalis)*

✔ Malaysian box turtle *(Cuora amboinensis)*

✔ Radiated tortoise *(Geochelone asterochelys radiata)*

✔ Red-footed tortoise *(Geochelone* or *Chelonoidis carbonaria)*

✔ Star tortoise *(Geochelone elegans)*

✔ Sulcata tortoise *(Geochelone sulcata)*

✔ Yellow-footed tortoise *(Geochelone* or *Chelonoidis denticulata)*

Even those turtles and tortoises that don't hibernate usually have in their natural geographical area a winter cooling period. Check a travel tour guide for normal winter temperatures; that will give you some guidelines for what your turtle or tortoise needs.

Some turtles and tortoises have a summer hibernation of sorts. When summer heats up too much or when the humidity drops, some turtles and tortoises dig into the ground and become dormant until conditions change. The Russian tortoise (*Testudo* or *Geochelone horsfieldi* — see Chapter 9) and the African helmeted turtle (*Pelomedusa subrufa* — discussed in Chapter 6) are two well-known species that routinely *estivate* (hibernate in summer) during hot, dry seasons.

Should You Allow Your Turtle or Tortoise to Hibernate?

Only healthy turtles and tortoises should be allowed to hibernate. If your pet has health problems of any kind — disease, infection, fungal or bacterial problems, injuries, or illness — don't allow it to hibernate. Granted, hibernation is a natural process, but so is death, and weak or unhealthy chelonians are more apt to die during hibernation.

Most experts don't advocate hibernating hatchling turtles and tortoises. Give the young a head start of at least one year, if not two, before allowing them to hibernate. Juvenile turtles or tortoises that are 2 or 3 years old, healthy, and eating well may hibernate for a short period — perhaps a month or two.

You can usually keep a turtle or tortoise from hibernating by keeping the ambient temperature high and using lights to create artificial, summerlike photoperiods (see Chapter 16). Keep feeding the turtle or tortoise, but don't be surprised if the animal still slows down, loses some appetite, and tries to hibernate.

Caring for a Hibernating Turtle or Tortoise

Your turtle or tortoise will give you signs that it wants to hibernate: refusing food (even favorite foods!) and becoming quite sluggish. Your pet will look for a place to hibernate and may start burrowing or hiding more often.

About two weeks before hibernation, stop feeding your turtle or tortoise and offer only water. Soak your pet for an hour every day in lukewarm water; you want the digestive system cleaned out so that no undigested food remains in its system through hibernation. At the same time, start decreasing your turtle's daylight photoperiods (discussed in Chapter 16). Shorter days (ten hours) and longer nights tell the turtle that winter is approaching.

When you're ready to put your turtle or tortoise away for the winter, fill a box with bedding. Potting soil works well, as does shredded bark. The bedding should be deep enough that your turtle or tortoise can dig in and cover itself. Put the box in a cool, dark place in the house where the temperature remains above freezing but lower than the 60s. Check on the turtle once in a while to make sure that everything appears normal.

If you have turtles or tortoises that live outside, they may be able to hibernate outside. Supply an ample pile of straw, hay, or leaves where they can burrow into the ground. The bedding should be sufficient to protect them during the worst of winter.

If your turtles or tortoises are outside, make sure that you know where they are. If your turtles haven't dug themselves deep enough, if temperatures plummet, or if the area floods, you may need to dig up your pets and bring them inside to a cool closet, the garage, or your basement to continue their hibernation.

A winter warming could be dangerous to your turtle or tortoise. If the turtle warms up enough to awaken from hibernation but not enough to eat, it could lose weight, weaken, and perhaps even die. Make sure that after your turtle goes into hibernation, it stays in hibernation until spring. If a warming trend awakens your turtle, bring your pet inside to finish the winter's hibernation. If your tortoise wakes up due to warm weather or because it has been disturbed, and you can't continue the hibernation due to various factors (including the temperature inside your house), let the tortoise wake up, warm it up to normal temperatures, and begin feeding and watering. Keep it warm inside and plan on keeping it awake for the rest of the season.

Coming Out of Hibernation

When spring arrives, or when you decide to simulate spring inside, your turtle will wake up. Heat and light are vital to bringing a turtle out of hibernation. The temperature needs to be a consistent 68 degrees or more. A reptile incandescent heat lamp over the inside cage or in the turtle's or tortoise's shelter outside helps raise the chelonian's body temperature.

The daylight photoperiods (discussed in Chapter 16) also need to be extended if your turtle is housed inside. Gradually increase daylight from 10 hours a day (winter) to 12 hours of daylight (spring).

When your turtle or tortoise awakens, either inside or outside, it needs to soak in clean, lukewarm water. A few drops of a liquid reptile vitamin added to the soaking water won't hurt. Let it soak for an hour every day for three or four days. Also make sure that drinking water is available daily.

Heat and light help hibernating turtles and tortoises awaken and then, once awake, stay awake. After your pet is awake and has warmed up and rehydrated, offer some food. Red or yellow flowers or foods often stimulate herbivores to eat. Live, wiggling foods catch a carnivore's or omnivore's attention. Offer a variety of foods daily with a vitamin/mineral supplement added.

When your turtle or tortoise is awake and rehydrated, checked for symptoms of illness. Check for signs of a respiratory infection — a bubbly, running nose or gasping for breath (see Chapter 20). Make sure that both eyes are open and are free from matter or discharge. If your turtle appears ill or has a problem you can't treat, don't hesitate to call your veterinarian.

After your turtle has recuperated from hibernation and has eaten, it will be invigorated, active, and probably (if the chelonian is an adult) ready to breed. Watch for escape attempts!

Part V
The Part of Tens

The 5th Wave   By Rich Tennant

In this part . . .

This part contains tidbits of information that you can read in just a few minutes. You can discover which species are the easiest to keep and which are the toughest, how to keep your pet healthy for a lifetime, and how to avoid common mistakes. In just a few minutes, you can quadruple your knowledge of turtles and tortoises!

Chapter 23

Ten Turtles and Tortoises That Make Great Pets

S ome turtle and tortoise species are much better suited to life as pets than others. In fact, even though some species are bred in captivity, they don't always thrive in captivity, and failure to thrive can make chelonian ownership frustrating and difficult.

The species in this chapter, which do thrive in captivity, can provide you with an exciting, rewarding life as a turtle and tortoise owner. You can find out more about each species in Part II.

Eastern Box Turtle (Terrapene carolina carolina)

These high-domed, golden-colored, hardy turtles do better in an outdoor enclosure and in northern climates, where they hibernate during the winter. However, in the spring, summer, and fall, they make fun pets. Most quickly learn to recognize their feeders and come running (yes, running!) to be fed. Many also learn to eat from their owners' hands. These turtles, with good care, also live a long time: 75 to 100 years is within the range of possibility. They also breed readily in captivity, and I have seen nothing quite as cute as a tiny hatchling box turtle.

Gulf Coast Box Turtle (Terrapene carolina major)

The Gulf Coast box turtle is often much plainer in color than the eastern box turtle — often a plain dark brown or black with no or few markings — but in personality, this species shines. These turtles quickly learn to recognize their owners and will eat from the hand. They're active, and after they acclimate to a new home, they will pursue normal behaviors while being watched — something many turtles don't do. They also dig in the dirt or compost for insects and catch earthworms or goldfish in the water.

Like the eastern box turtles, these turtles do better in an outdoor enclosure.

Wood Turtle (Clemmys insculpta)

The wood turtle is fascinating, often called the most intelligent turtle in the world. Some scientists have seen these turtles learn to find their way out of a maze, the same way mice and rats can do. When provided with a large cage or enclosure with both land area and water, these turtles are quite active and will explore the enclosure, dig, hunt, swim, and climb. They're great fun to watch. As an added benefit, the wood turtle is also quite hardy and long lived.

Red-Foot Tortoise (Geochelone or Chelonoidis carbonaria)

The red-foot tortoise is a very popular species. As the name suggests, these tortoises have red feet; in some adults, the red is bright and pronounced. Red-foots thrive inside or outside, although even tortoises kept indoors need some sunshine and outdoor grazing on nice days. Red-foot tortoises are hardy, active, and friendly.

Pancake Tortoise (Malacochersus tornieri)

The pancake tortoise is a strange-looking creature. It has a flat profile and a relatively soft *carapace* (top shell). This allows the tortoise to squeeze between rocks in its native habitat to escape from predators.

Although wild populations are severely reduced and threatened, the pancake tortoise is being bred in captivity, and captive-bred tortoises are friendly, hardy, and healthy. Potential owners beware, however; this species can climb and is escapist in nature — the cage or enclosure must be securely covered! And at $500 to $850 each, you want to hang onto your pancake tortoise.

Russian or Horsfield's Tortoise (Testudo or Geochelone horsfieldi)

A captive-bred Russian tortoise is a friendly, active, and appealing little tortoise. These tortoises should be kept outside, however, because they will beat themselves against the sides of a cage when kept inside. Outdoors, however, they run to greet you, climb on your feet, and nibble on your pant leg. In addition, a group of several tortoises of this species can live together quite well. The males may battle during breeding season, but they rarely harm one another.

North African or Moorish Tortoise (Testudo graeca)

These tortoises are hardy and healthy when kept in the proper conditions, although some keepers refer to them as somewhat delicate. Keepers also say that these tortoises are quite personable. Although they eat a standard herbivorous tortoise diet (see Chapter 19), flowers are a preferred food, and most of these tortoises quickly learn to beg for rose or hibiscus blooms. They breed readily in captivity, and the hatchlings are very cute!

Hermann's Tortoise (Testudo hermanni)

This European tortoise, which is losing its natural habitat in the wild, is now seen frequently in captivity and is attracting quite a fan club of admirers. Captive-bred Hermann's tortoises are quite friendly and react to their feeders. In good conditions, which include a nice basking spot in the sun, these tortoises make hardy, long-lived, undemanding pets.

Leopard Tortoise (Geochelone pardalis)

The leopard tortoise is one of the most attractive species, with a yellow or cream background and black markings. As large tortoises (fourth in the world behind the sulcatas — see the following section), they need to be kept outside. Very few leopard tortoises past the hatchling stage will thrive indoors for any length of time.

Leopard tortoises have a shyer personality than many other tortoises, but they do recognize and respond to their feeders. Becoming friends with a leopard tortoise is much like a romance; you must handle it delicately and with care, but the rewards are wonderful!

Sulcata Tortoise (Geochelone sulcata)

Although this species is the third largest in the world, it is still an appealing pet tortoise. Sulcatas are friendly, follow their owners around the yard the way dogs do, and accept petting with apparent pleasure. With good care, they're very hardy, and their large size attracts a lot of attention. Their size is their downfall, too; potential owners must be aware that these tortoises grow to a large size in a short period of time!

Chapter 24

Ten Turtles and Tortoises That May Be Difficult to Care For

In This Chapter

▶ Getting to know some tough-to-keep species

▶ Discovering why these species may be difficult to care for

*J*ust as some chelonian species thrive in captivity, others do not. Some species just don't do well in captivity no matter who keeps them. Because it's heartbreaking to lose a treasured pet, in this chapter I take a look at some of these species and explain why they often don't thrive. Avoid these species when you're looking for a potential pet.

Some species listed in this chapter can do well in captivity when given the proper care, but they're difficult to care for properly. For example, Galapagos tortoises do quite well in captivity and even breed readily in captivity. However, it's very difficult to keep a 500- to 600-pound tortoise!

Except for the common snapping turtle, all the species listed in this chapter are discussed in detail in Part II.

Common Snapping Turtle (Chelydra serpentina)

This is a common aquatic turtle from North America. It's not threatened or endangered, although some of its habitat has been destroyed. Although the snapping turtle is quite hardy — even in captivity — it has two characteristics that make it difficult to keep. First, as its name suggests, this species bites quite readily. The turtles move very quickly, bite hard, and can cause damage with their bite. The second characteristic is their size. Snapping turtles are quite large, many reaching 20 inches in length. A large aquatic turtle needs, as you may assume, a large swimming area — a pond or lake is best — and this is difficult for most pet owners to supply.

Bog Turtle (Clemmys muhlenbergii)

This attractive little turtle is facing a loss of habitat in the wild and is therefore threatened and legally protected. Prior to obtaining this species, if you decide to do so, make sure that you have all the applicable permits.

Although they're being bred in captivity, even captive-bred bog turtles have specific needs for their continued good health and survival. As a semi-aquatic turtle, a bog turtle needs land, water, and room to move around. The enclosure should be damp and well planted to simulate bog conditions and provide hiding places for the turtle. An open enclosure or cage will stress the turtle, and it won't survive.

Indian Snail-Eating Turtle (Melanochelys trijuga)

Most snail-eating turtles are quite fragile, are difficult to keep, and often die in captivity. Not only is an access to snails required (snails are this turtle's favorite food), but this semi-aquatic turtle also needs an aquarium or enclosure with very, very clean water. It has a low tolerance of water pollution.

Malayan Snail-Eating Turtle (Malayemys subtrijuga)

Like the Indian snail-eating turtle, this turtle can be delicate and difficult to keep. Although it will eat other live foods, such as earthworms, small fish, and small crabs, it prefers snails. This turtle doesn't tolerate fast-moving or polluted water, so you must provide clean, slow-moving water. Keeping the water clean while creating a slow-moving current can be tough to do. If you decide to keep this turtle, a long talk with a filtration expert at your local tropical fish store is in order.

Western Pond Turtle (Clemmys marmorata)

This semi-aquatic turtle can be quite hardy under the right conditions, primarily a semi-aquatic enclosure with plenty of swimming room. However, because this species is known as an escape artist (it has been known to climb 6-foot-tall fences!), it's difficult to keep. An enclosure has to have a roof or ceiling, or the fence must have an inward-facing top so that the turtle can't climb out. These turtles are protected, so make sure that you have all the applicable permits prior to obtaining this turtle.

Star Tortoise (Geochelone elegans)

The star tortoise is one of the world's most attractive tortoises, but it's also one of the most delicate. A shy tortoise, it can be kept in small groups with other star tortoises, but no more than three or four. Larger groups increase stress levels. This tortoise has been bred in captivity, but captive-bred individuals appear to be just as difficult to keep. Because these tortoises are legally protected, if you do get one, make sure that it's captive-bred and that you secure any applicable permits.

Bell's Hingeback Tortoise (Kinixys belliana)

Two characteristics of this species have caused it to perish in captivity. First, most tortoises are herbivorous, and tortoise keepers expect their tortoises to eat plants. The bell's hingeback, however, is an omnivore, eating plants but also insects, including snails, as well as carrion and rodents. (See Chapter 19 for more on feeding your chelonian the proper foods.) In captivity, this tortoise eats baby mice, aquatic turtle food, insects, and dog food.

The second characteristic is the species' attraction to water. Tortoises are land chelonians; turtles are aquatic. However, the bell's hingeback is often found in swamps and bogs; it is almost always close to water. In captivity, this tortoise needs an enclosure with mud and access to water. If you can satisfy these needs, you may find this species to be an appealing pet.

Desert Tortoise (Gopherus agassizii)

Thousands of these tortoises are kept in backyards throughout southern California, Nevada, and Arizona. Many thrive and even reproduce, but unfortunately, many also die. Desert tortoises need a warm, dry climate. A humid climate (such as near the coast) or a cool climate can contribute to an early death. Desert tortoises need a heated tortoise house for protection from rain, dew, and backyard sprinklers and need grass for grazing.

In addition, a contagious upper respiratory disease is running rampant throughout captive tortoise populations. Without treatment, thousands of tortoises will die from it. A runny nose is usually the first symptom of this disease. If you detect it, seek immediate veterinary care.

Sulcata Tortoise (Geochelone sulcata)

This tortoise is listed in Chapter 23 as one of the best tortoises to keep, so why is it also listed here as a difficult tortoise? Although sulcatas have many positive characteristics — they're friendly, extroverted, and hardy — they're also quite large. When full-grown, this tortoise can reach 200 pounds, and a 200-pound tortoise is capable of knocking down fences and potted plants.

Sulcatas are also known for their ability to dig large, long burrows. Many have actually dug their way out of yards or undermined the foundations of their owners' homes. To successfully keep a sulcata, you must be aware of this tortoise's physical strength and prepare for it ahead of time.

Galapagos Tortoise (Geochelone or Chelonoidis elephantopus)

The various surviving subspecies of the Galapagos tortoises are the largest tortoises in the world. In adulthood, some reach 500 to 600 pounds or more. Although these tortoises thrive in captivity (many are even breeding prolifically), they're difficult to keep. Tortoises this large need a large yard with an ample grazing area and a strong, secure wall (a Galapagos tortoise would knock down a fence). They need a heated tortoise house for protection from the weather. These tortoises also have a tremendous appetite; your food bill could be staggering! And keep in mind that what goes in must come out. The cleanup will be extensive, too.

Chapter 25

Ten Ways to Keep Your Pet Healthy

In This Chapter

▶ Finding out what your chelonian needs for good health

▶ Making a veterinarian your partner in good health

Many turtle and tortoise species are blessed with the ability to live a long time. When you compare a North American box turtle's potential to live 125 or more years with a dog's potential to live perhaps 12 to 15 years, it's absolutely amazing! However, to live a long, full life, your turtle or tortoise needs good care and the correct environment. Many, many chelonians die much too soon because they haven't received the proper care. This chapter looks at ten simple things you can do to make sure that your pet lives a long life; Chapter 20 shares in-depth tips on maintaining your turtle's or tortoise's health.

Begin with a Healthy Chelonian

It's much easier to start with a healthy turtle or tortoise and keep it in that condition than it is to try to save a turtle or tortoise that already has some health problems. If you're buying a turtle or tortoise, make sure that it's healthy: Its eyes are clean and bright, its shell is hard (except for those species with a naturally soft shell!), and the turtle or tortoise is alert and aware of its surroundings. The nose should be dry with no discharge or bubbles. The turtle should breathe through its nose, not its mouth. Make sure that the shell and skin don't have any wounds. The *cloaca* (anal area) should be clean, with no caked-on feces.

If you have any doubts about a turtle's or tortoise's health, ask if you can have a veterinarian examine the turtle or tortoise prior to or immediately after you purchase it. Ideally, the seller will offer you a guarantee of the chelonian's health. If not, don't purchase the chelonian.

Conduct Research, Research, and More Research!

Do as much research as you can concerning your turtle's or tortoise's needs. Because you're reading this book, you're on the right track; however, you can do even more research. The Internet is a good source of information: Use a search engine and search for your turtle's or tortoise's species, or join a message board for your species. Keep in mind, however, that you'll find a variety of opinions as to how certain species should be kept; don't take each opinion as fact. Instead, do as much research as you can and then decide what the majority of chelonian owners agree with or what the majority of veterinarians believe is correct. Let common sense prevail.

Use a Correctly Sized Enclosure

When you set up a cage or enclosure for your turtle or tortoise, make sure that it's large enough. Your turtle or tortoise needs room to move around. A cage or enclosure that's too small creates a great deal of stress for the chelonian. It needs to be able to regulate its temperature in various areas of the cage, and it needs to be able to get away from its feces after it relieves itself. I often hear reptile owners say that a reptile will only grow to fit its cage and then stop. This isn't true: Your turtle or tortoise will continue to grow as long as its health dictates. However, if the cage is too small, your pet's health will suffer.

Maintain the Correct Environment

Your turtle's or tortoise's species came from a specific type of environment, discussed in Part II of this book. North American eastern and three-toed box turtles, for example, are terrestrial turtles but are almost always found near water. A very dry, desertlike cage environment is inappropriate for these turtles and will eventual cause their health to suffer (or the turtles could even die). On the other hand, leopard tortoises originated in a much drier climate in eastern and southern Africa. A humid, damp environment stresses these tortoises and leads to disease, poor health, and, eventually, death. It's vital to your turtle's or tortoise's continued good health that you set up the cage or enclosure to mimic (as much as possible) the correct environment for its species.

Recognize That Heat Is Healthy

Turtles and tortoises are cold-blooded, which means that they can't produce their own body heat and, instead, rely on external sources for warmth. Because heat is necessary for many bodily functions — especially for the metabolism of food — you must supply heat to your turtle or tortoise in a way than it can use the heat. Most aquatic turtles need a water heater in the aquatic section of their cages, and most will also bask under a heat (incandescent) light. Tortoises can utilize a basking light but also enjoy an under-cage heater. Outdoor tortoises need a heated tortoise house. Without heat, your turtle's or tortoise's bodily functions will slow, food will rot in its intestinal tract, and death will follow. Chapter 17 gives you the lowdown on keeping your chelonian warm.

Understand That Light Is Life

Have you ever gone for a walk near a pond or river and seen an aquatic turtle basking on a log near the water? These turtles usually find a dark-colored log or rock, perch on it so that their bodies (and *carapaces,* the top shells) get the sun straight on, and then stretch out all four legs and their necks. They just soak up the sun. The sunlight warms the turtles, but the sunlight is also healthy in itself as an excellent source of vitamin D3, which chelonians need to metabolize calcium and phosphorus (both of which are necessary for good health). If your turtle or tortoise can spend some time — at least several hours each week — outside, that's enough. However, if your turtle or tortoise is inside, use a fluorescent light manufactured specifically for use over reptile cages. These lights produce UVB rays, which mimic the positive effects of the sun. See Chapter 16 for more on lighting.

Remember That You Are What You Eat

Good nutrition is an important element in your turtle's or tortoise's continued good health. Good nutrition means that the food is appropriate to your chelonian's species (whether omnivorous, carnivorous, or herbivorous — see Chapter 19) and is given in the correct amounts. In addition, the food must be of good quality. That means plants and vegetables are clean, free of pesticides and fertilizers, and fresh without wilt or rot. Make sure that insects or feeder fish are well fed so that they pass along their good nutrition to the turtle that eats them. Commercial turtle or tortoise foods must also be appropriate to the species being fed and given according to manufacturer's directions. Chapter 19 gives you plenty more information on nutrition.

Know What's Normal

Watch your turtle's or tortoise's actions and behaviors so that you know what's normal. Does your pet normally eat from your hand? Does it usually eat as soon as you put food down? How active is it during the day? How much time does it spend hiding?

By understanding your chelonian's normal actions and behaviors, you can notice changes in behaviors that may indicate something is wrong. If your turtle is normally a food hog, eating as much as it can as soon as you put the food down, you know something's wrong when it doesn't charge to the food. Turtles and tortoises are usually creatures of habit, so learn those habits. Then, when you see a change, you can try to solve the problem immediately.

Pay Attention

It's important to pay attention to your pet. Each and every day, spend some time looking at your turtle or tortoise so that you see any variations from normal behavior. Although understanding normal behavior (discussed in the preceding section) is important in its own right, you won't see changes or problems if you don't spend time watching your pet. Most people watch their pets after feeding them: You can see whether they're walking or swimming well, whether their appetite is normal, and whether they display any health problems. Pay attention to the details; they give you clues to your pet's over-all health.

Keep a record of your chelonian's weight — weekly for hatchlings, monthly for others. Any decline in weight is a cause for concern.

Make a Vet Your Partner

Make your turtle's or tortoise's veterinarian a partner in your pet's health care. Establish a good working relationship with a vet before your pet gets sick. Introduce yourself to your vet, introduce her to your chelonians, and have her examine them and check them for parasites. Find out about her office policies, her emergency routine, and her payment policies. One day, when you need her services, she'll be there for you. In addition, if she has seen your pet in good health, she will be better able to evaluate it if it does get sick.

Chapter 26

Ten Common Mistakes to Avoid

In This Chapter

▶ Finding out what some common mistakes are

▶ Preventing mistakes from happening

Many turtle and tortoise owners make mistakes when caring for their pets. Sometimes, a mistake is quickly over and done with no lasting harm. Other mistakes can cause problems for your pet. In this chapter, I take a look at ten common mistakes and help you prevent them from happening in your home.

Thinking Your Pet Isn't Worth a Visit to the Vet

Some turtle and tortoise owners think that a $10 pet isn't worth taking to the veterinarian's office. Although a visit to the vet will run considerably more than your purchase price, the value of your pet isn't based on what you paid for it. When you bought, accepted, or adopted your turtle or tortoise, you took it into your home as a pet and family member. Granted, your pet isn't a person, but it does deserve all the help you can give it to live a normal life. If that requires a visit to the veterinarian, well, then that cost is part of your pet's care.

Being Complacent

Too many owners bring home a turtle or tortoise, care for it as the pet store or seller recommended, and never do any additional research. Unfortunately, not everyone selling chelonians is an expert, and a great deal of incorrect information is given out to unsuspecting new owners. Don't assume that the initial information you were given is correct. Instead, do some research and then do some more. The more you know, the better. Your pet is the one that will benefit.

Using Glass-Sided Tanks

Aquariums were made to hold fish and are not always the right enclosures for chelonians. Many turtles and tortoises don't understand the concept of glass and beat themselves against the sides of the tank, sometimes to the point of hurting themselves. When you can, avoid glass-sided tanks, especially if your turtle or tortoise is one of those that fights the glass (see Part II for details). If you must use a glass-sided tank, tape colored paper or a cloth to the outside of the tank at a point above the turtle's or tortoise's eye level so that the tank's sides are no longer see-through.

Using the Wrong Substrate

Substrate is the stuff you put on the bottom of your turtle's or tortoise's cage or enclosure. The primary use of substrate is to soak up wastes, keep the cage clean, and look nice. Unfortunately, the wrong substrate can cause problems. Sand, which is commonly used in cages for many desert reptiles, can cause an intestinal blockage if it's swallowed with food. Bark, which is used for forest reptiles, can also cause problems when swallowed. In addition, for desert reptiles (including chelonians), bark is too damp and doesn't hold heat well. Alfalfa pellets are used for many tortoises but can mold quickly when wet.

So what should you use? Choose a substrate that works for your individual chelonian, which may mean that you use different substrates in different cages. I use alfalfa pellets for my leopard and sulcata hatchlings (and other desert and herbivorous species) because it's good food if they eat it. I just watch for mold and change the pellets when they're soiled. I use bark (a nonaromatic variety) for my box turtles because it holds moisture, and they need dampness.

See Chapter 14 for more information on substrates.

Feeding the Wrong Foods

Did you know that iceberg lettuce has no nutritional value, except for a minute amount of fiber? Many people, however, still feed it to their herbivorous tortoises. The foods you feed your turtle or tortoise are vital to your pet's quality of life, longevity, and good health. Feeding incorrect foods or foods of poor nutritional value shortens your pet's life span. Make sure that you know — through your ongoing research — what foods you should feed your pet to achieve the best health for it. And then do it! Chapter 19 has more information on nutrition.

Putting Large and Small Species Together

Don't house hatchlings and adult turtles and tortoises together. The hatchlings need to be protected from their larger relatives. Chelonians don't understand family bond; that is, adults don't look upon hatchlings as treasured offspring. Instead, a hatchling is simply a much smaller chelonian. With tortoises, larger ones may climb on or over smaller ones, sometimes doing physical harm. More likely, though, the larger ones simply get more of the food. With turtles, larger ones may even look upon a smaller one as a meal! To prevent potential disasters, keep turtles and tortoises of like size together, and don't mix sizes.

Mixing Species

If you have turtles and tortoises of different species, don't house them together. Each species should have its own cage or enclosure. Not only do chelonians from different species have their own individual housing, environmental, and nutritional needs, but turtles and tortoises from different species can potentially pass diseases or parasites to a different species that may have no immunity to them. In addition, some species are more extroverted than others and often become bullies when housed with a shyer species.

Being Unprepared for Emergencies

What will you do if you lose electricity? How will you keep your tortoises warm? How much tortoise food do you have in the house? Can you feed all your pets if you get snowed in? Being prepared for emergencies is part of being a smart pet owner. Several years ago, a friend of mine who lives in New England lost four star tortoise hatchlings because the power went off during a snowstorm and she didn't think to have an alternate power source. You may not live in an area where blizzards are common, but emergencies of some sort can happen anywhere. It's smart to be prepared for anything that can happen.

- A generator is always a good idea.
- Commercial turtle and tortoise food stays fresh in the freezer for quite a while; keep some on hand.

✔ Bottled water can replace tap water in an emergency.

✔ Plastic dog crates and sweater boxes can be used to transport turtles or tortoises if you need to evacuate.

Think and plan ahead; doing so could save your pet's life.

Finding Out Too Late That Fido Isn't Turtle-Friendly

I've been doing turtle and tortoise rescue for over 20 years. I take in abandoned, strayed, neglected, hurt, and sick turtles and tortoises; treat them; and try to adopt them to new homes. And I see more turtles and tortoises chewed by dogs than any other single cause of injury or illness. Many dogs seem to think that turtles and tortoises are chew toys — ones that wiggle and try to get away. Unfortunately for the turtle or tortoise, dogs can cause tremendous harm!

Make sure that your turtle or tortoise cage or enclosure is securely fenced so that the turtles and tortoises can't escape and a dog can't get in. Don't assume that your dog won't harm your shelled pets; instead, assume that he will! All my dogs have been raised with turtles and tortoises, and none of the three has ever tried to harm a turtle or tortoise. However, when I'm not supervising the dogs, they are away from the chelonians.

Getting Addicted

Many first-time chelonian owners are so smitten with their shelled friends that they bring home another one, and another, until they realize that the house and yard are overflowing with chelonians! It's easy to become excited about turtles and tortoises; they are fascinating pets. However, resist the temptation to keep bringing home more. When I found myself getting to the addicted stage, I decided to restrict myself to three species I knew I could care for. I couldn't have one of everything! I also set a limit on how many chelonians I could house inside and out, how many cages I could clean, and how many turtles or tortoises I could care for properly. Then, when I reached that limit, I couldn't bring home any more. This way, I know that I can care for my pets as they need me to.

Appendix A

Chelonian Terms and Scientific Names

· ·

*T*urtles and tortoises aren't complicated, but the jargon that humans have created about them may be. In this appendix, you can find a glossary of terms that can help you wade through the jargon you may hear from pet stores and other pet owners. In addition, this appendix provides a section listing the common names and scientific names of a variety of chelonian species.

Glossary of Terms

Although this book was written so that people other than scientists studying chelonians can understand it, terms can be confusing. If you find a term in the text that you don't understand, it's probably listed here.

abdominal scutes: Scutes located third from the front on the plastron; usually very large. See also *scutes.*

anal scutes: Scutes at the rear of the plastron.

annuli: Pattern of growth on the scutes; often called growth rings.

aquatic turtle: A turtle that spends most of its time in water.

basking: Behavior that allows a turtle to soak up heat from the sun or another overhead heat source.

beak: The hard, horny forward part of the jaw, similar to a bird's beak.

brackish water: Water with a high salt content.

bridges: The vertical sides of the shell where the carapace and plastron join.

carapace: The top shell.

carnivore: A chelonian that eats animal matter.

carrion: Eating rotten flesh; a natural diet for some turtles, but a danger in captivity.

central or vertebral scutes: Scutes running down the center of the carapace. See also *scutes.*

chelonians: Turtles and tortoises as a group.

cloaca: Where the body's wastes are excreted and the reproductive processes take place.

clutch: All the eggs laid by one female at one laying.

costal scutes: The scutes on either side of the central or vertebral scutes on the carapace. See also *scutes.*

Cretaceous: A geological period extending from approximately 140 million to 65 million years ago. Dinosaurs died out at the end of this period.

diurnal: A term for chelonians that are active during the day.

ectotherm: Cold-blooded; relying on outside sources for body heat.

Eocene: A geological epoch from approximately 55 million to 35 million years ago.

estivation: Inactivity during hot weather or drought.

femoral scutes: Located next to the anal scutes on the plastron, near the hind legs. See also *scutes.*

genetic: Pertaining to genes or inheritance.

gular scutes: At the front of the plastron, near the head. See also *scutes.*

habitat: The environment in which an animal lives.

hatchling: A turtle just after it leaves the egg.

herbivore: Eating plants rather than animal matter; a vegetarian.

herpetology: The study of reptiles and amphibians.

hibernation: Winter dormancy.

hinge: A mobile suture; specifically seen on hingeback tortoises, box turtles, and many other turtles and tortoises.

humeral scutes: Just behind the gular scutes at the front of the plastron. See also *scutes.*

incubation: The development of an egg after laying but prior to hatching, requiring warmth.

Jurassic: A geological period from approximately 200 million to 140 million years ago.

juvenile: Not sexually mature.

keel: A ridge on the carapace.

keratin: A fibrous protein found in scutes, beaks, and claws.

marginal scutes: The small scutes located around the edges of the carapace. See also *scutes.*

Mesozoic: A geological era, often referred to as the age of reptiles, encompassing the Triassic, Jurassic, and Cretaceous periods.

nocturnal: Active at night.

omnivore: Eats both plant and animal matter.

plastron: The lower or bottom shell.

Pleistocene: A geological epoch from 2 million to about 11,000 years ago.

Pliocene: A geological epoch ranging from 5 million to 2 million years ago.

scutes: The individual sections of shell on both the top (carapace) and bottom (plastron); fingernail-like sections of keratin that cover the underlying bone.

sea turtle: A marine turtle with flippers.

semi-terrestrial turtle: A turtle that spends some, but a minority, of its time on land and the rest in water.

serrated: Having a saw-tooth type of edge, usually at the rear of the carapace.

side-necked turtle: A turtle mainly from the southern hemisphere that folds its head to the side rather than retracting it completely into the shell.

subspecies: An identifying third scientific name. For example, the eastern box turtle is *Terrapene carolina carolina*.

substrate: Bedding material or floor covering for a cage or enclosure.

suture: The jagged patterning where skeletal bone fuses together, especially the shell bones underneath the scutes. See also *scutes.*

temperate: A latitude at which well-defined summer and winter seasons are experienced.

terrapin: A name applied to some species of freshwater turtles.

terrarium: A closed container housing land animals and plants.

terrestrial: Living on the ground; on land.

tortoise: An exclusively land-dwelling chelonian; family scientifically classified *Testudiniae.*

tubercle: The spur on a tortoise's leg; usually a rear leg. A small elevation on the skin.

turtle: An aquatic, semi-aquatic, or terrestrial turtle.

vent: Cloaca; the anal opening.

vertebral or central scutes: Scutes running down the center of the carapace. See also *scutes.*

vivarium: An indoor, artificial environment, usually with both water and land areas.

List of Scientific Names

A turtle's or tortoise's common name is much like a person's nickname. I'm Liz, so to my friends and people who know me, Liz is sufficient. However, the name Liz alone is not my legal name, and a lot of people go by the name Liz. So my legal identification has my first name, a middle name, and a last name. A species' scientific name is much like my legal name — it removes doubt as to what the species actually is.

In this section, I list the common names for many turtles and tortoises, followed by the Latin or scientific names in parentheses. Note that scientific names are always in a state of flux. New research changes the way scientists look at a particular family or animal, and names are then redone. These names are correct as of this writing according to the majority of experts and common usage. However, they may change tomorrow!

African forest turtle *(Pelusios gabonensis)*

African helmeted turtle *(Pelomedusa subrufa)*

African mud turtle *(Pelusios subniger)*

African spur-thigh tortoise *(Geochelone sulcata)*

Alabama map turtle *(Graptemys pulchra)*

Aldabran tortoise *(Geochelone or Aldabrachelys gigantea)*

alligator snapping turtle *(Macroclemmys temmincki)*

American box turtles *(Terrapene carolina)*

angulated tortoise *(Chersina angulata)*

Asian leaf turtle *(Cyclemys dentata)*

Asian yellow pond turtle *(Mauremys nigricans)*

Barbour's map turtle *(Graptemys barbouri)*

Bell's hingeback tortoise *(Kinixys belliana)*

big-headed turtle *(Platysternon megacephalum)*

black-breasted leaf turtle *(Geoemyda spengleri)*

black marsh terrapin *(Siebenrockiella crassicollis)*

Blanding's turtle *(Emydoidea blandingii)*

bog turtle *(Clemmys muhlenbergii)*

Bolson tortoise *(Gopherus flavomarginatus)*

bowsprit tortoise *(Chersina angulata)*

brown wood turtle *(Rhinoclemmys annulata)*

Burmese black tortoise *(Manouria emys phayeri)*

Burmese brown tortoise *(Manouria emys emys)*

Burmese star tortoise *(Geochelone platynota)*

California desert tortoise *(Gopherus agassizii)*

Chaco side-neck turtle *(Acanthochelys or Platemys pallidipectoris)*

Chaco tortoise *(Geochelone or Chelondoidis chilensis)*

Central American wood turtle *(Rhinoclemmys punctularia)*

chicken turtle *(Deirochelys reticularia)*

Chinese box turtle *(Cuora flavomarginata)*

Chinese three-striped box turtle *(Cuora trifasciata)*

Coahuila aquatic box turtle *(Terrapene coahuila)*

common cooter *(Pseudemys floridana)*

common map turtle *(Graptemys geographica)*

common snapping turtle *(Chelydra serpentina)*

crowned river turtle *(Hardella thurjii)*

desert box turtle *(Terrapene ornata luteola)*

desert tortoise *(Gopherus agassizii)*

diamondback terrapin *(Malaclemys terrapin)*

eastern box turtle *(Terrapene carolina carolina)*

eastern mud turtle *(Kinosternon subrubrum)*

eastern painted turtle *(Chrysemys picta picta)*

Egyptian tortoise *(Testudo kleinmanni)*

elongated tortoise *(Indotestudo* or *Geochelone elongata)*

European pond terrapin *(Emys orbicularis)*

Florida box turtle *(Terrapene carolina bauri)*

Florida cooter *(Pseudemys floridana)*

Florida gopher tortoise *(Gopherus polyphemus)*

Florida red-bellied turtle *(Pseudemys nelsoni)*

Florida softshell turtle *(Trionyx ferox)*

flowered box turtle *(Cuora galbinifrons)*

forest tortoise *(Geochelone* or *Chelonoidis denticulata)*

furrowed wood turtle *(Rhinoclemmys areolata)*

Galapagos tortoises *(Geochelone* or *Chelonoidis elephantopus)*

geometric tortoise *(Psammobates geometricus)*

giant Asian pond turtle *(Heosemys grandis)*

gopher tortoise *(Gopherus polyphemus)*

Greek tortoise *(Testudo graeca ibera)*

Gulf Coast box turtle *(Terrapene carolina major)*

Hermann's tortoise *(Testudo hermanni)*

Horsfield's tortoise *(Testudo* or *Geochelone horsfieldi)*

Indian black turtle *(Melanochelys trijuga)*

Indian snail-eating turtle *(Melanochelys trijuga)*

Indochinese box turtle *(Cuora galbinifrons)*

jagged-shelled turtle *(Pyxidea mouhotii)*

Japanese turtle *(Mauremys japonica)*

Klauber's box turtle *(Terrapene nelsoni klauberi)*

leopard tortoise *(Geochelone pardalis)*

Malayan box turtle *(Cuora amboinensis)*

Malayan snail-eating turtle *(Malayemys subtrijuga)*

marginated tortoise *(Testudo marginata)*

matamata *(Chelus fimbriatus)*

Mediterranean turtle *(Mauremys leprosa)*

Mexican box turtle *(Terrapene carolina mexicana)*

Mexican red wood turtle *(Rhinoclemmys rubida)*

Mississippi map turtle *(Graptemys pseudogeographica)*

Moorish tortoise *(Testudo graeca)*

Nayarit box turtle *(Terrapene nelsoni nelsoni)*

New Guinea side-necked turtle *(Chelodina parkeri)*

North African tortoise *(Testudo graeca)*

ornate box turtle *(Terrapene ornata ornata)*

painted terrapin *(Callagur borneoensis)*

painted turtle *(Chrysemys picta)*

pancake tortoise *(Malacochersus tornieri)*

Plymouth red-bellied turtle *(Chrysemys rubiventris)*

radiated tortoise *(Geochelone asterochelys radiata)*

red-bellied side-necked turtle *(Emydura subglobosa)*

red-eared slider *(Trachemys scripta elegans)*

red-footed tortoise *(Geochelone* or *Chelonoidis carbonaria)*

Reeve's turtle *(Chinemys reevesi)*

Russian tortoise *(Testudo* or *Geochelone horsfieldi)*

serrated hingeback tortoise *(Kinixys erosa)*

smooth softshell turtle *(Trionyx muticus)*

South American wood turtle *(Rhinoclemmys pulcherrima)*

speckled tortoise *(Homopus signatus)*

spiny softshell turtle *(Trionyx spiniferus)*

spiny turtle *(Heosemys spinosa)*

Spix's snake-necked turtle *(Platemys spixii)*

spotted box turtle *(Terrapene nelsoni nelsoni)*

spotted pond turtle *(Geoclemys hamiltonii)*

spotted turtle *(Clemmys guttata)*

star tortoise *(Geochelone elegans)*

striped mud turtle *(Kinosternon baurii)*

striped-neck leaf turtle *(Cyclemys tcheponensis)*

sulcata tortoise *(Geochelone sulcata)*

Texas tortoise *(Gopherus berlandieri)*

three-toed box turtle *(Terrapene carolina triunguis)*

travancore tortoise *(Indotestudo travancorica)*

twist-necked turtle *(Platemys platycephala)*

Vietnamese turtle *(Pyxidea mouhotii)*

Vietnam wood turtle *(Geoemyda spengleri)*

western painted turtle *(Chrysemys picta belli)*

western pond turtle *(Clemmys marmorata)*

wood turtle *(Clemmys insculpta)*

yellow mud turtle *(Kinosternon flavescens)*

yellow-footed tortoise *(Geochelone* or *Chelonoidis denticulata)*

yellow-headed temple turtle *(Hieremys annandalei)*

yellow-headed tortoise *(Indotestudo elongata)*

yellow-spotted Amazon turtle *(Podocnemis unifilis)*

Yucatan box turtle *(Terrapene carolina yucatana)*

Appendix B

Sources of Things Chelonian

● ●

Turtles and tortoises are addictive — not just the creatures themselves, but all things chelonian. I have shelves full of turtle and tortoise statues made of stone, glass, ceramic, pewter, and even plastic. Books on turtles and tortoises line my office walls. In this appendix, I offer you a wide selection of all things chelonian so that you can feed your addiction, too.

Sources of Live Foods

A steady, reliable supply of good-quality feeder insects is critical for keeping insectivorous or carnivorous chelonians well fed. If your local pet store can supply you with insects, great. However, if you're feeding several insect eaters, you may get a better price by buying in bulk directly from one of the following suppliers:

- **Arbico:** Crickets, mealworms, and other products; 800-827-2847
- **Bassett's:** Crickets and mealworms; 800-634-2445
- **Fluker Farms:** Crickets and mealworms; 800-735-8537
- **Grubco:** Crickets, mealworms, and other products; 800-222-3563
- **Manchester Farms:** Earthworms; 800-497-8067
- **Nature's Way:** Mealworms, waxworms, and other products; 800-318-2611
- **Rainbow Mealworms:** Mealworms and more; 310-635-1494

Suppliers of Foods and Supplements

Some turtle and tortoise keepers are very enthusiastic about commercial foods, saying that they make keeping reptiles significantly easier. Other experts are less than enthusiastic, saying that the foods have yet to be proven in the long term. The majority of turtle and tortoise keepers use commercial foods as an added ingredient to a more natural diet, feeding it once, twice, or three times a week, or feeding it when the cupboards are bare.

Following are some suppliers of commercial foods and supplements:

- **Five Star Diets:** 800-747-0557
- **Kaytee:** 800-KAYTEE-1
- **LM Tropical Magic:** 800-332-5623
- **Mardel:** 630-351-3557
- **Nekton Rep:** 813-530-3500
- **Nutri Grow Reptile Diets:** 800-737-8465
- **Ocean Nutrition T-Rex:** 800-275-7186
- **Petty Pets:** 800-356-5020
- **Rep-Cal:** 408-356-4289
- **Sticky Tongue Farms:** 909-672-3876
- **Zoo Med:** 805-542-9988
- **Zupreem:** 800-345-4767

Internet Suppliers

Reptile supplies are a retail specialty, so many pet stores stock few reptile supplies. However, the Internet has become a wonderful source of reptile supplies. The following are a few of the sites I've found; you can find others by searching for specific items.

- **ATV Habitats:** www.herp.com/atv/
- **The Bean Farm:** www.beanfarm.com
- **Bibliomania:** www.sisna.com/bibliomania/home.html
- **Big Apple Herpetological:** www.herp.com/ba.html
- **Central Florida Reptile Farm:** www.herp.com/cfrf/cfrf.html
- **Ecological Technologies:** www.herp.com/ecotach/ecotech.html
- **Energy Saver's Unlimited Inc.:** www.coralife.com
- **Fluker Farms:** www.flukerfarms.com
- **Grubco:** www.herp.com/grubco/grubco.html
- **Harford Reptile Breeding Center:** www.pythons.com
- **New England Reptile Distributors:** www.herp.com/nerd/
- **Pet Station:** http://petstation.com
- **Reptile Solutions:** www.reptiles.com
- **Zoo Med Laboratories:** www.herp.com/zoomed/

Index

Notes

Notes